The Sunni Tragedy
in the Middle East

The Sunni Tragedy
in the Middle East

Northern Lebanon from
al-Qaeda to ISIS

Bernard Rougier

PRINCETON UNIVERSITY PRESS
PRINCETON AND OXFORD

Adapted from Bernard Rougier, *L'Oumma en fragments: Contrôler le sunnisme au Liban*

Copyright © 2011 by Presses Universitaires de France

English translation copyright © 2015 by Princeton University Press

Requests for permission to reproduce material from this work should be sent to Permissions, Princeton University Press

Published by Princeton University Press, 41 William Street, Princeton, New Jersey 08540

In the United Kingdom: Princeton University Press, 6 Oxford Street, Woodstock, Oxfordshire OX20 1TW

press.princeton.edu

All Rights Reserved

Library of Congress Cataloging-in-Publication Data

Rougier, Bernard.
[Oumma en fragments. English]
The Sunni tragedy in the Middle East : Northern Lebanon from al-Qaeda to ISIS / Bernard Rougier.
pages cm.—(Princeton studies in Muslim politics)
Includes bibliographical references and index.
Translated from French.
ISBN 978-0-691-17001-5 (hardcover : alk. paper) 1. Ummah (Islam)—Lebanon. 2. Sunnites—Lebanon. 3. Islam and state—Lebanon.
I. Title.
BP173.6.R6813 2015
956.9204'53—dc23

British Library Cataloging-in-Publication Data is available

This book has been composed in Sabon

Printed on acid-free paper. ∞

Printed in the United States of America

1 3 5 7 9 10 8 6 4 2

Contents

Introduction

This book aims to explain how and why jihadism wove its way into a Sunni social fabric in the throes of a leadership crisis. It shows how this new phenomenon is both exploiting and provoking a deep crisis of authority within Sunni Islam. The setting is the predominantly Sunni Muslim city of Tripoli, Lebanon's second largest city, with a population of 350,000 inhabitants. Yet the story also encompasses other parts of North Lebanon, as well as western Syria, especially since the outbreak of the Syrian crisis in 2011.

When Lebanon's civil war ended in 1990, the country's north fell under the firm grip of the Syrian *imperium*. For the ensuing fifteen years it remained essentially marginalized from both national and regional politics. However, with the 2005 assassination of former Prime Minister Rafiq al-Hariri and the subsequent end of the Syrian military occupation of Lebanon, the North has become an arena in which various forces struggle to impose hegemony over Sunni political and religious expression. This book's ambition is to show how, why, and under what circumstances North Lebanon has produced different kinds of jihadi militants over the last fifteen years.

Backed by the West and Saudi Arabia, Rafiq's son, Sa'ad al-Hariri, used his seat in Beirut to construct and lead a broad anti-Assad coalition and champion Lebanon's sovereignty. This bloc became the March 14th Movement, named after the date of a mass demonstration against the Syrian regime that took place in downtown Beirut on that date in 2005 (a few yards away from the place where Rafiq al-Hariri had been assassinated one month before). His opponents were Bashar al-Assad's regime and its local allies, including the powerful pro-Iranian Hezbollah—named March 8th after the date of their earlier demonstration reaffirming Lebanese solidarity with the Syrian regime and the goal of "Resistance" against Israel.

But al-Hariri and his allies also confronted a number of amorphous Sunni religious networks that were vying to become the new leaders of Lebanon's Sunni community. The fact that all of these forces had ties with political power bases or religious hubs outside Lebanon—political bureaus in Riyad, Damascus, or Teheran; religious centers in Medina or Mecca; Iraqi militant networks in al-Anbar; charities in Doha; even cells meeting in mosque basements in Copenhagen or Sydney—turned North Lebanon into a cauldron in which competing and often irreconcilable regional and transnational interests clashed.

During this period, jihadism emerged and held the ground against a host of foes. At first it took the form of an underground network, then evolved into an armed movement that threatened to upset the internal equilibrium of the Sunni community. North Lebanon thus offers the first example of how jihadism, revolutionary by nature, contrived to seize control of the Sunni community by sidelining its political elite and frightening its middle classes. Each chapter of this book explores, in detail, the importance of interactions between local, regional, and transnational realities in the birth and development of this dynamic.

Since the outbreak of civil war in Syria in 2011, thousands of Syrians have sought refuge in the northern Lebanese cities of Tripoli, Akkar, and Dinniyeh. Volunteers from the Free Syrian Army (FSA) also sought a safe haven, but quickly came to the realization that they would have to remain underground if they were to escape the reach of the Syrian regime's local allies. At the end of 2013, Islamist rebels from the Syrian "Islamic Front," as well as radical jihadis from Jabhat al-Nusra (al-Qaeda in Syria) and from the Islamic State of Iraq and Syria (ISIS), followed the FSA fighters to North Lebanon. Hezbollah's massive intervention in the Syrian civil war starting from 2012, combined with the influx of Syrian refugees in North Lebanon, rendered the border between Lebanon and Syria more and more irrelevant, which in turn facilitated the enrollment of young Sunni Lebanese into ISIS's so-called caliphate.

This book also aims to describe how sociocultural dynamics and the strategic objectives of various actors interact and together generate processes of political mobilization in the Levant. Understanding these sociocultural dynamics requires an exploration into the mechanisms fueling Islamist radicalism, including tools of socialization, living conditions, external influences, and regional and transnational solidarities. Strategic dynamics come into focus once we understand the modes of action in which local and regional powers engage—be they the Hariri family, Bashar al-Assad's regime, or the pro-Iranian Hezbollah—as they seek to co-opt and exploit this Islamist militancy, while at the same time shielding themselves from it.

The book thus tries to connect the micro and the macro, the local and the regional, the peripheral and the central, the sociological and the strategic. Only by addressing all of these essential dimensions of Middle Eastern politics—with the aid of exceptional sources and an intimate knowledge of the terrain—does it become possible to decipher, over a period of study of more than ten years, the nature of the profound changes at work in the region.

Analyzing the social and strategic logics that underlie the Sunni predicament in the region, this book reveals the difficulty—but not *impossibility*—of building a liberal Sunni constituency in this part of the Levant. By exploring these issues in their historical, social, and political contexts, this book also endeavors to identify conditions under which such a constituency might emerge, despite the challenges it faces as a result of being caught between, on the one hand, the propaganda of the Syrian regime and of its Iranian allies, who are intent on justifying the scale of their repression, and, on the other, charges of treason from jihadis and many Salafi clerics. As a privileged vantage point for observing the controversies and contradictions at the heart of Sunni Islam, the story of North Lebanon also presages the severe political and social fragmentation that the Syrian civil war has wrought across the region.

What makes North Lebanon such an interesting and troubling setting is what it lacks, or only weakly possesses. It is not an intellectual hub generating new political rhetoric and local innovation.

The region is instead a locus of hybridization, a crucible for multiple influences, and a cradle for mobilization—factors that give it exceptional relevance. The wealth of the region's external connections means that it is not a passive recipient of influences, for these connections run in both directions. The actors who occupy this space are not only at the receiving end of influence, but also themselves influence a range of external communities. To understand the importance of studying such a space, one must attempt to trace the richness of its connections by inductively following how the actors themselves move across these boundaries. By highlighting the paths they follow and the uses they make of various linkages, this book will construct a multidimensional map, depicting both the areas that act as catalysts of influence, and North Lebanon as a whole, as an arena in which a plethora of militant and political agendas intersect.

These regional and transnational influences melded with the preexisting structure of Lebanese politics. In Lebanon, community leaders depend on demographic cores dominated by their confessional group—such as Mount Lebanon, a traditional Christian stronghold, or South Lebanon, home of many Shi'ite Muslims—to exert influence on the national stage. For the Sunni elite, political control over their own community depends very much on the control of the northern Lebanese social and geographic space, where Sunni are more numerous than anywhere else in Lebanon. This book highlights the most significant episodes in this struggle for the control of a geographic and political space that has become the Sunni community's center of gravity in Lebanon. At stake is the ability of Sunni Islam in the Levant to create a unified civilian leadership in a highly fragmented political and religious environment. The region has been particularly important to the Sunni community since the end of the Lebanese civil war, when the influence of Sunni notables who had previously enjoyed local powerbases in the cities of Sidon, Beirut, and Tripoli precipitously declined. The confessional fabric of the area is more complex than Sunni Islamists would have us believe. The dominant demographic is Sunni, certainly, but this observation obscures more than it reveals. The governorate (*muhafaza*) of North Lebanon, whether we are speaking of its urban center, the city of Tripoli, or its rural and mountainous areas, the subdistricts (*cazas*) of Akkar and Dinniyeh, is also a heterogeneous space: consider the many Christian villages in Akkar; the proximity of the Maronite town of Zghorta; and the existence of the Alawite minority neighborhood of Ba'al Mohsen. This relative confessional and political diversity results in an internal division of space, with militarization arising in mixed areas where invisible borders now separate Sunni villages controlled by Salafi militants from Alawite villages under the sway of militias backed by the Syrian regime.

Methodology

This book is an augmented and updated version of my *Oumma en fragments* (A Fragmented Umma) published in French in 2011 by the Presses Universitaires de France. Two new chapters have been added, as well as other hitherto unpublished material. It is the result of many years of research. My first contact with North Lebanon was in the late 1990s. At the time, I was studying the development of a jihadi identity in the Ayn al-Helweh Palestinian refugee camp for my doctoral dissertation.[1] Relations between the camp sheikhs and religious figures in Tripoli later oriented me toward the unexplored field of Sunni religious circles in North Lebanon.[2] While teaching political science in French universities, I devoted the time between school sessions to investigating the various "Sunni worlds" from a most propitious vantage point—the city of Tripoli and its environs. On each subsequent trip, I tried to preserve the ties made in the previous years and to further broaden my circle of relations. I collected the first data at the beginning of the 2000s and completed the fieldwork in May 2014. This extended period of research was critical, for it enabled me to gain the trust of my various sources, and to familiarize myself with the factors shaping their particular social, political, and economic

---

[1] See Bernard Rougier, *Everyday Jihad: The Rise of Militant Islam among Palestinians in Lebanon* (Cambridge: Harvard University Press, 2007).

[2] Only the anthropologist Michael Gilsenan had studied the relations between forms of violence and power among the feudal lords of Akkar in North Lebanon, in his fine book, *Lords of the Lebanese Marches: Violence and Narrative in an Arab Society* (London and New York: I. B.Tauris, 1995). For an in-depth look at Tripoli's religious and political history, see Tine Gade, "From Genesis to Deintegration: The Crisis of the Political-Religious Field in Tripoli, Lebanon (1967–2011)," PhD diss., Ecole Doctorale de Sciences Po, April 2015.

environments. Repeated trips to Tripoli made it possible to analyze shifts in the positions of different actors that took place as the regional situation evolved and to understand, from within, the constant negotiation between beliefs and opportunism, between strategy and tactics, and between risk taking and preservation. To account for the competition for influence that occurs between different levels of decision-making, I tried to consider individuals of different social backgrounds, searching out the mosque preacher and the former militant, the local notable and the petty criminal, the minister and the local security official.

Among my various institutional interlocutors, I met several times with Wissam al-Hassan, the former head of the Information Branch (*fara'al-ma'lumat*) of the Internal Security Forces (ISF). His able investigations played an important role in uncovering the murderous network behind the assassination of Rafiq al-Hariri, making it possible for the Special Tribunal for Lebanon to issue an indictment incriminating members of Hezbollah. Despite the numerous precautions he took, Wissam al-Hassan was himself assassinated in 2012 in the Christian neighborhood of Ashrafieh in East Beirut. There is no doubt that he tried to influence my analysis of regional events in general, and North Lebanon in particular—such is the nature of any interview between a researcher and a leading actor. It is part of the researcher's job to understand the factors that might lead such an actor to assume a particular stance in his account of events. Nonetheless, al-Hassan had no doubts as to the sincerity of the religious figures he came to deal with. When asked if he trusted the Salafi sheikhs of the North, his answer was "No!"—illustrating the complexity of power relations within the multifaceted and divided Sunni world that the contradictions of the North encapsulate. In his windowless office at the ISF, he continuously received phone calls soliciting a favor or an intervention, each time engaging his phenomenal memory so as to identify the possible plan and the beneficiary of such an intervention.

In addition to Wissam al-Hassan, many people gave me their trust (or part of it). Like al-Hassan, some were assassinated, Kamal Madhat, representative of Mahmud Abbas in Lebanon, among them. On the other side of the regional political spectrum is Sheikh Sa'ad al-Din al-Ghiyyeh, himself at the crossroads of Jihadi Islamism and collaboration with the Syrian intelligence services, who was assassinated shortly before this book went to press. As I was recommended to him by Rif'at Eid, Ali's son and the new chief of the Alawite community in Ba'al Mohsen, Ghiyyeh welcomed me several times into his home in the Qubbeh neighborhood, and he provided increasingly dramatic revelations about his intersecting relationships with heads of Syrian intelligence and Syrian jihadi militants. As a combatant who had trained in Abu Nidal's group in the late 1980s, as a jihadi volunteer in Iraq with Zarqawi in 2003, and with close ties to the Alawite community of Ba'al Mohsen (his mother's denomination), the "sheikh" was clearly a man of action, but he was also a seasoned adventurer in the arena of politics. Fearing for his safety (and rightly so), he always carried a miniature revolver in the pocket of his three-piece suit. During one of our last meetings, he claimed that he wanted to submit for approval to his Syrian contacts a "made in the Iranian embassy in Damascus" plan that would make him the leader of Hezbollah in North Lebanon. In 2011, with no explanation, he abruptly put an end to our meetings. I never knew if he took this decision on his own, or if his superiors instructed him to stop talking to me out of fear of his volubility.

I was immersed in work that would serve this book not only time-wise, but geographically as well. In Australia, I made new connections and studied transnational solidarity networks, without which my fieldwork in Lebanon would have been unintelligible. The material for this book encompasses a broad array of documentary sources—hundreds of interviews, sermons, flyers, and legal documents. Chapter 1 in particular is informed by legal documents supplied by lawyers acquainted with the "McDonald's network" affair—over one hundred handwritten pages recording the "confessions" of arrested persons. Likewise, for chapters 4 and 5, I had access to part of the report of the prosecutor in charge of investigating the Fatah al-Islam affair, as well as to the record of the interrogations led by the Popular Committee of the Baddawi camp in Tripoli, after the arrest of suspects in the camp previous to the establishment of the group.[3] Wissam al-Hassan had also

[3] The posting online on July 20, 2012, of the full indictment, "Bill of Indictment in the Case of Fatah al-Islam," drafted by the judge for the Judicial Council (al-Majlis al-'Adli), Ghassan Munif 'Awaydat, has provided an additional source of valuable information on the founding and development of the jihadi group. See "Bill of Indictment in the Case of Fatah

overseen the writing of a memoir entitled "Fatah al-Islam: From the Cradle to the Grave" (*fatah al-islam: min al-mahad ila al-lahd*), a few pages of which he let me read during an interview in the summer of 2008. On the other side, I also received from Hamas militants testimonials by the families of the group's fighters, which underlined the presumed responsibility of those close to Hariri in North Lebanon. Thanks to the sum of knowledge accumulated patiently over the years, I was able to make both an external and internal critique of these various documents. As the French historian Antoine Prost writes, "One must first be a historian to make a critique of a document, since in essence, it means confronting that document with everything one already knows about the subject it deals with, the place and the time it concerns."[4]

Such a critique thus demanded a certain number of methodological precautions so as to take possible distortions into account: the data obtained may have been extracted under duress, with the result that the "testimonies" of the accused persons were *a priori* to be regarded with caution unless they were confirmed by other sources or, at least, proved consistent with the overall narrative framework that emerged from the questionings. Far from any normative judgment of one person or another's responsibility, I was above all concerned with trying to discern, in concrete terms, how a jihadi group had constituted itself, and gave priority to understanding the conditions that made possible the successive play of encounters between individuals from different backgrounds and professional pathways. The main preoccupation of the officials in charge of the inquiry, by contrast, was to establish the degree of responsibility of persons directly involved in carrying out terrorist acts. They had to gather a maximum number of names as well as practical information on the military materiel used (arms, explosives) in order to reconstitute channels and broaden investigations. For that purpose they employed the action semantics proper to their domain. My work as a researcher was to recreate a part of the social, political, and religious universe, so as to shed light on the circumstances underlying the creation of a

---

al-Islam" (*al-qarar al-itihami fi qadiya fatah al-islam*), https://journalismnl.wordpress.com (accessed July 20, 2012).

[4] See Antoine Prost, *Douze leçons sur l'histoire* (Paris: Seuil, 1996), 59.

terrorist network in North Lebanon, which required a very different vernacular.

It will be up to the reader to judge whether the interpretation given here reflects the respect for objective criteria that has always guided this research. Contrary to postmodern epistemology, the author of these lines believes that social reality *exists*, and that it is possible to objectively reconstruct the perceptions that actors have of it at diverse moments of their actions.

These documents, like the interviews with the lawyers of the accused, are nonetheless of exceptional value. They provide a wealth of information and detail, once one has calibrated the weight of the private code that saturates the text with its own "language game." Pieced together, these documents reveal a progression of events that enable one to follow, over roughly a decade, the evolution of the different categories of actors that "make" Middle Eastern politics today.

Summary

CHAPTER 1: NORTH LEBANON IN *BILAD AL-SHAM*

The first chapter retraces the main events in the political history of Tripoli, from the period of the French mandate (1920–1943) to after the civil war (1990).[5] Severed from its Syrian hinterland with the advent of modern Lebanon, the city long dwelled in nostalgia for its bygone grandeur until it joined Lebanese political life under the leadership of the al-Karami family. The subsequent civil war put an end to the "politics of the notables," replacing it with the

---

[5] *Bilad al-Sham* is a geographic term that denotes what is now Lebanon, Syria, Jordan, and Palestine. Etymologically, the expression means "the left-hand region." It goes back to an ancient usage in central Arabia, where Arabs, standing in front of the rising sun, saw Syria on their left and Yemen on their right. See C. E, Bosworth et al., "al-Shām, al-Sha'm," in the *Encyclopaedia of Islam*, 2nd ed., ed. P. Bearman et al. Brill Online, 2015, http://referenceworks.brillonline.com/entries/encyclopaedia-of-islam-2/al-sham-al-sham -COM_1031 (accessed April 18, 2015).

According to historian Jean-Paul Pascual, "Before the twentieth century, the expression refers to the geographic area stretching from the Taurus Mountains to the north, the Sinai Peninsula to the south, the Mediterranean Sea to the west, and the Syrian desert to the east." J.-P. Pascual "La Syrie à l'époque ottoman," in *La Syrie d'aujourd'hui* (Paris: Editions du CNRS, 1980). For ideological uses of this notion, from King Abdallah of Transjordan to Hafez al-Assad of Syria, see Daniel Pipes, *Greater Syria: The History of an Ambition* (Oxford: Oxford University Press, 1992).

hard politics of street militias. One of the latter even dreamed of establishing an Islamic republic in Tripoli, until the Syrian army crushed it in 1985. This historical detour helps us gauge the weight of the massacres in local memory and understand the peculiar relationship that the city has with the Syrian authorities, who view it as an extension of their own society. It is also important to understand that different spheres of authority coexisted, represented by various types of figures: government officials (members of parliament, ministers), street leaders, and sheikhs in the mosques. The concomitance of these spheres of activity persisted into the 1990s, when Sunni businessmen with close ties to the Syrian government became involved in politics, while a new generation of sheikhs attracted a segment of the youth into religious institutes financed by the Gulf countries and the Lebanese diaspora in the West.

Chapter 2: Defending an Imagined Umma: The Path to Terrorism

North Lebanon under Syrian tutelage served as prime territory for the establishment of a transnational jihadi movement, run by expatriate Lebanese communities in Europe (particularly in Denmark) and Australia. With reference to previously unpublished documents, this chapter describes how a jihadi network was established in Tripoli after September 11, 2001. In a restrictive, Syrian-controlled political context rife with ideological agitation, young, restive militants were provided with a motive—defending an imagined Islamic community (umma)—to justify their attacking symbols of Western presence in the city. The formula of "regional domination + political repression" that the Syrian regime concocted to prevent the emergence of a Sunni leadership also facilitated a type of transnational religious identification conducive to terrorism. This chapter highlights and explores this dynamic by illustrating how the local jihadi network managed to increase its destructive power by establishing a relationship with al-Qaeda.

Chapter 3: The Anti-Syrian Movement: Rebuilding a Political Scene

The second chapter describes North Lebanon's transformation after the assassination of former Prime Minister Rafiq al-Hariri and the April 2005 withdrawal of Syrian troops from Lebanon.

This chapter turns to al-Hariri's party (the Future Movement), which, though once banned from the "northern capital" of Lebanon, tried to take back Tripoli with the help of the militant networks that had defended the city against Syrian occupation in the 1980s. Thus, a collective memory of militancy that once saw Yasser Arafat's Fatah, the Syrian Muslim Brotherhood, Saddam Hussein's Iraq, and Saudi Arabia unite in opposition to Hafez al-Assad was reactivated. With Sunni political and religious expression freed from Syrian chains, Tripoli once again became an open threat to the regime in Damascus.

CHAPTER 4: THE SYRIAN REGIME REACTS: BUILDING UP A JIHADI NETWORK

This chapter analyzes the Syrian regime's reactions to what it considered a threatening and unacceptable situation: the presence of an extremely polarized, Sunni-dominated territory at its borders, one that hosted political and religious networks highly critical of its rule. The chapter uses material gathered from exclusive interviews (some of which were conducted with clerics very close to the Syrian security apparatus) to draw a detailed picture of Syrian dealings with religious actors, as well as with smaller militant groups that had proved their worth in Iraq before arriving in Lebanon in the summer of 2005. It also describes, based on previously unpublished information, how the Syrian regime pressured its proxies to ensure an obedience indispensable to the implementation of the regime's regional policies. Saydnaya prison, on the outskirts of Damascus, played a particularly important role in the recruitment of "volunteers" to serve the regime. This chapter also seeks to clarify how the Syrian regime functions, both inside and outside its borders.

CHAPTER 5: JIHAD AND RESISTANCE IN NORTH LEBANON: THE HISTORY OF FATAH AL-ISLAM

Chapter 4 looks at the consequences of Syrian policy in North Lebanon through the story of the establishment of Fatah al-Islam, a jihadi group in the Palestinian refugee camp of Nahr al-Bared, north of Tripoli. Here we attempt to explain the contradictions and frictions this group raised, both within its own ranks and within local Islamic circles. These conflicts help explain how local dynamics influence the way in which actors fighting for their survival read and interpret the religious corpus. While some Sunni religious leaders hoped to use this jihadi organization as part of a negotiating process with the Hariri family, in reality the organization represented a grave threat to the March 14 anti-Syrian coalition. The group's true aim was to shatter the Sunni, anti-Syrian confessional movement from within by turning its own militants against the Hariri family—accused of betraying Islam by allying itself with the West. The chapter concludes with a description of the different phases that marked the vicious war between the jihadi militia and the Lebanese army.

CHAPTER 6: THE FAILURE TO CREATE A LASTING SUPPORT BASE FOR THE SYRIAN INSURRECTION

Chapter 5 showed how Sa'ad al-Hariri, with the support of Saudi Arabia, aided the Syrian revolt in the hope of toppling the Assad regime. Sunni networks close to the former prime minister set up a supply line from Tripoli to Akkar, making it possible for the city of Homs—consecrated by some as the "capital of the Syrian revolt"—to resist in face of the soldiers of Bashar al-Assad and the Shi'ite militiamen of the Lebanese Hezbollah. However, by the end of 2013, Syrian pressure on the Lebanese state apparatus succeeded in cutting Homs off from its support base in North Lebanon, thus enabling the Assad regime to take over the city in May 2014. Sa'ad al-Hariri, isolated and faced with the combined tactics of the Lebanese army and Hezbollah, was compelled to abandon his policy of supporting the Syrian revolt. The impossibility of exercising Sunni leadership in Lebanon thus opened the door to a plethora of religious networks avid to proclaim themselves the "defenders of Sunni Islam" in the region.

The Use of Weberian Ideal Types to Better Understand Mobilizations

Rather than impose the very broad and imprecise category of "Islamism" on the communal and regional divisions within North Lebanon, we have forged three Weberian-inspired ideal types—the *muqatil* (local combatant), the *muqawim* (resistance fighter), and the *mujahid* (jihadi)—that enable us to get a better grasp of the situation.

The 1978 Iranian revolution promoted the *muqawim* as a representative of revolutionary, third-worldist Islam aiming to oust Western influence in the region. The *muqawim* built a power system linking Tehran to the eastern Mediterranean, taking as his Lebanese representatives the pro-Iranian Lebanese Hezbollah. In concert with the Pasdaran (the Iranian Revolutionary Guard), Hezbollah has been fighting in Syria since January 2012 in defense of the Assad regime.

The *mujahid* emerged from the Afghan jihad of the 1980s that attempted to build a power base in Greater Syria. Through informal networks, he claims to defend the whole Islamic community (umma) against the West and against secular Muslims. Beyond the al-Qaeda organization, the *mujahid* is currently exploiting the Syrian civil war to build an underground organization and base of power.

Finally, the *muqatil* symbolizes an attitude of local defiance toward external aggression. He lacks a sophisticated ideology, drawing his identity instead from his concrete environment and conceptualizing his fight as against an alien intruder. While the *muqawim* and the *mujahid* attempt to impose their reading of religion on other Muslims by force, thus defining themselves as Islamic militants, the fighter assumes an Islamist or non-Islamist outlook depending on his political socialization and preferences.

These categories are only meant to function as an aid in understanding the political reality of the Arab Middle East. Obviously, they do not correspond to the more complex reality on the ground, where individuals and groups may even pass from one form to another as shifting circumstances dictate.

Journalists and observers have noted the spillover of the Syrian crisis into Lebanon. This observation works in reverse as well, for the conflicts that underlie the civil war in Syria were already present in Lebanon in the 2000s. During the Independence Intifada of 2005, segments of the population staged a peaceful demonstration to express their desire for emancipation from Lebanese leaders organically tied to the regime in Damascus and the Syrian-Iranian alliance. This dual aspiration for national sovereignty and political liberalism was stalled in Lebanon by the Hezbollah's counter-mobilization, as it would be also in Syria by the same organization beginning in late 2011, a few months after the start of the first peaceful demonstrations.

In 2006 a jihadi movement, Fatah al-Islam (FAI), began at a decisive moment to undermine the dynamics of emancipation from Assad from within the Sunni community itself. In 2012 and 2013, Jabhat al-Nusra, and then the Islamic State of Iraq and Syria (ISIS), in turn came to blur the message of opponents to the Bashar al-Assad dictatorship. The resemblance between these two forms of Sunni jihadism goes further, however, than the mere fact of being exploited by the Syrian regime. Through its territorialization of North Lebanon in 2007, jihadism, which until then had preferred underground operations, foreshadowed a strategic transformation that would be confirmed, ultimately, by the declaration of an Islamic caliphate in April 2013.

The two movements also display internal similarities. Each at its core is made up of former members of secular organizations who were won over by radical Islam—volunteers from Palestinian factions in one case, and former soldiers of Saddam Hussein in the other. In the religious bodies of the two movements one remarks a high proportion of youths from the Gulf, an instance being the role played by the Bahraini Turki al-Benali in ISIS's religious structure.[6] A resemblance is also apparent in the internal structure of Fatah al-Islam and ISIS, both having an extremely hierarchical and bureaucratized *modus operandi* based on a multitude of committees—a religious committee, a security committee, a military committee, a coordination committee, and so on.

These points of convergence did not come about by chance. FAI was the Lebanese-Syrian branch of a tree planted by Zarqawi in Iraqi soil. FAI leaders were former companions of the founder of al-Qaeda in the Land of the Two Rivers, established by proclamation (and with Osama bin Laden's benediction) in October 2004. Some of them fought the American army in Iraq, in one of many jihadi groups reunited within a Mujahidin Advisory Council (Majlis

---

[6] A Bahraini born in September 1984, Turki al-Binali is considered ISIS's main religious ideologue. Early in the first decade of the 2000s, he studied for a year and a half at the Faculty of Islamic Studies in Dubai until his arrest and expulsion from Bahrain. He continued his religious studies in Lebanon at the small Imam al-Awzai Institute in Beirut, from which he graduated. He rounded out his education at the Bahrain Legal Studies Institute. Biographies available on the Internet say that he studied with Saudi Sheikh Abdallah bin Jibrin and the jihadi Sheikh Abu Muhammad al-Maqdisi. See Cole Bunzel, "The Caliphate's Scholar-in-Arms," *Jihadica*, http://www.jihadica.com/the-caliphate%E2%80%99s-scholar-in-arms/ (accessed July 23, 2014).

Shura al-Mujahidin) set up in late 2005. After al-Zarqawi's violent death on June 7, 2006, in an American air raid, the Egyptian Abu Hamza al-Muhajir—whose name will recur throughout this book—came to replace him. In October 15, 2006, the council announced the creation of the Islamic State in Iraq, with al-Qaeda as its main component. This was the first attempt by jihadis in the Arab world to govern a territory—at that time, the Islamic State's dream map included the main Sunni Iraqi provinces, as well as less homogeneous territories such as Diyala and Baghdad, but it did not extend beyond the Sykes-Picot border. In 2007, perhaps bowing to council pressure, al-Muhajir swore allegiance to Abu Umar al-Baghdadi, "emir" of the Islamic State in Iraq.[7] This move was approved neither by Bin Laden, nor by his deputy Ayman al-Zawahiri, signifying a divorce between jihadism in the region and the "historic" or central al-Qaeda organization.[8] Abu Umar al-Baghdadi and Abu Hamza al-Muhajir were killed in April 2010, and Abu Bakr al-Baghdadi became the new emir. On April 9, 2013, al-Baghdadi declared himself the caliph of the Islamic State in Iraq and Syria—a clear sign that the Jabhat al-Nusra that appeared in Syria a year before was a mere emanation of the Iraqi matrix.[9]

Two significant differences, however, distinguish the two experiences. In 2007, institutional and political Sunnism in Lebanon counterbalanced jihadism, preventing contagion from spreading from North Lebanon to the rest of the country. Discredited by the events of May 7, 2008, when Hezbollah attacked the offices of the

[7] In an online audio recording, Abu Hamza al-Muhajir, who succeeded Abu Mus'ab al-Zarqawi as head of al-Qaeda in Iraq, swore allegiance to Abu Umar al-Baghdadi in 2006. https://www.youtube.com/watch?v=2WG7l03tgcA. (accessed in 2006).

[8] In a video recording one year later, in 2007, Ayman al-Zawahiri admitted that al-Qaeda no longer existed as such in Iraq and that the Islamic State group was henceforth independent. https://www.youtube.com/watch?v=iwzvUQtTNoo (accessed May 2007).

[9] The Jabhat al-Nusra (Salvation Front) leader, Abu Muhammad al-Jolani, refused to swear allegiance to the new "caliph" of the Islamic State in Iraq and Syria. According to jihadi groups specialist Romain Caillet, "The Nusra Front leader, Abu Mohammad al-Julani, did not respond favorably as he was anxious to maintain his leadership of the organization. He admitted that he had . . . benefited from funds, weapons, and fighters sent by ISI. He also sought to preserve the jihadi identity of the Nusra Front, ending his statement with a 'renewal of allegiance' to Ayman al-Zawahiri" (who supported al-Julani against al-Baghdadi's claim). See R. Caillet, "The Islamic State: Leaving al-Qaeda Behind," *Carnegie Endowment for International Peace*, http://carnegieendowment.org/syriaincrisis/?fa=54017, December 27, 2013.

Future Movement in the capital, institutional Sunnism would be hard put to do the same Lebanon today.

The second distinction, internal to the jihadi sphere, has to do with the definition of the enemy. Faithful to Zarqawi's teaching, ISIS espoused a hatred of Shi'as just as ardent as the enmity it directed against Westerners and secular Muslims, whereas the leader of Fatah al-Islam did not dare to take the same stand in Lebanon, for reasons explained in this volume.[10] His Lebanese and Syrian successors in North Lebanon have jettisoned this reticence, leaving us fearing the worst for the future of the country and the region.

A Note on the Transcription of Arabic

An attempt has been made to follow a simplified version of the guidelines used by the *Encyclopedia of Islam*. For ease of reading no 'ayn is used at the beginning of Arabic given names (thus Abdallah, *not* 'Abdallah). For proper names already familiar in English, current usage has been followed (e.g., Frangieh, *not* Farandjiyya; Absi, *not* 'Absi). Similarly, for place names ending in the Arabic *tamarbuta*, an "h" has been added better to reflect the pronunciation of the Syrian-Lebanese dialect (as in the cases of Ayn al-Helweh and Dinniyeh).

---

[10] Prior to the first legislative elections in Iraq, Zarqawi broadcast a speech in January 2005, in which he not only stated his principled opposition to democracy, but went on to warn the Sunnis of the risk of Shi'a hegemony: "You should be aware of the plan carried out by the enemy by installing a so-called democracy in your country. He wants it so as to deprive you of what you hold dearest. He is setting up like a fatal trap to install the Rafida [Shi'as] in power. Four million Rafida have come from Iran to take part in the elections. They will thus take the majority of seats in the pagan parliament (*al-majlis al-wuthni*) and will be able to form a powerful government that will control the state's primary strategic, economic and security sectors. This will all be done on the pretext of 'preserving the homeland and citizens' and 'advancing the democratic process,' and 'liquidating the cadres and symbols of the bygone (*al-ba'id*) Ba'ath Party, Saddam's fedayin and terrorists.' This is how the Rafida will settle their sectarian score to liquidate Sunni cadres, be they *'ulama'*, preachers or elites in general." See the jihadi site www.tawhed.ws/r?i=oz6rva5q (accessed January 2005)

The Sunni Tragedy
in the Middle East

CHAPTER 1

North Lebanon in *Bilad al-Sham*

Before the Lebanese Civil War—Karami's Leadership in the North

The city of Tripoli began to decline in the mid-nineteenth century.[1] In less than a hundred years, it had become the "always less" city—less economic activity due to the growth of the port of Beirut, less prestige with the loss of its status as an Ottoman provincial capital, and less regional influence following the creation of Greater Lebanon in 1920. With the French mandate, Tripoli experienced the same phenomenon as did *Bilad al-Sham* in general—a weakening of power through territorial amputation and a loss of influence. Its marginalization was complete when its hinterland was appended to Syria and its trade links with Lattaqiyyeh, Homs, Hama, and Aleppo severed. Isolated, its inhabitants' self-perception was that of a Sunni minority outpost in the Lebanese state. At a time when the Sunni elite of Beirut foresaw the pragmatic benefits they could gain from the new state,[2] the notables of Tripoli sought to regain their majority status in the political framework of Greater Syria. To this end, they would have to recreate the space known as *Bilad al-Sham*.

[1] For a history of Tripoli up to 1947, see Nur al-Din al-Miqati, *Trablus fi al-qarn al-awwal min al-qarn al-'ashrin* [Tripoli in the first half of the twentieth century] (Tripoli: Dar al-Insha, 1978).

[2] For a detailed study of Sunni Beirut elites' strategy in that period, see Carla Eddé, *Beyrouth. Naissance d'une capitale (1918–1924)* (Paris: Acte Sud/Sindbad, 2009).

The son of a large family of Muslim legal scholars (*'ulama'*), Abd al-Hamid Karami was the very embodiment of a rebel figure during the mandate. In 1912, at the age of twenty-four, he became a mufti, and in 1918 Faisal's short-lived Arab government appointed him governor of Tripoli. Rejecting the idea of a Lebanese state separate from the rest of Syria, he became one of the champions of the Arab union with Syria. His unionist stance helped turn the city into a bastion of Arab militancy. He financed the first rebellion in northwest Syria in 1919–1922, was briefly arrested by the mandatory power for supporting the Hashemites in 1924, and then once again aided the Syrian revolt of 1925.[3] Desire for unification with Syria gradually gave way to aspirations of national independence. In November 1943, after being taken prisoner by the French along with the other prominent figures of the independence movement, he was able to rally to the Lebanese cause without losing face. He became a member of parliament and then later prime minister for a brief period in 1945. An old rule of political survival took hold of this Arabist leader of Tripoli: all notables, regardless of their degree of ideological radicalism, must participate in national politics, or else lose their status as "notable." The political leader (*za'im*, pl. *zu'ama'*) rewards his political base with state money.[4] Accordingly, a *za'im* cannot hold a grudge against the state for too long, lest he lose access to the financial resources by which he retains his power on the ground.

When Abd al-Hamid died in 1950, his son Rashid inherited his position as notable. In 1955 Rashid became, at the age of thirty, the youngest prime minister in Lebanese history. From 1951 to 1972, he won every legislative election in Tripoli, even facing down a serious challenge from President Camille Chamoun, who had attempted in 1957 to rig elections against him. In the context of the United Arab Republic, the short-lived union between Egypt and Syria that had been declared a few months before under Nasser's authority, the Nasserist-leaning streets of Tripoli played a key role in the

[3] See Nadine Méouchy, "Les temps et les territoires de la révolte du Nord (1919–1921)," in *Alep et ses territoires. Fabrique et politique d'une ville 1868–2011* (Beirut and Damascus: Presses de l'IFPO, 2014).

[4] Naomi Joy Weinberger rightly observed that the "socioeconomic basis of a *za'im*'s influence, derived from landed properties or clannish enterprises in the towns, was increased through his ability to provide patronage while holding public office." *Syrian Intervention in Lebanon: The 1975–76 Civil War* (Oxford: Oxford University Press), 92.

outbreak of the mini-civil war of 1958 that provoked Chamoun's departure. During that conflict, Karami was one of the leaders of an insurgency that lasted almost four months. His fighters, firmly entrenched in the old town, withstood a siege by security forces loyal to President Chamoun. For historian Khaled Ziadeh, Tripoli thus took its revenge for all the humiliations it had suffered during its decline. The insurgents' "confrontation with armored vehicles revived memories of the 1943 clashes when the French tanks plowed through crowds protesting for independence on the main square and its vicinity."[5]

Ten years later, the failure of Nasserism following the June 1967 defeat weakened Rashid Karami's *zu'ama'* to the advantage of leftist political organizations favoring the Palestinian cause. The *effendi* of Tripoli would pay a high price for the loss of Nasser's Arab leadership, for the latter's powerful though distant charisma helped preserve the autonomy of local elites, mobilizing the masses for rather than against them. After 1967, however, it was not a politically united Tripoli that decided, on its own, to influence its regional Arab sphere and assert itself against the Lebanese state. Instead, the increasing polarization of Arab politics gradually encroached on Tripoli—penetrating the privacy of its social fabric, changing the local equilibrium, bypassing the increasingly outdated traditional leadership—all factors that risked throwing the entire city and its surroundings into a much more violent state of upheaval than in the past.

Tripoli's Military Resurgence from the Late 1960s to the War

In the late sixties, Tripoli was the scene of intense militancy. An amalgam of Marxist references, slogans backing the Palestinian cause, and a desire for social reform shaped the political discourse of the period. After the defeat of June 1967, portraits of Nasser disappeared from the urban scene. In 1968, Palestinian commandos established bases in southern Lebanon along the border with Israel.

[5] Khaled Ziadeh, *Yuwm al-jum'a, yuwm al-ahad. Maqati' min sirat madinat 'ala-l-bahr al-abyad al-mutawassit* [Friday, Sunday. Fragments of the biography of a Mediterranean city] (Beirut: Dar al-Nahar, 1994), 127.

In North Lebanon, Arafat and his deputy commander-in-chief in Fatah, Khalil al-Wazir (Abu Jihad), relied on the politicized segment of Tripoli's population to penetrate Lebanese society more generally. After Black September (1970) and the PLO's military defeat in Jordan, the Palestinian leadership began to prioritize harmonious relations with the local community. In executing this strategy, they exploited the numerous pockets of resentment in Lebanese society—especially among Muslims—in order to create the local alliances they had lacked in Jordan. In a climate of social tension and political clamoring, this was relatively easy to achieve.

Fatah helped Faruq al-Muqaddem, the son of an illustrious Tripolitan family (rivals to the Karami family),[6] establish the first training camp in the North, the "Hittin Base." The camp was near the town of Jeyroun, on the steep slopes of Dinniyeh, an area accessible only by donkey. Al-Muqaddem coordinated with Fatah to provide military training to volunteers from the refugee camps and the poor neighborhoods of Tripoli. Hittin provided a setting where those engaged in the Palestinian struggle could meet those excluded from the Lebanese "miracle," who exhibited the social rage that is felt by all disfranchised people. As in the other main coastal towns, part of the population lived in tune with the "Palestinian revolution," in an atmosphere of high tension and frequent run-ins with the army.

After clashes between the army and Fatah in October 1969, and despite the ban imposed by the government then headed by Rashid Karami, Faruq al-Muqaddem committed his group to participate in a demonstration of solidarity with the Palestinians on October 24, 1969. Violence between demonstrators and the army resulted in four deaths, and the seventeen days of fighting that followed paralyzed the city. Muqaddem's supporters, aided by Fatah, occupied the citadel of Tripoli in Abu Samra and set up a radio station. Very quickly, the movement found Arab legitimization. In solidarity with al-Muqaddem, the Syrian government closed its northern border

---

[6] Faruq al-Muqaddem's grandfather had been an ally of the French during the mandate period. His father, Nafiz al-Muqaddem, a parliamentarian, was assassinated in Tripoli during a nationalist riot on May 14, 1948, the day that the State of Israel was proclaimed. For a more detailed description of this period in Tripoli, see Joumana al-Soufi, "Lutte populaire armée. De la désobéissance civile au combat pour Dieu" (PhD diss., New Sorbonne University, Paris-III, 1988).

with Lebanon. Nasser then offered to mediate, and the urban insurrection ended on November 2. The same day, the government and the PLO signed the Cairo Agreement, which included a provision for the dissolution of the Jeyroun base. Faced with this perceived "betrayal," al-Muqaddem and his supporters refused to return the citadel to state control. Nasser again intervened to obtain legal guarantees for the insurgents and officially invited al-Muqaddem to Cairo, recognizing his new role as Tripoli's *za'im*. Things calmed down and al-Muqaddem's "group" went on to become the Progressive and Socialist October 24 Movement—better known as the October 24 Movement.

Another of Rashid Karami's adversaries was a physician, Abd al-Majid al-Rafi'i. Born into a large family of ulemas scattered across Palestine, Syria, and Egypt, al-Rafi'i was a notable engaged in social justice. The head of the Iraqi Ba'ath party, he was best known for his humanitarian activities, which included establishing many clinics in poor Lebanese neighborhoods. No doubt buoyed by support from those he had aided, he was elected to parliament in 1972, obtaining more votes than Rashid Karami.[7]

Al-Muqaddem and al-Rafi'i were populist leaders hailing from highly respected upper-class families. They challenged Karami's leadership in order to reinstate their previous leadership. There were also leaders of low birth, who were often despised by the upper-class populists. In the underprivileged neighborhood of Bab al-Tabbaneh, Ali 'Akkawi, a baker's son, began to organize an antiestablishment revolt in the late sixties to denounce the shortage of hospitals, schools, vaccination programs, and the like. He also tried to encourage a peasants' movement in the Akkar against the landowning class supported by the state. While he was in prison (where he died in 1974), his brother Khalil took up the torch of the revolt that Ali began. In 1972, with support from Fatah, Khalil founded the Popular Resistance (al-Muqawama al-Sha'biyya), which was at the forefront of social dissent before the outbreak of the 1975 war. More than the great ideologies of the moment—Nasserism, the

---

[7] He was not only elected with fewer votes than his opponent al-Rafi'i, but for the first time in his electoral history he also failed to get four candidates from his list elected. In Lebanon, voters are called to elect their representatives on a communal basis and may compose their own list by deleting names. The authority of a *za'im* is measured by his ability to bring all of his fellow candidates to office.

Palestinian cause, Islamism—what drove Khalil 'Akkawi was the simple wish to defend his neighborhood.[8] The Popular Resistance was organized on an urban militia model, whereby youth would acquire basic military training in the neighboring Fatah-run Baddawi camp. In the early seventies, Palestinians also played a part in setting up an Islamist fighting group in Abu Samra, which would be known in 1975 by the name "Jund Allah" (the Army of God).

Right from the beginning of the war, in 1975, rebel groups in Tripoli besieged police stations and declared "civil disobedience." The October 24 Movement retook the citadel, where it established its headquarters and a radio station broadcasting in Arabic and French. Fatah took control of the more lucrative enterprises—the port and the oil refinery. Old tensions with the mountain suburb of Zghorta erupted into armed clashes between Sunni "progressives" from Tripoli and "conservative" Christians regrouped into President Suleiman Frangieh's Christian militia.[9]

Beginning in January 1976, Palestinians from the PLA under Syrian army control deployed into the region as a peacekeeping force. When the Syrian army entered the region in November 1976, all of these militant activities came to an abrupt halt. The effervescent atmosphere of partisan fervor vanished, and all political parties were banned except the Syrian Social Nationalist Party (SSNP). The October 24 Movement evacuated the citadel, and its radio station ceased broadcasting. Fatah cautiously retreated to its natural bases—the Palestinian camps of Nahr al-Bared to the north of Tripoli, and Baddawi on the city's outskirts.

The Rise of the Alawites

The Lebanese Alawites, who lived in certain villages of Akkar and in the Ba'al Mohsen neighborhood of Tripoli, came originally from the Jabal Ansarieh (still called the "Alawite mountain") to the northwest of Syria, and they belong to the same tribes as their Syrian

[8] See the classic text by the late Michel Seurat, "Le quartier de Bâb Tebbâné à Tripoli (Liban): étude d'une 'asabiyya urbaine" in *Mouvements communautaires et espaces urbains au Machrek* (Beirut: Centre d' Etudes et de Recherches sur le Moyen-Orient Contemporain, 1985.)

[9] Suleiman Frangieh was himself originally from Zghorta. He was a friend of Assad and a proponent of a military solution against the Palestinians.

coreligionists. In 1972, a movement of young Alawites, the Movement of Alawite Youth (Harakat al-Sha'biyya al-Alawiyya) formed in Tripoli to reclaim the status of a "religious community"—a *sine qua non* for political existence in a country where citizenship is mediated by the confessional community (at the time, an Alawite had to convert to Sunnism to become a civil servant). At the end of the year, a certain Ali Eid, originally from Ba'al Mohsen, "the very figure of these political adventurers that the region got us accustomed to,"[10] took control of the movement with a goal of mobilizing the Alawite community of the city and the Akkar plain—an area with a population of around 30,000 inhabitants at that time. This undertaking was made possible by Eid's privileged relationship with President Frangieh's family—which was very close to the Assads in Syria. This proximity allowed him to incorporate his community into the regional system and to turn it into a kind of satellite for the Syrian regime in North Lebanon. He thus obtained, in the early 1970s, the naturalization of 20,000 Alawites originally from Syria, then consolidated his confessional hold by becoming the patron of his community.

The Alawites of North Lebanon also indirectly helped to provide the Hafez al-Assad regime with Islamic legitimacy through the most charismatic figure of the Lebanese Shi'ite community, Imam Musa al-Sadr. In July 1973, speaking from a hotel in Tripoli in his capacity as chairman of the Supreme Islamic Shi'ite Council (SISC), as-Sadr recognized the Lebanese Alawites as belonging to Twelver Shi'a Islam.[11] As a Shi'ite religious leader, he was acceding to a request from President Assad, who was threatened by Sunni protests in Homs, Hama, and Aleppo following the January 1973 publication of a constitutional draft in which the drafters "forgot" to grant Islam the status of state religion.[12] The initiative by the Shi'a imam might also be read as an attempt to gain control over the Alawites of Lebanon and thus to subvert the political ambitions of Ali Eid. The latter then developed a close relationship with Rif'at al-Assad, brother of the Syrian president and chief of the defense

[10] Seurat, "Le quartier," 138.

[11] Martin Kramer, "Syria's Alawis and Shi'ism," in *Shi'ism, Resistance, and Revolution*, ed. Martin Kramer (Boulder, CO: Westview Press, 1987), 237–54.

[12] For the Sunni protestors, the stakes mostly involved preventing a non-Islamic minority from imposing its hegemony over the Syrian state.

brigades (*saraya al-difaʿ*), who was also a proponent of a community mobilization of all the Alawites of the region in defense of the Syrian regime. During the Syrian army's invasion of Tripoli in November 1976, Ali Eid allowed one of Rifʿat al-Assad's sons to plunder the port and the refinery. Others among Eid's supporters specialized in various mafia-like activities, such as setting up protection rackets, carrying out assassinations, and kidnapping for ransom. Under the supervision of its new leader, the community gained a vehicle for expression with the 1982 formation of the Arab Democratic Party. They added an armed militia as well, the Red Knights, to whom the Alawite soldiers in the Syrian army always offered a fighting hand. The Baʿal Mohsen neighborhood, which overlooks Bab al-Tabbaneh, became the symbolic heart of this community, which was now unified both politically and geographically. All throughout the Lebanese conflict, Ali Eid's militia served as an auxiliary corps, supporting all of the actions carried out against the Syrian regime's enemies in North Lebanon—among them Fatah, the Islamists, the Iraqi Baʿath, and the combatants of Bab al-Tabbaneh. At the war's end in 1990, with Lebanon completely under Syrian hegemony, Eid's zeal would be rewarded. The Alawites received recognition as the country's eighteenth religious community.

The Struggle between the Syrian Regime and Fatah

From the early 1970s until the 1990s, North Lebanon served as the key battleground in the conflict between the Palestinian Liberation Organization (PLO) and the Syrian regime. Once Syria began to see itself as a regional power, it could no longer tolerate the risk of Palestinian self-affirmation in neighboring Lebanon. First because the creation of a Palestinian power at its border might provoke an Israeli military intervention—a threat to the stability of a regime still fragile since Assad's 1970 takeover. Even more important, the consolidation of Palestinian power in Lebanon would instill a climate of revolutionary discord that would inevitably reverberate inside Syria, where the new Alawite president held little legitimacy in the eyes of the majority Sunni population. Finally, if the PLO acquired a territorial base in the Middle East, it might develop an independent diplomatic policy favorable to a peace treaty with Israel—eventually isolating Syria within the region. Whether moderate or radical, the mere idea of autonomous Palestinian leadership was extremely worrisome to Syrian leaders.

Faced with these threats, Syria had to obtain control over the PLO in order to enhance the regime's Arab legitimacy and gain crucial regional influence in the Middle East. This Syrian desire for control would clash with an opposite desire, the principle of the "independence of the Palestinian decision" that was promoted by Yasser Arafat, president of the PLO and leader of Fatah—his strongest constituency. Indeed, escaping Syrian tutelage was one of Arafat's main goals. Not only did he strive to frustrate the hegemonic ambitions of the Syrian regime, but he also knew how to leverage internal Syrian affairs so as to weaken Hafez al-Assad. North Lebanon has always served as a geographic launching pad for such initiatives.

When the Lebanese civil war broke out in 1975, Syrian intervention (in June 1976) prevented a likely military victory by the "Islamo-progressive" camp—consisting of an alliance between Kamal Joumblatt's Lebanese National Movement and the PLO—over the Christian forces self-identified as champions of the Lebanese cause. Thereafter, political and military struggle between the Syrian regime and the PLO was the only constant throughout a conflict that would last fifteen years and witness constantly shifting alliances.

In the spring of 1983, the Syrian regime fomented an anti-Arafat rebellion within Fatah. Their goal was to eliminate Arafat because of his recognition of UN Security Council Resolution 242 and his support for the Fez Initiative a few months after the Israeli invasion of Lebanon and the PLO's departure from Beirut. During the summer, Palestinian dissidents joined by Ahmad Jibril's Popular Front for the Liberation of Palestine-General Command and Saiqa (both organic allies of the Damascus regime), and aided by the Syrian army, stormed Fatah loyalists' positions in the Bekka valley. Colonel Qaddafi's Libya joined Hafez al-Assad and funneled financial and military support to the dissidents. In September, Arafat went from Tunis to North Lebanon and organized a "sea bridge" between Cyprus and Tripoli through which "a steady flow of PLO personnel, weapons, vehicles, and non-combat supplies was arriving by sea."[13]

The Palestinian dissidents' offensive, led by Syrian officers, began on November 2. Fatah was forced to leave camp Nahr al-Bared on November 6 in order to regroup in Tripoli. From Fatah's Zahriyya headquarters, protected by the old city and the Bab al-Tabbaneh district, Arafat mobilized supporters in Tripoli by evoking the Syrian army's destruction of Hama in February 1982. Camp Baddawi would fall on November 9, thanks to a decisive intervention by Syrian commandos. On December 20, Arafat evacuated North Lebanon through the port of Tripoli, under the protection of the French army.[14] Forced to flee Syrian bombing by taking to the sea, Arafat would nonetheless continue to take action against his most formidable Arab enemy. Meanwhile, Damascus's Palestinian allies occupied the camps Arafat left behind, where they continue to exert a very strong influence, despite their patron's withdrawal in April 2005.

The Struggle between the Syrian Regime and the City of Tripoli

In 1985 and 1986, North Lebanon was home to another kind of struggle—just as violent—which pitted the Syrian regime and its Lebanese allies against the rebel districts of Tripoli. Although these districts retained relationships with, and continued to receive covert aid from, Fatah, they had by this point mixed their support for the Palestinian cause with a zeal for militant Islamism very much inspired by the 1979 Iranian revolution.[15]

On August 25, 1982, when the country had suffered the brunt of the Israeli invasion, an imam from a mosque in the old city, named Sayyid Sha'ban, proclaimed the birth of the Islamic Unification Movement (Harakat al-Tawhid al-Islami)—more commonly

[13] Yezid Sayigh, *Armed Struggle and the Search for State: The Palestinian National Movement, 1949–1993* (Oxford: Oxford University Press, 2000), 570.

[14] A few months after this event, the Syrian vice president, Abd al-Halim Khaddam, confided in the French minister of foreign affairs, Claude Cheysson: "The one thing for which we cannot forgive you is allowing Arafat to leave. We *had* him!" In Gilles Ménages, *L'oeil du pouvoir*, vol. 3, *La France face au terrorisme moyen-oriental* (Paris: Fayard, 2001), 228.

[15] On Islamism in Tripoli, see Muhammad Abi Samra, *Tripoli: Sahat Allah wa al-Mina' al-Haditha* [Allah Square and the modern port] (Beirut: Dar al-Nahar, 2011).

known as Tawhid. He federated the activities of three groups, all from neighborhoods with proximity to Fatah: Khalil 'Akkawi's Popular Resistance, Kana'an Naji's Jund Allah, and Ismat Mrad's Movement for an Arab Lebanon. Because of the experience they had gained since 1976 from the city's Syrian occupation, their personal and ideological ties to Fatah, and above all, their keen desire to retain local sovereignty over "their" neighborhoods, these groups provided military support to Arafat during his confrontations in the autumn of 1983.

Yet, the movement experienced much internal strife. Sheikh Sha 'ban benefited from a privileged relationship with the heads of the Islamic Republic of Iran, never missing a single anti-imperialist conference. He aimed to duplicate the Iranian model in Tripoli by forbidding alcohol and imposing strict Islamic rules on the population. In October 1983, Hashem Minqara, emir of the local al-Mina (port) district, murdered twenty-eight communist militants on charges of atheism, which prompted Khalil 'Akkawi and Kana'an Naji to withdraw from the Tawhid.

On a regional level, Syrian leaders could not allow Tripoli to fall out of their military and political control, because it might later be used as a bridgehead for a new Arafat strategy. So in the fall of 1985, they mobilized their local allies to attack Tripoli. Faced with this external menace, the Tawhid regrouped and began fighting on September 14. The battle—which resulted in over five hundred deaths and thousands injured—ended on October 6, when four Syrian army battalions entered Tripoli.[16] Negotiations between revolutionary Iran and Syrian leaders allowed Sheikh Sha'ban and his organization to survive, on the condition that they cooperate with the Syrian regime or suffer a new wave of repression. According to the terms of a political and military accord signed in Damascus on October 3, 1985, the movement surrendered its heavy weaponry to the Syrian army and placed its light weaponry in a depot under Syrian army surveillance. Sheikh Sha'ban was prepared to give up all political autonomy in order to remain leader of a militia, although he would retain no power other than that of approving the Syrian regime's or Hezbollah's positions in Lebanese politics. Although the October 3

[16] For more on this part of the war, see Jubin M. Goodarzi, *Syria and Iran: Diplomatic Alliance and Power Politics in the Middle East* (London and New York: Tauris Academic Studies, 2006), 152–57.

agreement officially recognized the principle of freedom of expression for all parties, the Syrian army continued its campaign of mass arrests of Tawhid members.

In January 1986, Samir Ja'ja' ousted Elie Hobeika from the Christian Lebanese Forces, annulling the tripartite accord signed in Damascus on December 28, 1985, by Hobeika, the Amal militia, and the PSP. The Syrians, the only power with the authority to designate enemies on Lebanese territory and have such designations endorsed by others, asked Tawhid's most respected leader and the head of the Popular Resistance, Khalil 'Akkawi, to take their side against the Christian Lebanese Forces, headed by Samir Ja'Ja'. 'Akkawi refused, and on February 9, 1986, he was assassinated in the Abu Samra neighborhood of Tripoli following a stormy meeting, during which a Syrian intelligence officer accused him of treason. After this incident, several hundred Tawhid members sought refuge in Sidon, where Fatah protected them in the Miye-Miye and Ayn al-Helweh camps.

Former Tawhid members helped create a new clandestine military organization called the February 9 Movement (Harakat Tis'a Shbat—the anniversary of Khalil 'Akkawi's death), which grouped all those opposed to Sheikh Sayyid Sha'ban's pro-Syrian path. Members of the February 9 Movement were present in North Lebanon, East Beirut, and Sidon, where Fatah hosted them in the Abra neighborhood and the Ayn al-Helweh camp. They announced themselves by executing deadly attacks against Syrian soldiers at different checkpoints, particularly at Rmeileh, the entrance to the capital of southern Lebanon. Acting on instructions from Yasser Arafat, the February 9 Movement also attempted to obstruct a Syrian "security plan" in West Beirut in July 1986.

During the same period, part of the organization moved from the Dinniyeh mountains to Tripoli in hopes of regaining control of the Bab al-Tabbaneh neighborhood. Syrian forces knew of the plan, however, and preempted it with a helicopter assault on Bab al-Tabbaneh. After two days of fighting, Tawhid members were forced to retreat despite Hashem Minqara and Kana'an Naji's attempt to distract Syrian forces by attacking them in Dinniyeh. On December 19, 1986, Syrian soldiers and several of their auxiliaries from Ahmad Fakhr al-Din's Tripoli Resistance Group and Ali Eid's Arab Democratic Party took revenge against residents of the neighborhood, reportedly indiscriminately killing at least 250 people.[17] The "massacre of Bab al-Tabbaneh" (*majzarat bab al-tabbane*) as it became known in local Tripolitan memory, was the height of a campaign to "root out the weeds," in the words of the chief of Syrian intelligence in Lebanon.[18] Two sieges (1983 and 1985) and one massacre (1986) explain why "Tripoli residents developed a special hatred of Syrian Ba'athists and Syrian-aligned groups."[19] From the mid-1980's, "Syrian intelligence monitored the city scrupulously, using blackmail to acquire local informants, and Sunnis felt threatened by Alawite immigration."[20]

North Lebanon after the Lebanese Civil War
Setting Up Transnational Salafism in North Lebanon

The second occupation of Tripoli by Syrian troops in 1985 induced a wave of departures to what would later become the three main poles of influence over North Lebanon: the Gulf, the city of Peshawar in Pakistan, and certain Western capitals.

Dozens of young people from the Islamist movement were able to enroll in Saudi Universities, especially the Islamic University of Medina.[21] Under the influence of their Wahhabist teachers, they learned a Salafi Islam that advocated a return to the "pious ancestors" (*al-salaf al-sahih*). Using the sayings and actions (*hadith*) of the

---

[17] Officially led by a Sunni businessman from Tripoli, Tareq Fakhr al-Din, the Tripoli Resistance Group (*muqawamat trablus*) was a militia formed by the Syrian intelligence services to provide them with a military instrument within the local Sunni community that would prevent their having to rely solely on Ali Eid's Alawite group to do their dirty work. Protected by his powerful backers, Fakhr al-Din is today a prosperous businessman who owns the Palma Beach Resort, "a haven of serenity on the shores of North Lebanon," according to its Facebook page.

[18] Syrian General Ghazi Kana'an used the expression in a press conference on December 31, 1986, in Tripoli. Quoted in the Chronological Series of the Center for Studies of the Modern Arab World (CEMAM) of the University of Saint Joseph 10 (1993): *Évolution socio-culturelle au Proche-Orient. Les faits et les idées* (1986).

[19] William Harris, *Faces of Lebanon: Sects, Wars and Global Extensions* (Princeton, NJ: Markus Wiener Publishers, 1996), 209.

[20] Harris, *Faces of Lebanon*, 213.

[21] Some seventy years before, in the 1920s, Sheikh Rashid Rida (1865–1935), an important reformist figure born in Qalamoun near Tripoli, had transformed himself into an enthusiastic proponent of the Wahhabi creed. See *al-Wahhabiun wa al-Hijaz* [The Wahhabites and the Hijaz] (Egypt: al-Manar Publishing, 1925), a compilation of articles published in *al-Manar* and *al-Ahram* in support of the Saudi dynasty.

Prophet and his companions, the Salafi sheikhs staked their owner-
ship over Islam, claiming to understand the religion exactly as it
had been understood and applied by the first generations of Muslims. On campus, in Medina, the young Lebanese and Palestinians from North Lebanon learned of the importance of the notion
of divine unity (*tawhid*). Having been socialized in conditions of
excessive war and militancy, this notion became the filter through
which their religious beliefs (*'aqida*) became cleansed of the impu-
rities of their pasts.

At the end of the Lebanese civil war, these students of Lebanese
and Palestinian origin, freshly graduated from the Islamic University, returned to North Lebanon with countless Salafi connections
worldwide.[22] Upon their arrival in Lebanon, they would take it
upon themselves to spread the "true Islam" they had learned in the
Arabian Peninsula. Thanks to their extensive networks, they considerably influenced the religious landscape of Tripoli and North
Lebanon, working to extend Salafism by promoting Islamic standards of morality. Women wearing *niqab* or *khimar* walked down
Tripoli streets, something that had never been seen before. The
larger teaching network at that time was founded by Da'i al-Islam
al-Shahhal, the son of a local sheikh who had been close to Abd
al-Aziz Ibn Baz, the former mufti of Saudi Arabia. Graduated from
Medina University in 1984, Da'i came back to Tripoli in 1990 to
establish a religious association, the Association for Islamic Guidance and Charity (Jama'iyya al-Hidaya wa al-Ihsan al-Islamiyya),
which was responsible for a *madrasa* of the same name (Ma'had al-
Hidaya wa al-Ihsan). Much more in tune with the Saudi religious
establishment, his cousin, Hassan al-Shahhal, directed the Institute
for Preaching and Orientation (Ma'had al-Da'wa wa al-Irshad),
which was closely associated with the Saudi Ministry of Education.

After the Gulf War in 1991, Salafi circles of North Lebanon mir-
rored the divisions in Saudi Salafi circles. Da'i al-Islam al-Shahhal
and a few others followed the Saudi Sahwa Islamiyya (Islamic Awakening), which strongly criticized both the king and the religious es-

[22] See Zoltan Pall, *Lebanese Salafis between the Gulf and Europe: Development, Frac-
tionalization and Transnational Networks of Salafism in Lebanon* (Amsterdam: Amsterdam
University Press, 2013). On the history of Salafism's implantation in North Lebanon and its
diverse expressions, see Robert G. Rabil, *Salafism in Lebanon: From Apoliticism to Transnational Jihadism* (Washington, DC: Georgetown University Press, 2014).

tablishment for their decision to invite US forces to the kingdom after Saddam Hussein's invasion of Kuwait.[23] Da'i befriended the main protagonists of protest in the kingdom, such as Safar al-Hawali, Nasir al-'Umar, and Salman al-'Awda. Under their influence, he adopted the principle of the "comprehension of reality" (*fiqh al-waqi'*), according to which believers are required to understand the political questions and contexts that confront the umma instead of concentrating exclusively on moral issues relating to everyday existence. Critically, this attitude implied a potential challenge to the principle of blind obedience to those who wield political authority (*wali al-amr*)—a core principle of Wahhabi doctrine. Along with other sheikhs, Da'i became one of the main proponents of an activist (*haraki*) trend within local Salafism, one that is mainly concerned with the broader umma and attempts to avoid troubles with local authorities. The Saudi al-Haramayn Association financed this strain until the Saudi authorities dissolved the group on June 8, 2004. Afterward, the Qatari Sheikh Eid Charitable Institution (Mu'assasat al-Sheikh 'Id al-Khairiyya) took over the task of helping *haraki* networks and personalities in North Lebanon.[24]

In the 1990s, Tripoli also witnessed the return of those who had gone to fight in Afghanistan with the Palestinian sheikh Abdallah Azzam. Consistent with his territorial vision of the umma, Azzam considered that jihad for the "liberation of Muslim lands" was a vital duty for every Muslim. He created a recruitment structure called the Bureau of Services (Maktab al-Khadamat) to facilitate sending volunteers to Peshawar. One of these volunteers, a young Tripolitan named Bassam al-Kanj, resolved to continue Azzam's work when he returned from Afghanistan to Tripoli—after a stay in Bosnia—in 1996.

In 1997, al-Kanj created recruitment cells to prepare volunteers for war against Russia in Chechnya. To this end, he established a military training camp in the rugged mountains of Dinniyeh. This camp came into being nearly thirty years after Fatah established a similar camp nearby, with the notable difference that the training here was intended for military action in the Caucasus, not in

---

[23] On the role of the Sahwa movement within the Salafi religious field, see Stéphane Lacroix, *Awakening Islam: The Politics of Religious Dissent in Contemporary Saudi Arabia* (Cambridge: Harvard University Press, 2011).

[24] Pall, *Lebanese Salafis*, 36.

Palestine. On New Year's Eve, 2000, unexpected clashes with the Lebanese army halted completion of this project. After a week of fighting, the network was dismantled, and a wave of arrests decimated Islamist ranks in Tripoli and North Lebanon generally.

Haraki Salafism was also weakened by suspicions of collusion with jihadism and by the growth of rival Salafi institutions from Kuwait, both in Tripoli and elsewhere in the North. A local branch of the Kuwaiti charity called the Revival of Islamic Heritage Society (Jama'iyyat Ihya al-Turath al-Islami) benefited from Kuwaiti wealth to increase its activities. In contrast to *haraki* Salafism, which focuses on political action, this "scientific Salafism" (*'ilmi*) prioritizes preaching (*da'wa*) and avoids involvement in the umma's political affairs—except when preaching justifies political participation—and does not question the legitimacy of those in power. By relying on a network of mosques, religious institutes, and clinics, it furthered the integration of Salafism into the daily lives of the region's inhabitants.

A new element was also added in the cartography of Lebanese Salafism, one that connected it with the European continent. After Syrian troops entered Tripoli in 1986, followed by a crackdown especially aimed at the Islamic Unification Movement's militia (Tawhid), several hundred militants obtained political asylum in Denmark. Lebanese and Palestinian émigrés from North Lebanon met in basement mosques in Copenhagen, especially in the former working-class neighborhood of Norrebro in the capital's northeast, nicknamed "Little Arabia" due to its high Arab and Middle Eastern immigrant population. Some converted to the most radical forms of Salafism associated with the central al-Tawba mosque, sending all manner of things (fatwas, money, information) to North Lebanon. Others became quietist Salafi sheikhs, condemning the use of violence and instead devoting themselves to defending the faith conceived in all its purity.

Among them, a Salafi sheikh from North Lebanon, Ra'ed Hlayhel, became a Salafi imam in Aarhus, Denmark's second largest city, after having been granted political asylum in 2000. A graduate of the University of Medina, where he studied from 1989 to 1993, and known for his sermons inveighing against the West's moral decadence (described as hostile to Islam), Hlayhel strove to arouse indignation in the Muslim world over cartoons of Prophet

Muhammad that were published in the Danish daily newspaper *Jyllands-Posten* on September 30, 2005.[25] In this endeavor he was joined by Sheikh Abu Laban, an activist in Egypt's Gama'a Islami-yya, also a political refugee in Denmark, and Ahmad 'Akkari, a fellow Lebanese living in Aarhus. Hailing from Akkar, as his pat-ronymic indicates, he was able to obtain a humanitarian residency permit in 1994, through the intercession of Danish humanitarian organizations. Hlayhel became the president of the European Com-mittee for Prophet Honoring, founded by his associates and him-self. The group put together a forty-page dossier—"Dossier about championing the prophet Muhammad—peace be upon him"—to explain to the Muslim World the situation of Muslims in Eu-rope and the offense against Islam that publication of the cartoons represented.[26]

Returning to Tripoli at the end of 2005, Hlayhel was one of the organizers of the demonstration of anger that took place on Sunday, February 5, 2006, in front of the Danish consulate in the Christian neighborhood of Achrafieh, in East Beirut. Salafi insti-tutes in Tripoli and Akkar supervised free transportation of volun-teers to the capital by bus and van, including among them many determined participants from the Palestinian camps of Baddawi and Nahr al-Bared. In the course of this particular day, demonstra-tors not only set fire to the Danish consulate. They also vandalized automobiles and shops, to the great alarm of the neighborhood population, which remained trapped at home until the riot was over. The day before, in Damascus, an angry crowd had set fire to the Danish embassy in the Abu Ramaneh district. The mass dem-onstration, which the regime authorized in this exceptional case, also attacked the French and American embassies. After traveling to Cairo himself to meet senior al-Azhar dignitaries in December 2005, Sheikh Hlayhel did not neglect to send his associate Ahmad 'Akkari to preach the word of God in the Syrian capital—defense of the prophet being deemed more important at the time than the Salafis' principled hostility toward the Alawites (known as

[25] For the context surrounding the Muhammad cartoons issue, see Gilles Kepel, "The Propaganda Battle in Europe," in *Beyond Terror and Martyrdom: The Future of the Middle East* (Cambridge: Harvard University Press, 2008).

[26] A copy of the "Akkari-Laban dossier" can be found on Wikipedia. http://en.wikipedia .org/wiki/Akkari-Laban_dossier (accessed November 23, 2014).

"Nusayris" in the Salafi lexicon).[27] Syrian leaders seized the opportunity to put the Hariri camp and the pro-Western March 14 Movement in a tight spot. Only days prior to the second commemoration of the assassination of Rafiq al-Hariri, they could pose as champions of the Muslim religion and its offended prophet.

A POTENTIAL THREAT FOR THE SYRIAN REGIME

Since the mid-1980s, the Syrian regime has aimed to divide the population of North Lebanon. Its leadership long conceived of this part of Lebanon, with Tripoli as its capital, as an extension of its own society and therefore as warranting special treatment. The area's unique connections with Syrian cities, such as Homs and Aleppo, and its Sunni communal identity explain why North Lebanon has always been of keen interest to the Assad regime, both in Syria itself and in the context of Syria's lengthy occupation of Lebanon. Beginning in 2000, the Hariri family attempted to counter Syrian policy in the region by working to unify its control over the Sunni community—and over North Lebanon in particular. This strategy was crucial to the family's national and regional legitimacy, as part of their aspirations to free the Sunni community in Lebanon from the grip of powerful regional actors, such as Syria and Iran.

From 1976 to 2005, the Syrian security apparatus exercised direct control over North Lebanon. The region itself is of exceptional political and religious importance, hosting the full spectrum of militant Sunni Islamist ideological currents, including the Syrian and Lebanese Muslim Brotherhoods, Salafi networks, jihadi networks, al-Qaeda connections, the pro-Iranian Islamic Unification Movement (Tawhid), and others. Moreover, Sunni Muslims living in the area maintain close ties with Lebanese expatriate communities that left for Europe and Australia in the 1980s. These extended networks ensure the region's economic survival and also exert significant influence on the community. As for the Syrian secret services and their various Lebanese collaborators, including those within the Lebanese security apparatus, for them the region is simply a Lebanese appendage of "Greater Syria" and a threat to their domination of both Lebanese and Syrian societies.

[27] After the name of the founder of this esoteric sect, Ibn Nusaïr, who lived in the ninth century.

The Syrian regime also established and consolidated itself during, and by way of, the Lebanese civil war. The war did more than provide the regime with the regional legitimacy and economic rent essential to its survival. Lebanon also served as a laboratory that enabled the regime to accumulate savoir-faire in the art of "governing" a Levantine society. By leveraging this founding experience, the regime has become adept at manipulating religious fears, nourishing internal divisions, and eliminating "politics" from its deliberative dimension, that is, its ability to raise individuals and groups above their primordial attachments.

As such, the regime's unwavering willingness to control the Palestinian cause is not merely reflective of strategic calculations. It comes from a deeper, almost instinctive ferocity vis-à-vis the pluralism of opinions and currents that comprise the Palestinian political universe. Notwithstanding the differences between the Palestinian and Lebanese political scenes—including the existence of national integration without territory in the Palestinian case, and a territory without national integration in the Lebanese context—their respective corrupt, extraverted, voluble, and pluralistic natures were deemed by Syrian political elites to pose a threat. This perceived threat arose precisely because of the temptations and nostalgic longing the regime feared could be incited within the Syrian territory of *Bilad al-Sham*, whose population was presumed prone to enticement by that which it had not been able to experience within the authoritarian framework of the Assad regime.

North Lebanon as a Strategic Political Space
HARIRI'S ENDEAVOR

Since 2000, the Hariri family had sought to counter Syrian policy by unifying its control over the North, an objective crucial to the family's national and regional legitimacy. Close to the Saudi royal family, Rafiq al-Hariri became a construction tycoon in the kingdom during the seventies and eighties. Prime minister of Lebanon from 1992 until 1998, and again from 2000 to 2004, he clashed with new Syrian president Bashar al-Assad as the latter, through his proxies President Emile Lahoud and the pro-Iranian Hezbollah, reacted with great hostility to Hariri's political liberalism and international networks.

Hariri's arrival on the national stage was the result of a combination of strategic and systemic factors. Strategically, Syrian-Saudi cooperation throughout the 1990s explains why Hafez al-Assad accepted the French and American-backed Rafiq al-Hariri as Lebanese prime minister from 1992 to 2000. The Syrian president checked Hariri's international influence by helping Hezbollah's "resistance" against Israeli occupation in southern Lebanon, and by leaving no decisions on strategic issues to the Sunni prime minister. A more systemic explanation takes in the fact that, in the aftermath of the Lebanese civil war, the Lebanese Sunni community could not exist politically without unifying its ranks under a single leadership. Needless to say, in order to confine his ambitions, Syria did not allow Hariri to build a powerbase in North Lebanon. Rafiq al-Hariri was assassinated in February 2005, after reportedly helping to draft UN Resolution 1559 in September 2004, which called for Syrian withdrawal from Lebanon and the disarming of all militias (a clear reference to Hezbollah).

Hariri's death proved sharply divisive for Lebanese politics. Sa'ad confronted the same strategic problems as had his father. On the one hand, he needed to rely on the West to counter the regional system dominated by the Syrian-Iranian alliance. On the other, he had to attempt to win over a Sunni constituency largely hostile to the United States' policy in the Middle East. It is on the local level, in North Lebanon, that one can best measure the success (or failure) of the former prime minister's efforts to create these linkages, despite efforts by his strategic adversaries (Hezbollah, Iran, and the Assad family) or ideological enemies (jihadi groups) to thwart them.

For these reasons, Sa'ad al-Hariri decided, in utmost secrecy, to come to the aid of the Syrian revolution at the end of 2011. By focusing most of his humanitarian and military support on the city of Homs—the Sunni city closest to the Syrian capital, tied by both blood and business to Tripoli—Rafiq al-Hariri's heir bet on the fall of the Syrian regime. The Assad family's demise would allow him to consolidate his status as the official political representative of Sunni Islam in Lebanon. Al-Hariri's decision seems to stem as well from a desire to outflank the Islamist groups also fighting the Syrian regime, whose religious demands could destroy the possibility of a civil political alternative for post-Assad Syria.

This policy has not been risk-free. Since the end of 2011, Bashar al-Assad has repeatedly called for the Lebanese army and Hezbollah to reestablish control of Lebanon's northern border with Syria, and to limit the activities of Sunni groups fighting in Syria's civil war. Along the way, North Lebanon has become a merciless battleground between supporters and opponents of the Syrian regime.

North Lebanon's susceptibility to external influences should be understood in conjunction with the Lebanese state's limited role there during the first two post–civil war decades. The North lacked a strong political backer during this period, and it had no leader figure (*za'im*) powerful enough to attract a significant portion of public funds to the region, or even with the wherewithal to reward a client network for electoral loyalty by providing basic public services. In Lebanon, public developmental structures are, first and foremost, structures of political patronage. Any political actor seeking to consolidate local power must control these services. Thus, the difference between a national leader and a local one is the former's capacity to demand the creation of a public developmental structure, and then to maintain control of it until he dies or passes his authority to a son or other relative. The first prime minister of the post–civil war period was Umar Karami, the brother of Rashid who had been assassinated in 1987, a *za'im* from Tripoli, close to Syrian president Hafez al-Assad. In spite of this proximity, by the time he was removed from this position in 1992 he had not established in his own region an institutional equivalent of the Council for the South (Majlis al-Janub), the public patronage structure that nurtures Nabih Berri's leadership among part of the Shi'a constituency. Umar's successor, Rafiq al-Hariri, focused postwar reconstruction efforts on the capital, and Syria prevented him from exerting political and financial influence in the North.

In this vacuum arose a few Tripolitan strongmen, most often Sunni billionaires from the northern capital, such as Najib Miqati and Muhammad Safadi, who had leveraged their financial resources for political gain. Only they had the private financial means necessary to establish clientele networks via charities and foundations, such as al-Azm wa al-Sa'ada (Miqati), and the eponymous Safadi Foundation. Their entry into parliament, and the connections they then established with certain government ministers, gave them opportunities to recoup the cost of the initial investment that had enabled them to enter the political sphere—just as Rafiq al-Hariri had done some ten years before them in the city of Saida.

Najib Miqati is emblematic of this brand of politician.[28] Appointed public works minister in December 1998—right after Bashar al-Assad ousted Rafiq al-Hariri from his post as prime minister—Miqati was elected to parliament in September 2000. The conditions of his election—his list won fourteen of his constituency's seventeen seats—made him a major political figure in North Lebanon. An ally of Bashar al-Assad, he had just before the election convinced the Syrian president to release two former Tawhid leaders, Hashem Minqara and Samir al-Hassan. A shrewd politician, cultivating an image of moderation, he was appointed caretaker prime minister in March 2005, after Rafiq al-Hariri was assassinated. He returned to parliament after the 2009 legislative elections, in which he had agreed, under pressure from the Saudis, to join a consensual list of candidates with representatives of the Future Movement. In January 2011, he nevertheless voted along with the March 8 coalition to bring down the Sa'ad al-Hariri government. The coalition was demanding that Sa'ad reject the Special Tribunal for Lebanon. Miqati resigned from the post of prime minister in March 2013, due to the increasing polarization between Assad supporters and opponents, amplified by the Syrian crisis.

Today, the giant propaganda posters of these strongmen adorn building façades in Tripoli's poorer quarters, in the old town, and further east in the neighborhoods of Qubbeh and Abu Samra. These men provide services that function as a "safety net" for the many people whose only survival option is to rely on a local

---

[28] Miqati made his fortune in telecommunications. He had started by selling walkie-talkies to the various armed groups during the final decade of the war. Investcom, which he founded with his brother Taha in 1982, became a huge mobile phone holding corporation in the 1990s, owning a number of companies around the world, including Cellis in Lebanon. In 2001, through its special ties with the Assad family, the group won a fifteen-year BOT (Build, Operate, and Transfer) contract in Syria. After having sold Investcom in 2005 to the South African concern TNM for 5.5 billion dollars, the Miqatis founded the M1 group in 2007. Its multiple and varied investments range from a Swiss bank to brand-name clothing, and include consumer products, as well as the acquisition of prestigious real estate in London. Also eager to build intellectual legitimacy, Miqati finances a research facility and continues to enter into international scientific partnerships.

patron's generosity.[29] These *zu'ama'* thus draw most of their power from the region's poverty, and in light of the political benefits it brings them, they have every incentive to perpetuate that poverty.

A Disenfranchised Region

Today, the North is the poorest region of Lebanon. Its population comprises 21 percent of the Lebanon population, yet includes 38 percent of the "poor population" and 46 percent of the "extremely poor population," a larger proportion than any other governorate (region).[30] The city of Tripoli and the Akkar and Minniyeh regions are especially poor, with infant mortality rates far above those of Beirut.[31] Deteriorating economic conditions have coincided with social and cultural regression. Tripoli lost any significant Christian population after the civil war. The "contented modernity" of the 1960s, which historian Khaled Ziyadeh described in his "urban biography" of the city, gave way to a constellation of urban islands, enclaves increasingly withdrawn from each other and increasingly parochial.[32] The economist Charbel Nahas evoked several instances of "spatial trauma" to explain the city's geographic evolution and its shrinking sphere of influence. After 1976, the civil war's rifts deprived Tripoli of its trade relationships with Christian areas, including Zghorta, Bsharre, and Batrun.[33] During the civil war, these areas were directly connected to Beirut via a road network designed to bypass Tripoli. On the coastal road from the capital to Tripoli, militia checkpoints discouraged trade flows, leaving the ill-named "Capital of the North"

[29] See Bruno Dewailly, "Foncier et Immobilier, régime de gouvernementabilité urbaine et spatialités. Le cas de Tripoli el-Fayhâ'a (Liban)" (PhD diss., University of Tours, 2015), 967.

[30] Heba Laithy, Khalil Abu Ismail, and Kamal Hamdan, *Poverty, Growth and Income Distribution in Lebanon*, International Poverty Center, Country Study, http://www.undp-povertycentre.org/ (accessed January 13, 2008). The poverty line for Lebanon is measured in terms of expenditure on a basket of goods necessary to feed a household, and set at US \$4 per person per day; the "extreme poverty" line is set at US \$2.4 per person per day.

[31] According to the UNICEF representative in Lebanon, the infant mortality rate is 52 percent in Akkar and Minniyeh, compared to 21 percent in Beirut. *L'Orient Le Jour*, October 1, 2010.

[32] Khaled Ziyadeh, *Yuwm al-jum'a, yuwm al-ahad* (Beirut: Dar al-Nahar, 1994), 135.

[33] Charbel Nahas, "La Foire internationale et Tripoli, quel avenir?" Lecture given at the Safadi Foundation, in Tripoli, on December 15, 2007. http://charbelnahas.org/textes (accessed January 2008).

on its own to bear the pressure of an influx of migrants from the furthest villages of its mountainous hinterland. Finally, the city suffered from the opening of the Lebanese economy to the Syrian market. Flooded with cheap goods and labor, it was unwillingly integrated "into a partial regional market, different from the national market in terms of prices." This led to the "decline of craftsmanship and industry" in the city, as well as to a "fall in agricultural investment and revenue."[34]

Tripoli's present-day social and physical geography bears witness to that period. The avenue that crosses the city from north to south, skirting around al-Tell Square, divides Tripoli into two urban segments: the wealthy and middle classes live in the west, the poor inhabit the east. Following the flood of the Abu Ali river in 1955, the poor, rural population poured into the historic city center, which housed the administrative center of the Ottoman *vilayet* (province) of Trablus al-Sham, with its Mamluk mosques, khans and markets, and stately French and Ottoman buildings. The ancient olive groves of Qubbeh and Abu Samra sheltered the residents of the old town when they fled the flood; the more affluent residents moved out and settled on the western side of the city. In the early 1970s, these two neighborhoods underwent a similar phase of impoverishment, and soon afterward, the civil war accelerated their economic deterioration. For example, the neighborhood of Bab al-Tabbaneh, with over 50,000 inhabitants, has the chiaroscuro of a medieval city—towering buildings, crowded homes (seven people per household on average), and unsanitary, damp, dark apartments, often at risk of collapse. In 2008, 60 percent of the neighborhood's families lived below the "extreme poverty" threshold.[35]

This "Tripoli of the poor" connects to the rural areas of Akkar and Dinniyeh, but it has few links with the western side of the city, built around broad avenues that link al-Tell Square and the al-Mina neighborhood on the seafront. Yet it is the former district, along with its geographical extensions into the countryside, that provided a setting for the processes of mobilization analyzed

[34] Ibid.

[35] Laithy et al., *Poverty, Growth*. See also Catherine Le Thomas, *Pauvreté et Conditions Socioéconomiques au Liban: une Etude sur la Situation de Tripoli al-Fayhâ'*, Agence française de développement, 2010.

in the last four chapters in this book. In fact, the dynamics of "enclosure" underscored by geographers and urban planning experts have not prevented this area from forming connections both within the region and across the world. There was a time when Tripoli envisioned itself as a new Arab version of modernity, when it welcomed, for example, the bold projects of avant-garde Brazilian architect Oscar Niemeyer, who designed its international fairground. The war put an end to those progressive dreams. Now it is a broken town, fragmented into multiple militant spheres, capturing, in a way, a larger process that is going on across the Levant.

CHAPTER 2

Defending an Imagined Umma

THE PATH TO TERRORISM

Throughout 2002 and 2003, Lebanon experienced a wave of terrorist attacks directed at American fast-food restaurants and a supermarket belonging to a British chain. Six successful bombings occurred in Tripoli and on the coastal road between Beirut and Tripoli. The last attack, carried out on April 5, 2003, was carefully crafted to maximize casualties. Its target was the McDonald's restaurant at the entrance of the Dora neighborhood, in the eastern suburbs of Beirut, and it was timed for a Saturday afternoon, when the restaurant would be at its busiest. The first charge, planted in the bathroom, was calculated to provoke panic and send customers rushing to the exit, where a car bomb was waiting. Fortunately, a short circuit saved dozens of customers from near-certain death.

This scenario was made possible by new forms of transnational solidarity between Tripoli and certain radicalized groups of the Lebanese diaspora in Australia. Somewhat ironically, the network's obsession with destroying restaurants franchised to American fast-food chains reflects an interesting form of symmetry: this terrorist group on Lebanese soil had actually been established in coordination with internationalist al-Qaeda militants. Thus, "ideological franchising" manifests as an obscure counterpart of commercial franchising—

both being products of an internal contradiction of globalization, without which neither could have existed.

The McDonald's attack happened as the Syrian regime began to reinforce its authoritarian structures within Lebanese society. In Tripoli, politics amounted to parochial rivalries between local strongmen and pro-Assad Islamists celebrating Hezbollah "resistance" and Syrian "steadfastness" against Israel and the West. Between this gloomy local reality and vibrant transnational networks, something was missing: there was no national political scene where grievances could be freely expressed. With local and national politics thus hobbled, changes could take place only at the transnational level.

In the early 1990s, those who supported a Salafi conception of Islam hostile to both national divisions and cultural specificities set their sights on Tripoli and its vicinity as a site for missionary activity. Their insistence on the prophetic tradition (*sunna*) and their rejection of politics (which they thought divisive), helped establish a new religious universality among disenfranchised and disillusioned Lebanese. The architects of these transnational Salafi networks were the young people who fled Tripoli when Syrian troops occupied the city in 1985. After studying at the University of Medina in Saudi Arabia, these sons of the soil returned with sufficient money and connections to open religious institutes across the region. Others went further afield, to Western countries such as Denmark, Sweden, and Australia, known for granting residence permits to Palestinian refugees and Lebanese nationals requesting political asylum. In these countries the former partisans of the Tawhid Movement also adopted a Salafi form of Islam, some even becoming jihadis linked to their hometowns. Finally, Bassam al-Kanj, a Tripolitan veteran of the 1980s Afghan jihad, established military training camps in the mountains of Sir al-Dinniyeh to the west of Tripoli. In December 1999/January 2000, al-Kanj's forces clashed with the Lebanese army. Against that background, conditions were ripe in the early 2000s for poor young men to rise up and speak on behalf of the whole Islamic umma.

Muhammad al-Ka'keh and Capitalizing on Personal Contacts

Muhammad al-Ka'keh was born in 1976 in Tabbaneh to a family of shopkeepers. In 1996–97, at around the age of twenty, he completed military service close to his hometown and to the Tripolitan neighborhood of Abu Samra, where he then settled. Military conscription—instituted after the war in support of the new official ideology—did not produce the desired "melting pot" effect of national integration, least of all in al-Ka'keh. During a period of training in a gendarme police station in the Fawwar area, near Tripoli, he befriended Sergeant Nasir al-'Umar:

> We exchanged opinions on Muslims and what they are exposed to in the world, in Chechnya, in Bosnia. I felt he was a fervent believer and that our views coincided on the necessity of helping Muslims in every way. He told me that he knew someone originally from al-Burj in Akkar, by the name of Bilal Khaz'al, known as Abu Suhayb, who had emigrated to Australia out of fear of the Lebanese authorities.

This meeting was decisive because it marked a change from a still-superficial attitude of Islamist solidarity in the face of current events to the gradual embrace of a structured jihadi ideology. Al-'Umar maintained an archive of paper copies of the jihadi journal *Nida'u al-Islam* (The Call of Islam), which Bilal Khaz'al published in Sydney. Lebanese émigrés had brought these copies with them on visits to the country, because sending them by mail was potentially dangerous for the recipient. The journal could not otherwise be found in the Middle East, and it was only later made available on the Internet. Al-Ka'keh was enthused by the issues that al-'Umar secretly gave him, in particular those condemning the impious nature of the Syrian regime and the anti-Sunni dimension of Syria's policies in Lebanon. These discussions likely gave both men a measure of relief from any anxieties occasioned by the contradiction between their participation in an "impious organization" and the nature of their religious orientation. For the Islamist sergeant, guiding his new recruit toward reading a jihadi publication was likely a means to reconcile this apparent dissonance.

After completing his military service, al-Ka'keh worked in his father's shop, where al-'Umar would frequently visit him when he was on leave. The bond between the two was by then strong enough for the sergeant to give him Khaz'al's telephone number, facilitating the development of an ever-closer relationship between the Sydney-based magazine publisher and al-Ka'keh. The situation did not change until the clashes at Sir al-Dinniyeh in December 1999–January 2000. Al-Ka'keh was entertaining the idea of supporting the families of survivors of Bassam al-Kanj's network when he heard from a neighbor that a sheikh in his late forties, Ahmad al-'Attar, known as Abu Abd al-Qadir, was undertaking a similar effort. Al-Ka'keh decided to meet the sheikh and join forces. A meeting took place in a mosque in the neighborhood of Qubbeh, and al-Ka'keh and al-'Attar decided to create a joint solidarity fund for these families.

Throughout 2000, every Thursday evening after *maghrib* prayer, al-Ka'keh attended al-'Attar's *halaqat* (sessions) in the al-Aweysiyyat Mamluk mosque on Bab al-Hadid Square in the old quarter of Tripoli. A carpenter by profession, al-'Attar lacked any religious credentials. According to Muhammad al-Ka'keh, his "lessons" took place without the knowledge of the appointed imam. During this period, he recommitted to the ritual obligation of prayer, learned the rudiments of Islamic jurisprudence (*fiqh*), and absorbed the basics of the creed (*'aqida*). Al-'Attar's meetings gathered various militants who had taken different paths to activism. Their encounters reshaped a new and shifting field of bonds, experiences, and potential contacts. During al-'Attar's first lesson in Islamic jurisprudence, al-Ka'keh met a former detainee from Dinniyeh, Fadi Tayyiba, whose parole terms obliged him to attend the sessions of the Judicial Council (Majlis al-'Adli), the exceptional judiciary body responsible for the Sir al-Dinniyeh affair.[1] Al-Ka'keh benefited from this broadening of intellectual and human horizons:

> My relationship with Ahmed al-'Attar became stronger. He told me that he was guiding a group of pious youth in religious matters without mentioning any details. He asked me if I would join this group, and I agreed. We had several meetings at different times and places, mostly in Baddawi, in the homes of Ahmed al-'Attar or others. During these meetings,

[1] While on parole, Fadi Tayyiba was once again detained from the 12th to the 28th of August 2002 by the military intelligence services. According to his lawyer, he was subjected to various tortures (food deprivation, electric shocks, beatings) in various military intelligence premises (Tripoli, Baabda). See Amnesty International's report, "Lebanon: Torture and Unfair Trial of the Dhinniyyah Detainees" (in Arabic), MDE 18/005/2003 2010. http://www.amnesty.org/en/library/info/MDE18/005/2003 (accessed March 17).

we decided to form a fund for group member contributions, each according to his means. We then began to buy weapons and to practice using them. We decided that the fundamental objective of the creation of this group was to assassinate political figures, without specifying which ones, in order to pressure the Lebanese state to release the Dinniyeh prisoners.

The idea of supporting the families of Dinniyeh prisoners that prompted the establishment of the solidarity fund should be understood in a purely military, not humanitarian, sense. Concurrent with their religious lessons and discussions about potential human targets for a terrorist attack, the members of the group undertook physical training in a gym in the Abu Samra neighborhood.

Al-Ka'keh worked in his father's hardware shop, which sold construction supplies. Tripoli then resembled a *Khaldunian* Arab city, with its mosques, souks, and a foreign political power, embodied by the Syrian intelligence services whose premises were deliberately located in a working-class neighborhood on the eastern side of town. As the group treasurer, al-Ka'keh bought a Kalashnikov as a "first step toward arming the group." During one of al-'Umar's visits to the store, they discussed the possibility of Khaz'al providing external help. The Islamist sergeant then informed al-Ka'keh that the Australian imam's brother—Maher Khaz'al—had arrived in his hometown of Akkar. Al-Ka'keh then notified al-'Attar of Maher Khaz'al's arrival, and the two decided to meet him. This was the first step in the group's efforts to connect with international jihadism. It was hoped that a link with the Sydney-based imam would provide recognition and material assistance.

The first tensions within the group appeared during discussions pertaining to the use of money collected for the solidarity fund. During a closed-door meeting, al-'Attar appealed to Maher Khaz'al for financial support. For al-'Attar, it was urgent to purchase an isolated plot of land in the mountains where they could toughen up the recruits through outdoor physical training, as Bassam al-Kanj had done a few years earlier. Al-Ka'keh, on the other hand, thought they should follow their original plan: use the money to buy weapons and explosives for political assassinations.

These two schemes were clearly incompatible. Purchasing a plot of land was reminiscent of a stylized image of the Afghan jihad of the 1980s, when the figure of the *mujahid* was inextricably linked to a physical environment for military and religious training. From this perspective, the training of *mujahidin* appeared to be an end in itself, and the group's consolidation was not linked to a specific objective from the start. Conversely, the purchase of lethal weapons steered the group into the realm of political assassinations and deadly action. Al-Ka'keh backed this option:

> Later on, Fadi Tayyiba and I headed to al-Burj in Akkar [to meet Maher Khaz'al]. I told him that al-'Attar had misspoken, and that we were asking only for financial support for security operations, consisting of assassinations. I told him, literally: "the money [will come] from you, the manpower from us" (*minkum al-mal wa-minna al-'amal*). I clarified things for him, telling him that the attacks would be aimed against state officials to pressure them to release Dinniyeh political prisoners. Maher seemed to agree and promised us success.

Al-Ka'keh justified this divergence during private discussions with other members of the group, which still consisted of a network of contacts centered on al-'Attar. The Weberian ideal type of the *mujahid* lent itself to two different modes of action. The first was a continuation, within the Levantine context, of the saga of the Arab *mujahidin* in Afghanistan, and left open the possibility of taking action outside of Lebanon. In fact, during a meeting shortly after the beginning of the October 2001 US offensive in Afghanistan, al-'Attar mentioned the possibility of sending volunteers to support the Taliban. The second mode of action involved prioritizing the purchase of weapons and explosives, steps that would limit the field of action to Lebanon.

The jihadi ideology worked symbolically: real people were treated as mere symbols, stripped of their historical, national, and anthropological substance. The Maronite patriarch, a potential target for assassination, was no longer viewed as the leader of one of the oldest Christian communities of the Middle East. He was disembodied, labeled, and assimilated to a representative of America, the West, or Christianity. As such, he was to be fought against and eliminated if possible. Similarly, Fatah was not a Palestinian organization struggling to recover its territory, but a secular entity despised for politically acknowledging impious entities, including the West, Israel, and Arab regimes. Jihadi symbols were used to destroy religious systems deeply rooted in the political and religious history of the region. Whereas Islamic religious law was designed to set boundaries on the arbitrary actions of Men, in its jihadi guise it left open the possibility for actions unconstrained by any limits.

Through his acquaintance with Fadi Tayyiba, Muhammad al-Ka'keh met another fugitive, Ahmad al-Miqati, then hiding in Ayn al-Helweh:

> I also learned from Tayyiba that he was in contact with the fugitive Ahmad al-Miqati of Ayn al-Helweh. He informed me that Miqati's financial situation was dire and that he needed money to live in the camp. I gave Tayyiba 300 dollars for him to pass to al-Miqati, to supply us with two machine guns with silencers and to carry out operations . . . as per our understanding.

Al-Miqati was only sixteen when he was arrested by the Syrian security forces in 1986, along with hundreds of other young Sunnis. He was suspected at the time of fighting with the Tawhid militia. Released in 1990 in a blanket amnesty granted by President Hafez al-Assad, unable to read or write, he got by doing odd jobs, such as flatbread vendor (ka'keh), building painter, and so on. In the late 1990s, he crossed paths with a Bosnian veteran of the Afghan jihad, Bassam al-Kanj, and his name appeared on the wanted list after fighting broke out in Sir al-Dinniyeh in December 1999/ January 2000, a clash in which his brother Umar was also involved. He then settled in the Palestinian refugee camp of Ayn al-Helweh, off limits to the Lebanese security forces. He regularly paid protection money to the local jihadi group Jund al-Sham in the area of Tamir, at the northern tip of the camp.

Al-Ka'keh's contact with the fugitive Ahmad al-Miqati, a survivor of the Sir al-Dinniyeh battle of December 1999, furnished a framework for establishing contacts with individuals who had participated in Bassam al-Kanj's undertakings a few years earlier. Those events may now be interpreted independently of their protagonists' initial intentions (to the extent that these were ever clearly articulated). Revisiting the Sir al-Dinniyeh affair allows interpretation of these past events as the inauguration of an inexorable conflict between the jihadis and the state. Relating a completed event to an evolving situation makes interpretation of the initial Sir al-Dinniyeh events even more uncertain.

As we shall see in the following chapter, other interpretations advanced since 2005 have attempted, as much as possible, to downplay a fundamental antagonism between Sunni Islamism and the state. They have instead offered an explanation derived from the malicious intent of contemporaneous leaders—who were all connected to those in power in Syria—to criminalize Sunni Islam in Lebanon, thus dividing the community and preventing Rafiq al-Hariri from imposing his hegemony over it. All sides were vaguely aware that victory depended on their capacity to impose one dominant reading of an Islamist discourse whose production had begun in the mid-1980s. Since then, this discourse has been growing progressively denser as new layers accumulated, each shedding a different light on the preceding ones, and each tending to controversial conclusions.

Since the 1990s, the Ayn al-Helweh camp had served as the crucible for new connections between militants and had begun to connect with other locations embedded in the jihadi geography of the time. Escaping to the south and seeking refuge in the Ayn al-Helweh camp, less than two kilometers east of Sidon, was nothing new in local history. In 1985, when the Syrian army entered Tripoli, several hundred militants relocated to the camp and to the suburbs of Sidon to escape mass arrest campaigns. But at this time, the southward exile was carried out under the protection of Yasser Arafat's Fatah organization. In order to continue his unrelenting struggle against the Syrian regime, Arafat had carefully retained his Lebanese allies. By virtue of the 1986 deal between the Christian Lebanese Forces militia and the Palestinian leaders of Fatah, Tawhid Islamists were authorized to leave Lebanon through the port of Jounieh (then controlled by the Lebanese Forces) and could even stop in the Christian regions safely. The combatants were determined to avenge their defeat by the Syrian army and had no qualms about forming alliances with the enemies of their enemies, so long as their urban identity prevailed over their Islamic discourse.[2] The Tawhid organization of which they were members was

[2] Seurat, "Le quartier" (see chapter 1, note 8).

a federation of local neighborhood militias defending Tripoli from intruders of all affiliations, including state forces, nearby Christian or Alawite groups, and the Syrian army. At the time, the Tawhid was the purest expression of the *muqatil*—young local combatants dedicated to defending their neighborhood. They were essentially an urban solidarity group (*ʿasabiyya*).

In the Syrian-controlled Lebanon of the 1990s, Tripolitans still found refuge in Ayn al-Helweh. But now the fugitives joined anti-Fatah jihadi enclaves established inside the Palestinian camp. The figure of the *mujahid* had replaced that of the *muqatil*.

Ahmad al-Miqati's role in connecting the Ayn al-Helweh camp with the Tripoli group made him emblematic of this transition. Al-Miqati invited members of al-Kaʿkeh's group to participate in ten-day military training sessions that al-Miqati had organized. Upon their return from the camp, two volunteers whom al-Miqati told about training programs in the Islamic Emirate of Afghanistan passed on this information to al-Kaʿkeh. Al-Kaʿkeh and others wished to make the journey as well. Naturally, travel entailed a number of expenditures, from forging passports to procuring safe houses along the way in Aleppo, Istanbul, Iran, and Afghanistan. Al-Miqati disseminated information and instructions to facilitate the passage of volunteers between Istanbul, Aleppo, Tripoli, and Ayn al-Helweh. In May 2001, he asked al-Kaʿkeh to buy falsified identification papers for Fadi Tayyiba so that the latter might meet Osama bin Laden.

By this point, the group seemed to be under the authority of al-Miqati. Interestingly, while al-Kaʿkeh was working to build mutual trust in his relationship with al-Miqati, Sheikh al-ʿAttar was similarly devoting himself to the creation of comparable ties with the leaders of the Palestinian jihadi militia ʿUsbat al-Ansar (the League of Partisans), which was well established in Ayn al-Helweh. During frequent visits to the al-Quds mosque in the Baddawi Palestinian camp in the northern suburbs of Tripoli, Sheikh al-ʿAttar had befriended a Palestinian originally from Ayn al-Helweh. This man offered to introduce al-ʿAttar to Abu Tariq, the leader of ʿUsbat al-Ansar:

> During our conversation, we talked about ʿUsbat al-Ansar and how we might get in touch with them. [The Palestinian]

then offered to take me to the camp himself and to introduce me to Abu Tariq. We met on the outskirts of the camp. He introduced me to Abu Tariq. I informed him that I was preparing some youth for jihad in God's path and the defense of Muslims.

In October 2001, during a meeting in Qubbeh, al-'Attar suggested merging the Tripoli cells with the 'Usbat al-Ansar jihadi militia in Ayn al-Helweh. Al-Ka'keh firmly opposed this proposal:

Al-'Attar asked us to unify the ranks and integrate them into 'Usbat al-Ansar, but I refused, since the entire group and I were under Ahmad al-Miqati's authority, and because all of us were hoping to join al-Qaeda. The meeting ended without us having reached an agreement.

In October 2001, al-'Attar circulated one hundred copies of a leaflet in which he condemned the American offensive against Afghanistan and called upon Muslims to join Bin Laden. He then penned a second pamphlet expressing his outrage that the "Arab and Muslim states have betrayed the Muslim cause and abandoned Bin Laden, even though he is working to spread the voice of Islam." In a third leaflet, he denounced the inequality between the prison sentences for militiamen of the Christian general Antoine Lahad after Israel's retreat from southern Lebanon in May 2000. Lahad's men, he reasoned, had colluded with the enemy, yet received sentences more lenient than those given to the Muslim prisoners of Dinniyeh.

Al-Ka'keh held a different opinion of the group's direction. He rejected setting up a training camp because it would be too noticeable and would likely delay any concrete action. He was also determined to deny al-'Attar a leadership role within the network, and he favored going underground immediately. Al-Ka'keh's ambition was to bypass any preparatory stage and to proceed directly to political assassinations. His authority was based on the international connection that allowed him to obtain funding.

In the autumn of 2001, al-'Attar, the group's imam and its embodiment of religious authority, eventually gave in, albeit unwillingly, to al-Ka'keh's aspirations. That al-Ka'keh finally managed to win most of the group's support for his plan was due no doubt to his contact in Australia and his access to sources of external funding. One final incident isolated al-ʿAttar even further from the rest of the group. He wanted to take money from the solidarity fund to purchase a weapon for someone unknown to the group, an initiative that was perceived as evidence of insufficient solidarity with the community. From then on, al-ʿAttar found himself excluded from the group's decision-making process, although he did remain on the periphery of the network.[3] Al-ʿAttar's departure attests to the interchangeability of interactions and therefore to the existence, in this case, of a social network as an objective form of organization in the sense that no single individual seems to have been indispensable to its proper functioning.[4]

The External Provider: The Role of Bilal Khazʿal

Born in Tripoli in 1970, Khazʿal was raised by his grandmother and aunt, as his parents lived in Australia. He spent part of his adolescent years as a militant in the branch of the Tawhid Movement that Hashem Minqara controlled in the al-Mina district. At the time, young recruits were initiated into Islam through reading Sayyid Qutb's texts.[5] In 1985, the Syrian army's invasion of the city forced the family into permanent exile in Australia.

There young Bilal lived in the Lakemba district, a southwestern suburb of Sydney. The main street, Lakemba Street, offers the casual visitor several miles of "Little Lebanon," with Arabic shop

---

[3] Although he was no longer the group's leader, al-ʿAttar did not cut himself off entirely from its main members. For example, he met with Khazʿal in Saudi Arabia during the Hajj to Mecca. In the fall of 2002, he was included in discussions regarding how to attack the American embassy in Beirut. He was impressed by the attacks organized by the group's engineer, Khaled ʿAli (see above), and asked the latter to provide him with explosives for a bomb intended for the Casino du Liban.

[4] Pierre Livet and Frédéric Nef emphasize the idea that a robust network must be "capable of repairing any breakdowns, which requires that its actions not be dependant on any single person or any single type of action. In other words, there must be an alternate plan in place for certain interactions (or all interactions, if the network is to be considered absolutely robust) if they cannot be carried out, either because the protagonist has proven to be defective, or because the environment has made it impossible. Thus, the existence of a social network requires that interactions be interchangeable." *Les Êtres sociaux. Processus et virtualités* (Paris: Hermann/Hermann Philosophie, 2009), 154.

[5] Interview with a former member of the Tawhid Movement, Tripoli, July 2008.

signs, a number of Lebanese cafés and restaurants, and several Islamic bookshops. The religious buildings of the district chronicle successive waves of immigration that have formed multiple strata in this neighborhood where human geography subtly recreates invisible borders similar to those inside Lebanon, the source of almost all the immigrants. Migration to Australia accelerated remarkably after the start of the Lebanese civil war, with the number of Lebanese born in Australia doubling after 1975. In the 1980s, a final wave consisted mainly of Sunnis from Tripoli or its surrounding areas. Most of these immigrants lacked both skills and resources, and they settled in the industrial districts west of Sydney. Khaz'al, still an adolescent when he arrived, had only completed a primary school education. He began religious studies in the Lakemba mosque, established in 1977 on the outskirts of the suburb.

After the Tawhid Movement had imposed an "Islamic social order" in Tripoli, and in the context of the ideological enthusiasm that followed Khomeini's Iranian revolution, Khaz'al's life underwent, within the Lebanese expatriate environment in Australia, a second accommodation to Islamic norms.

Sheikh Taj al-Din al-Hilali, his teacher in the mosque, was pivotal in this shift. Born in 1941 in Upper Egypt and trained by the Egyptian Muslim Brotherhood, Sheikh al-Hilali had arrived in Australia from Lebanon in 1982, four years before his young student. As a member of the University of al-Azhar's mission in Lebanon (which retreated to Tripoli after the Israeli invasion of June 1982), he had taken part in the foundation of the Tawhid Movement.[6] Soon after his arrival in Sydney, a group of worshipers from the Lakemba mosque encouraged him to stand for election to the post of sheikh of the mosque, in hopes of ousting the incumbent, Ahmad Zaydan, who was close to the Kata'ib Christian party and had the local Iraqi Ba'athist party's support. The new wave of immigration had significantly increased membership in the Lakemba mosque's congregation, which in turn facilitated al-Hilali's election as the sheikh.[7] Representatives of the Kata'ib party in Sydney, worried by

[6] See chapter 4 of this book.

[7] Michael Humphrey, *Islam, Multiculturalism and Transnationalism: From the Lebanese Diaspora* (Center for Lebanese Studies-Oxford/London and New York: I. B Tauris, 1998).

the influence an Islamist sheikh might have on their fellow Sunni countrymen, tried to have him deported by the federal government. But such moves only consolidated the sheikh's religious legitimacy in the eyes of a constituency eager to affirm its religious identity.

Al-Hilali's election marked a turning point in the way Lebanese immigrants organized and defined themselves in Australia. For the Sunnis, religion began to take on greater importance than one's village of origin, the identity marker that had mattered most to earlier generations of immigrants. Although the community association network was closely coupled to Lebanese identity, the choice of religious criteria of identification intrinsically implied the labeling and rejection of non-Sunni Lebanese as alien to the group. In addition, this new form of self-identification allowed religious elites to take advantage of a framework in which they could directly negotiate for public funds with national and local Australian government representatives. These representatives had become convinced since the 1970s that a "multiculturalist" policy toward religious and ethnic minorities was beneficial. Being accustomed to the Lebanese political scene, which was structured by the subtle linguistic codes of intercommunal dynamics, these new religious elites had no trouble mastering the discourse of "interethnic harmony" in their dealings with Australian officials, yet saw no contradiction between this mode of political action and their Islamist orientation.

Young Bilal's poor English prevented him from continuing his studies, and he took a job as a baggage handler for the national airline, Qantas. In doing so, he managed to avoid some of the social problems faced by the "third wave" of Lebanese immigrants, which in the early 1990s included unemployment for over a third of the working-age population. Those who had recently arrived were poorly integrated into Australian society due to their weak language skills, and they survived largely on welfare benefits. With an average of four to six children per household, Muslim families had the highest birthrate in the country at that time.[8] Khaz'al, on the other hand, was well integrated both socially and economically. He had little reason to embrace an Australian cultural

---

[8] Data quoted in Manal Suwaydan's article "Lebanese Muslims in Australia amass money and make babies as if they were in a 'war' to obtain citizenship" (in Arabic), *al-Balad*, July 22, 2004.

model that inflated the meaning and value of the esthetic, erotic, and athletic aspects of the body, since such an ethic ran counter to the strict teachings he had received from Sheikh Salem al-Rafiʻi during his adolescence in the Tawhid "emirate."

It is difficult to determine how Khazʻal became involved in jihadism at a time when no Internet or satellite television was available. At the beginning of the 1990s, the jihadi ideologue Abu Qatada toured the Islamic centers of Sydney and Melbourne, and it is possible that Khazʻal crossed paths with him.[9] In August 1992, at the age of twenty-two, he left Australia for almost two months. To this day, his destination remains unknown. Immediately after his return, he launched the monthly jihadi magazine *Nidaʾu al-Islam*. Its forty issues contained interviews and articles dedicated to the main figureheads of jihadism, including Osama bin Laden, as well as texts they had penned.[10] The monthly magazine was published in both English and Arabic and presented itself as the voice of the Islamic Youth Movement created by "Sheikh" Bilal Khazʻal. This association had a prayer room on the second floor of a modest building on Haldon Street (a side street off Lakemba Street).

The creation of the Islamic Youth Movement constituted a definitive rupture with al-Hilali. The Egyptian sheikh disapproved of those whose "short robes and long beards are their only assets in the science of religion," and stated that Abu Qatada had "excommunicated" him during the latter's visit to Australia.[11] The quarrel between the two men should be seen in the broader context of harsh criticism by the jihadi movement of the Muslim Brotherhood's behavior. Khazʻal had no choice but to give up all hope of taking control of the Lakemba mosque, which was attended by many worshippers during Friday sermons and enjoyed generous Libyan and Saudi funding. This failure in the conquest of local Islam incited Khazʻal to shift the focus of his action. In 1998, he met Osama bin Laden and Ayman al-Zawahiri at a jihadi training camp in Taliban-controlled Afghanistan. Khazʻal's path—the experience of military

[9] Interview with the Egyptian Sheikh Taj al-Din al-Hilali in the daily newspaper *al-Sharq al-Awsat*, August 7, 2003.

[10] On September 25, 2009, he was sentenced to fourteen years in prison by the Supreme Court of the State of New South Wales (Australia) for planning terrorist attacks on military sites and for his writings calling upon others to commit acts of terrorism.

[11] Interview with Sheikh al-Hilali, *al-Sharq al-Awsat*, August 7, 2003.

defeat followed by exile abroad—coincided with that of militants who had broken with national Islamist movements to refocus on a transnational struggle.

From Australia, Khaz'al would go on to affect the evolution of al-Ka'keh's group. He influenced its orientation, approved of the assassination strategy, and transmitted messages and money. In early 2001, for instance, Khaz'al contributed several thousand Australian dollars to al-Ka'keh's solidarity fund. Al-Ka'keh used these funds to buy a mobile phone for Fadi Tayyiba, giving the latter a direct line of communication to Khaz'al. The Australian imam asked Tayyiba not to attend the Judicial Council sessions (and thus to violate the terms of his parole).

The magazine publisher became a sort of interlocutor and facilitator of connections between different networks. Khaz'al was the person who provided the resources that made it possible to develop a network over a very short period, which in turn established links between jihadis whose experiences and backgrounds varied.

Khaz'al's decisive intercessions demonstrate how far-away actors can use new technologies to involve themselves in and influence local situations. In interpreting social situations, which Goffman saw as "environments composed of mutual monitoring possibilities," the fact that actors share a common intellectual framework arising from a shared ideological mindset seems more pertinent than their occupying the same geography.[12] Moreover, the technological component may considerably bend the institutional rules understood to govern face-to-face situations. The telephone, followed by the Internet, reduced differences in status within the movement between a twenty-something jihadi novice and an elder sheikh.

In September 2003, Khaz'al published a one-hundred-page jihadi manifesto—using the alias Abu Muhammad al-Tawhidi—entitled *Handbook of the Rules of Jihad: Essential Rules of Jurisprudence and Organizational Orientations Concerning every Fighter and Mujahid Who Fights Impiety.*[13] In the introduction, he explained that,

---

[12] Erving Goffman, "The Neglected Situation," *American Anthropologist*, New Series 66, nr. 6 (December 1964), part 2: "The Ethnography of Communication," 133–36.

[13] Abu Muhammad al-Tawhidi, *Al-za'id fi Ahkam al-Jihad. Ahkam fiqhiyyat mukhtasira wa Tawijhat Tandhimiyyat Tuhimm kull Muqatil wa-Mujahid lil-Kufrat.* [Handbook of the rules of jihad. Compiled with the help of God the all-powerful, the 21st of *Rajab*, 1424 Hijri (September 18, 2003).]

at the request of "several brothers involved in the victory of this religion," he wished to compose urgently a basic jihad manual for "any brother or group that wishes to work for the victory of this religion." The handbook is a compilation of texts penned by the chief ideologues of jihadism. It explains why it is acceptable to "fight against infidels" and what rules apply to "women, children, and elderly people who help the enemy." It also deals with potential penalties for those who "abandon jihad to live with the atheists." The fact that Khaz'al assigned paramount importance to assassinations—to which he devoted almost one third of the handbook—sheds some light *a posteriori* on Muhammad al-Ka'keh's insistence on adopting this mode of operation during initial discussions in Tripoli.[14] To legitimize assassination as a tactic, Khaz'al cited a hadith about a Jewish woman who was strangled for insulting the Prophet of Islam. By not intervening, the prophet Muhammad was said to have legitimized the murder of anyone who insulted the religion. According to Khaz'al, because the killer did not ask the Prophet's permission, all believers were justified in taking this kind of initiative when someone insulted Islam. No external authority was required, not even that of the Messenger of God.

Following the Palestinian ideologue Abu Qatada, Khaz'al established a distinction between the "original nonbeliever" and the "apostate nonbeliever." The latter category included Muslim elites—"emirs, presidents, ministers, policemen"—who had declared their apostasy by "no longer preoccupying themselves with what God has prescribed or with blasphemy against Him." As such, the Imams of unbelief could be killed legitimately, starting with "the head rather than the tail" and targeting "the prominent rather than the small."

Khaz'al included many comparisons between present-day Muslim leaders and famous traitors of Islamic history, including Abu Righal, "who offered his services" to the Ethiopian king Abraha when Abraha was endeavoring to conquer Mecca. He also cited Ibn al-Alqami and the religious scholar (*'alim*) Sadr al-Din al-Tusi, who served the Mongol invader Hulagu after he had killed "the Caliph and the statesmen, and destroyed the capital of the Caliphate of

---

[14] Ibid., 57–85.

Baghdad while exterminating from 800,000 to a million, or maybe even two million people . . . in what is known as the worst massacre in the history of humanity" (p. 58). History repeats itself, with its share of "defeats and *naqabat* (disasters)," because "this umma never encounters a single foreign enemy without someone appearing to assist them, to do them favors, to justify their crimes, to defend their policy, to spread their ideas and to show them their weaknesses, as did Abu Righal, Ibn al-Alqami, and Sadr al-Din al-Tusi." During the 2003 Iraq war, "Abu Righal became king and under his authority, religious sheikhs gave legitimacy to the Crusaders and Zionists."

Khaz'al believed that assassins had to meet very high standards. Enlightened by his "belief (*'aqida*) and way of life (*manhaj*)," "the brother knows why he fights, whom he fights, how [he fights] and when [he fights]" (p. 60). To evade the apostate regimes' surveillance, recruiters were to target persons involved in social activities. Within a cell, which should include no more than three people, volunteers had to undergo intense physical and military training, learn to kill with poison, a knife, a handgun, or a rifle, and to become familiar with remote explosion techniques and methods of kidnapping (p. 61). They were also exhorted to read espionage manuals, keeping in mind that God had put an end to the legend "of the heroes of the CIA, the FBI, and the Mossad" forged "by Hollywood movies," through the "successive operations of the mujahidin in Tanzania, Kenya, Aden, New York, Washington, Mombasa, etc." The assassination team was to monitor "the movements of the target, its usual appointments, its place of residence, its itineraries, its ideas, psychology and weaknesses (permanent or temporary)." Rigor was key, for "most of these individuals have mistresses or secret affairs, and take precautions as they do not wish the public to discover them" (p. 63).

Khaz'al also stressed the network's internal security. "The *mujahid* must know nothing of his brother's mission" and adopt a specific "cover (*al-satir*)" "to hide the reality of their clandestine work and to conceal the nature of their activities from the enemy" (p. 64). For further details, Khaz'al regularly referred the reader to the *Encyclopedia of Jihad* written by al-Qaeda operatives. The individuals "whose assassination must be encouraged" were, by order of importance, "all the diplomats, ministers, and military personnel among the Jews, Christians and the polytheists in the Arabian peninsula," as per "the texts which call for their expulsion from the peninsula" (p. 79). In decreasing order of enmity, those who were to be eliminated from the peninsula were "the Americans, the English, the French, members of other NATO states, what is left of the Christian presence, Hindu Indians, Buddhists, and finally, the Russians." Indeed, "these states are engaged—under the Jews' guidance and with their participation—in waging war on the people of Islam, shedding their blood, violating their honor, pillaging their wealth—all of it well known to anyone in the world who watches and listens" (p. 80).

Then came the "imams of apostasy and unbelief" in the Arabian peninsula and the "Arab states falsely called Islamic, like Abu Righal and his four brothers—Pervez No-Honor [al-la Musharraf: an Arabic pun based on the former Pakistani president's name], Hamid Karzai, Hosni Mubarak and Yasser Arafat." Khaz'al added to the list "journalists who insult Islam and its Prophet," as well as the "officers and individuals known for their hostility to Islam." A final category was composed of "people holding sensitive posts," such as "heads of state, defense ministers, ministers of foreign affairs, heads of intelligence services, prominent generals"—in the countries of the "original unbelief," that is, "the United States and Great Britain, and between the two, Israel"—preferably designated as "the Jews"—then "France, Germany, Australia, Canada, other NATO member states, Russia, and India."

Thus, a baggage handler for Qantas, with no more than elementary school education in his home country, contributed to a body of jihadi writings that has seen continual growth since the advent of the Internet in the mid-1990s. This corpus first appeared at the time of the first Afghan war in the 1980s, and expanded as subsequent Middle Eastern events generated additions. In unabashed ignorance of the different schools of Islamic jurisprudence's methodological traditions, Khaz'al justified the use of terrorism by equating prophetic precedents with the contemporary situation.[15] Thus, Khaz'al placed himself in the category of "hadith-shouters," who

---

[15] Salafi jihadis unduly ascribe these schools of Islamic jurisprudence to a cult of personality of the scholars for whom the schools are named; ironically, the goal of these schools was precisely to limit the risks of improper or dangerous interpretations by means of critical deliberation on the normative significance of religious sources.

use litanies of sacred narratives to drown out their critics.[16] "Religious law" is proclaimed generously throughout his manifesto in an effort to confer divine authority on and justify an anthology of prescriptions chosen for their usefulness for his cause.

The global scale of the struggle paradoxically allowed Khaz'al to reenter the Tripolitan scene from his Lakemba suburb of Sydney. He helped al-Ka'keh become more influential within the group by using the latter's voice to advocate assassination as the main mode of action. Nonetheless, before organizing a deadly operation, the group first proved itself in a more limited way, putting to use the do-it-yourself ingenuity of a skilled newcomer.

Khaled 'Ali, the Obstinate Engineer

In addition to al-Ka'keh, a second individual played a key role in structuring the network. The idea of collecting money to purchase weapons was circulating among other groups during the year 2000, but it was Khaled Muhammad 'Ali, a bricklayer born in 1968 in Tabbaneh, who decided with a few others to create a fund for buying weapons that would enable the group to "face"—as per the wording of his declaration—"any danger threatening Muslims, especially in Tripoli." He acquired a Kalashnikov and two boxes of ammunition.

Ali encountered al-Ka'keh by chance, in October 2001, when he went to Ka'keh's father's shop to buy construction supplies. The external signs of Salafi affiliation made it relatively easy for two individuals familiar with the "Salafi way of life" (*minhaj salafi*)[17] to recognize and trust each other. According to 'Ali's testimony, their first conversations were about the war in Afghanistan:

> During the American war against Afghanistan in 2001, I met Muhammad al-Ka'keh (Abu Yahya) following my visits to his father to buy construction supplies. Our relationship grew stronger when it became clear that we both followed the "Salafi way of life" and jihadi ideas. We began to talk about the

---

[16] This expression is borrowed from Khaled Abou El Fadl, *The Great Theft: Wrestling Islam from the Extremists* (San Francisco: Harper, 2005), 90.

[17] In addition to the beard—left untrimmed because of a hadith stating "let your beards grow out"—the Salafi dress code includes the wearing of the *qamis* (a light-colored, loose-fitting tunic that must not cover the ankles).

suffering and oppression of the Muslims, especially because of America. We exchanged jihadi ideas about the victory of Islam. During this period, I spoke to Muhammad al-Ka'keh about my organization—the one I belonged to in Tabbaneh. . . . Muhammad al-Ka'keh told me he belonged to another organization, along with Ahmad al-'Attar (Abu Abd al-Qadir) and Fadi Tayyiba. He told me he was able to get funding from a Lebanese man in Australia, known as Abu Suhayb.

In early 2002, al-Ka'keh informed Ali that a "brother" living in Australia, Bilal Khaz'al, had asked him to pass some money on to Ahmad al-Miqati. At the time, al-Miqati had taken refuge in the Ayn al-Helweh camp, and since then al-Ka'keh had been running errands back and forth between Tripoli and the camp. After Muhammad al-Ka'keh had let him in on this secret, he sent 'Ali to Ayn al-Helweh to meet al-Miqati.[18] There 'Ali and al-Miqati discussed potential targets. 'Ali favored fast-food restaurants, whereas al-Miqati preferred strikes against the American embassy, located in the Awkar district. Thanks to the latter's contacts in the camp, Ali had no trouble procuring materials to carry out the mission: electric cables, detonators, explosives, grenades, an M-72 Light Anti-tank Weapon (LAW) rocket launcher, and Kalashnikovs. This began a period of intense weapons procurement through purchase and trial-and-error manufacturing/experimentation that continued for almost two years.

From the beginning, the environment of the Palestinian camps (both Ayn al-Helweh and Baddawi) profoundly shaped these protagonists' behavior. Along the lines of James Gibson's theory, they found new sources of support that broadened the range of their possibilities.[19] To them, Ayn al-Helweh's significance lay not in its

---

[18] Incidentally, Badi' Hamadeh served as their guide during visits to the camp, a few months before he escaped a dramatic arrest attempt and fled to Ayn al-Helweh. On July 11, 2002, Hamadeh killed three soldiers who had come to his home in Sidon to question him about his alleged participation in the Sir al-Dinniyeh events. He then found refuge in Ayn al-Helweh. After several weeks of negotiations, 'Usbat al-Ansar agreed to turn him over to the Lebanese authorities, justifying this decision with a prophetic precedent: Muhammad himself gave the convert Abu Basir back to the Meccans, in virtue of a treaty with them. This apparently shocking decision was taken in the best interests of Islam.

[19] James Gibson, *The Ecological Approach to Visual Perception* (Boston: Houghton Mifflin, 1979).

intrinsic qualities, such as the highest concentration of Palestinian refugees in Lebanon. Rather, the camp was seen as a reservoir of potential for action, as it provided access to military equipment and practical opportunities to develop underground solidarity. Khaled 'Ali could not act on his own, and therefore endeavored to make use of such technical know-how as was available in his surroundings. First, the detonators—provided by Ahmad al-Miqati—promised a highly efficient way of destroying fast-food restaurants. After one of his companions had suggested the first target—the Kentucky Fried Chicken (KFC) restaurant in Tripoli, "because it is an American interest," 'Ali's sole concern became developing a timer mechanism to set off a delayed explosion.

Preparing this operation in March 2002 did not prevent Ali from informing al-Ka'keh of his desire to blow up a Hindu temple in Nahr Ibrahim, on the north coast road, near Jounieh.[20] According to al-Ka'keh's testimony, 'Ali wanted to "take revenge on [the Hindus] because they had burned several mosques in India." The two men took a taxi to case the temple, situated on the ground floor of a three-story building. Indifferent to their social and economic deprivation, the plotters viewed the Hindus through a strictly religious lens. To ensure that all would understand their act of vengeance, they decided to target the temple with a car bomb on Sunday, the only day when many of the worshippers would not be at work. 'Ali procured a 500-gram block of TNT from al-Ka'keh, but they postponed the attack because American franchised restaurants had by now become their priority targets.

Each member's technical skills were put to use to produce functional tools in assembly-line fashion. The task involved connecting various items—some common (electric wire, car batteries), and some more dangerous (detonators, explosives)—and finding an electrician who followed the "Salafi way of life," who could prep the makeshift timer and program the explosion:

> I asked an acquaintance who follows the "Salafi path" and who is also an electrician, to equip several alarm clocks for use in the bombs. When he agreed, we met at my home, and

---

[20] The temple's main clientele were Sri Lankan nationals whose working conditions as housekeeping staff, managed by unscrupulous recruitment agencies that sent them from one household to another, were hardly enviable in Lebanon.

I helped him to take one of the alarm clocks apart in order to connect its ringer to the wire. At my request, he modified the rest of the alarm clocks, too. Then I brought the explosives that Muhammad al-Ka'keh had given me.

At dawn on May 9, 2002, they placed a charge near the KFC wall. It exploded less than half an hour later, destroying part of the restaurant and injuring one worker. The timer allowed for distance between the action (placing the charges) and the result (the blast), thus sparing the group from having to be present at the scene and providing them some measure of security. Building in this way from a relatively vague objective of "striking American restaurants" to then obtaining equipment through chance meetings in a variety of locations became their standard mode of operation. As much as their initial intent, fortuitous interactions with their physical environment served as pragmatic guides to action.

It was not organizational efficiency, as Lenin theorized in the early twentieth century, that would multiply their power, but the technical efficiency with which they made use of tools of destruction. During al-Ka'keh and Ali's group deliberations about potential theaters of operation, it was always available weapons and techniques, as well the obstacles revealed by tests they had conducted, that determined new targets. Their level of mastery of their destructive equipment also played a fundamental role in determining the identity of those targets, which were by preference static. For instance, when the group members considered attacking the American ambassador's convoy as it passed through North Lebanon, they familiarized themselves with several bridges in Tripoli, evaluated the chances of success of an RPG (rocket-propelled grenade) attack on a moving target, and then decided to abandon the idea. Their decision was the result of an evaluation of possible modes of operation permitted by the equipment they possessed, applied to the characteristics of the area where the mission was to be executed.

The KFC bombing gave the group an objective existence. It was certainly not the first time a Tripolitan shop was bombed—several liquor retailers had been targeted since the early 1990s—but this was the first American business singled out. After the KFC bombing, 'Ali tried to adapt the timer mechanism to B7 anti-tank rockets. He also improvised launching pads using sawed-off, meter-long pipes to house the rockets. During the summer of 2002, he tested these contraptions several times—rather unsuccessfully—in the Akkar area, in Baddawi camp, and close to the Shekka tunnel, through which one must pass to enter Tripoli. The KFC precedent, however, seems to have continued to predispose him to static operations. Al-Ka'keh suggested that he place explosives near a Tripoli radio station accused of deriding the city's sheikhs, but he was advised to simply beat up the radio station's presenters. He also planned to place a hand grenade with a timer in a local liquor store of his Qubbeh neighborhood, but he failed because a driver let him down twice. This convinced him of the necessity of acquiring some means of transportation to continue his experiments. His meeting with Muhammad Taha gave him this opportunity:

> He [Taha] asked me to renovate the home of a member of his family. During the renovation, he asked me questions about jihad and its benefits. After he told me that somebody from my group had informed him about the KFC operation, I decided to trust him more; he was enthusiastic and promised to obey me. For this reason, I asked him to use his car to drive me to a place near Baddawi camp to detonate a B7 rocket with the help of a timer.

Just as happened with al-Ka'keh, "weak ties" led to core relationships. From a chance meeting through construction work, Taha entered the network and rapidly mastered the technique of manufacturing timers and explosive systems. Near the Baddawi camp, they successfully detonated a B7 rocket, using a timer and adding large quantities of gunpowder and benzene. 'Ali also suggested manufacturing explosives based on ammonium nitrate. They conducted tests in the Zeitun quarter of Abu Samra, in the Qalamoun district, and on the outskirts of the Baddawi camp, obtaining weapons and explosives from Palestinian factions in the Baddawi camp.

Now familiar with the manufacturing process, the two men decided to duplicate the KFC bombing at the Jounieh McDonald's restaurant on the Christian coastline. They sought more effective explosive materials, this time in the Baddawi camp. Some of al-Ka'keh's recruits were in charge of collecting a shipment of some twenty kilos of TNT, for which al-Ka'keh paid. Muhammad Taha equipped the explosive charge with his own homemade timer, connected to two electronic detonators. 'Ali and Taha then set the explosives in a window box meant for flowers and covered them with soil. After one failed attempt, they managed to detonate 1.5 kilos of TNT concealed in a flowerpot on the night of September 23, 2002—and heard about it later, through the press. The technical competency of Muhammad Taha influenced the decision-making process within the network. Indeed, it was this young electrician who advocated using the same method in three different American businesses on the same night in order to make a greater impact on the public.[21] Thanks to Taha's timers, the group successfully bombed three restaurants on the night of November 12, 2002, during the holy month of Ramadan: two Pizza Hut restaurants, one in Tripoli and one in Jounieh, and a Winners restaurant on the highway between Jounieh and Tripoli.

International Jihadi Backing: The Role of Ibn al-Shahid

One month later, Lebanese media reported the arrest of a network suspected of belonging to Osama bin Laden's organization, and al-Ka'keh's name surfaced in the reports. Before going into hiding, he notified Ali that their operations had impressed an al-Qaeda militant, originally from Yemen, named Ibn al-Shahid (son of the martyr) or al-Muhajir (the emigrant). Ibn al-Shahid expressed a strong desire to meet al-Ka'keh in Ayn al-Helweh, where the Yemeni had sought refuge in November 2001 after fleeing Afghanistan. As al-Ka'keh was no longer able to support Ali's activities financially, it was all the more urgent to connect with Ibn al-Shahid:

> I agreed and spoke to Muhammad Taha about it. A few days later, a person contacted me and introduced himself as Ibn al-Shahid. He asked to meet me inside the Ayn al-Helweh camp. Upon arriving in Sidon, I called Ibn al-Shahid who sent us a

[21] This shows the influence of al-Qaeda's signature tactic of striking several targets simultaneously: the two embassies of Nairobi and Dar es Salaam in 1998, the twin towers of the World Trade Center along with the Pentagon in 2001, and multiple trains in Madrid in 2003.

Palestinian named Abu Ibrahim who brought us by car to Ibn al-Shahid's home in the camp. Once we became acquainted, Ibn al-Shahid expressed his satisfaction about the attacks I had carried out. He asked me to continue such attacks against American interests in Lebanon, expressing his desire to see more victims fall, because this encouraged brothers abroad to send large amounts of money to finance these attacks.

Their meeting appears to have been fundamental: until then, Khaled 'Ali and his associates destroyed American establishments to make a statement. They did not kill people. In fact, their very mode of operation—attacks carried out at night when the restaurants were empty—foreclosed the possibility of a bloodbath. This time, looking for something like a larger-scale version of the aborted Hindu temple operation, they discussed killing civilians as a means to gain publicity and thus increase external aid to the group.

Ibn al-Shahid reportedly left Yemen for Afghanistan soon after the Taliban takeover of Kabul. According to investigation sources, he then "fought in Chechnya in the al-Qaeda organization," returning to Afghanistan to fight the Americans shortly after the beginning of the October 2001 offensive. At the end of 2001, he fled across the Syrian-Lebanon border and found refuge in Ayn al-Helweh with the partisans of 'Usbat al-Ansar. At Ahmad al-Miqati's suggestion, al-Ka'keh met al-Shahid in Ayn al-Helweh (later on al-Ka'keh asked Khaled 'Ali to procure forged identification papers for Ibn al-Shahid).

In Ayn al-Helweh, the meeting between Ibn al-Shahid—who introduced himself as a member of al-Qaeda—and Khaled 'Ali was interesting in itself, as an encounter between the second and third generations of jihadi terrorism. The first generation—that of the 1980s jihad in Afghanistan—constituted the contemporary matrix of jihadism. The second generation—that of Ibn al-Shahid—consisted of volunteers who came to Afghani camps after the Taliban's rise to power in 1996, and fought in Bosnia and Chechnya. The third generation, that of Khaled 'Ali, Muhammad al-Ka'keh, Muhammad Taha, and their companions in Tripoli, constituted a new form of jihadi terrorism that was autonomous, decentralized, and developed its modes of operation according to the means available.

In fact, third-generation jihadism did not always emancipate itself entirely from second-generation jihadism—in the case of the McDonald's network, the latter was, in a sense, caught up in it. Nevertheless, this form of jihadism asserted itself independently of the "al-Qaeda" label, and ascribing it to Osama bin Laden's organization would constitute a dangerous simplification. It was a phenomenon already in the process of emancipating itself from the global network and finding ways to spread more widely.

Initially, Ibn al-Shahid took over from al-Ka'keh and secured funding for a new operation Ali was planning: dynamiting the Spinneys supermarket in Tripoli. By choosing this supermarket, the members of the network sought to capitalize on a local dispute with inter-communal overtones: the store's management had laid off employees, who then accused management of ignoring Muslim-Christian quotas in their recruitment policy. Ibn al-Shahid authorized the operation and agreed to communicate with the actors via the Internet. As al-Ka'keh was about to leave Lebanon for Syria, he asked his brother—then completing his military service—to join the operation. On February 11, 2003, Ali and his henchmen rigged three explosive charges with timers and stashed them in the supermarket shelves. Only one exploded, but, as the bombers had hoped, suspicion initially fell on the establishment's former employees. Informed of the details of the operation, Ibn al-Shahid promised to supply state-of-the-art timer detonators "so that the next time, there would be no more technical malfunctions."

During their discussions in Ayn al-Helweh, Ibn al-Shahid and Khaled 'Ali also debated the best way to attack the American embassy, located on the northern road out of Beirut. They considered a car bomb, but Ibn al-Shahid judged the operation impossible due to embassy security measures, which a member of 'Usbat al-Ansar had already scouted and evaluated. Ibn al-Shahid was more inclined to favor a rocket attack and asked Ali to continue thinking about it and suggest plans at their next meeting.

Ibn al-Shahid tried to influence the group to attack American targets, or targets associated with the United States. However, this influence cannot be described as hierarchical. Rather, he motivated his fellow group members by pointing out the connection between a spectacular and deadly operation and possible access to significant external funding. Ali and al-Ka'keh do not seem to behave as his subordinates; their relationship with al-Shahid had more to do with coordination and exchange than obedience and hierarchy.

The Target of Violence

For an essentially local group, using violence risked state reprisal against their native neighborhood or city. Thus, when Ahmad al-Miqati, one of the leaders of the Sir al-Dinniyeh insurrection, met with al-Ka'keh in Ayn al-Helweh, he asked him not to carry out any assassinations, "to prevent Tripoli suffering repression at the hands of the security services afterward."

The members of the network perennially debated potential targets for their violence. They considered many possibilities drawn from different ideological and strategic referents:

- A geopolitical approach, sort of an extension of the Chechen conflict: targeting a Russian plane in Beirut airport (al-Miqati's idea).
- A moral approach on a local scale: bombing a local radio station that had broadcast irreverent comments about "a Tripoli sheikh" (al-Ka'keh's idea),[22] or destroying a bar in Tripoli's Qubbeh district. Sheikh Ahmad al-'Attar—who reappeared in 2003 after the three explosions on a Ramadan night—wanted to bomb the Casino du Liban (and asked Ali to teach him how to make explosives).[23]
- A religious approach with a transnational dimension: striking Hindu places of worship to avenge violence against Muslims in India.
- An "inner" approach directly focused on state authority figures: assassinating members of the Lebanese army intelligence services (Khaled 'Ali considered this option, and tried

[22] This sheikh's name was not mentioned, no doubt for reasons related to intercommunal tensions.

[23] Sheikh al-'Attar wanted to carry out an attack on the Casino du Liban with the help of an accomplice who would have placed the bomb without being noticed (without sporting the Salafi beard and garb). Khaled 'Ali refused to share his technical knowledge of bombing, but he agreed to give him the amount of explosives he needed. The source specifies that the sheikh showed Khaled 'Ali a timer connected to two 3-volt batteries with electrical wire.

to procure silencers for it). Such acts would avenge the young militants killed during the Sir al-Dinniyeh clashes or tortured after their arrest.

- An anti-imperialist approach, targeting symbols associated with American and British power. This framework explains the attacks against the KFC and Spinneys establishments in Tripoli. Targeting the US embassy in Lebanon had unanimous backing from all network members but, as mentioned above, there were disagreements over the best tactic. Al-Ka'keh, Ali, and al-'Attar considered three scenarios during several autumn 2002 meetings. The first, which Ali advocated, was a Lebanese version of the September 11 attacks, involving crashing an explosives-laden helicopter into the embassy. Ali volunteered to fly the helicopter himself on this suicide mission. Al-Ka'keh argued against this plan because, according to him, trainees for the operation would immediately be spotted when they went out on flight practice. The second scenario was to launch rockets on the embassy from a high vantage point. Finally, a third possibility involved sneaking a bomb into the compound by painting a van to match those used by a company doing construction work there. This last idea appealed to Ibn al-Shahid, and it was scheduled to follow the April 5, 2003 operation against the McDonald's restaurant in Dora.
- A denominational anti-Syrian approach: al-Ka'keh proposed attacking Syrian interests in Lebanon by, for example, firing rockets at the main Syrian intelligence services premises in Tripoli, in the Mar Maroun district. The details of this aborted operation are revealing for at least two reasons. First, there would be no public claim of responsibility for hostility toward the Syrian regime. The idea was to direct blame for the attack on partisans of the Christian general Michel Aoun, who were responsible for most anti-Syrian activism at the time, although they did not use violence. Second, al-Ka'keh gave an LAW rocket launcher to an aide and entrusted him with this mission, but the latter could not find the courage to carry it out. This bears witness to the terrifying effect of the mere mention of Syrian intelligence services on Tripoli's Islamists.

- A symbolic anti-PLO approach to weaken the Palestinian nationalist leadership, in order to lighten their constraints on Islamist activity in the camps. Thus, Khaled 'Ali wished to begin by "attacking Fatah's local offices in the Baddawi camp as retribution for Fatah's harassment of 'Usbat al-Ansar in the Ayn al-Helweh camp." It seems, however, that later on, 'Usbat's decision to surrender Badi' Hammade to the Lebanese army and the house arrest it imposed on Ahmad al-Miqati shocked Khaled 'Ali. As a result, he reportedly decided to launch an RPG at the Qubbeh army barracks and have the Palestinians of Baddawi camp blamed for it. However, he dropped the idea because too many people frequented the location where he intended to set up the launch pad.

The McDonald's Operation in Dora

The December 2002 decision to attack the McDonald's restaurant in Dora marked a substantial change for the group. They decided—probably under al-Shahid's influence—to act on April 5, 2003, around 4 pm, during Saturday afternoon peak hours. The location was not chosen at random. This particular McDonald's was situated in a working-class Christian suburb, right next to the Almaza brewery (makers of the national Lebanese beer). The attackers expected that the brewery too might be destroyed in the blast.

The lawyers' files indicate that Ibn al-Shahid sent Khaled 'Ali and his recruit, Muhammad Taha, a first payment to fund the preparations. Upon their return to Tripoli, they purchased a used Renault 18, had a mechanic in Tabbaneh change the license plates, and got a friend to repaint the vehicle. Without much difficulty, their network enrolled two conscripts, one of whom was al-Ka'keh's brother, barely nineteen years old at the time. Meanwhile, Ali had secured additional financial support from Ibn al-Shahid thanks to one of his aide's trips back and forth between the Ayn al-Helweh camp and Tripoli.

The day before the operation, Ali and Muhammad Taha drove into the Dinniyeh mountains, far away from prying eyes. There they positioned the explosives and electric timers inside the Renault.

They took care to erase identification numbers from its bumpers and doors.

On the day of the attack, their two-car convoy headed to Beirut. Muhammad Taha led the way in a Honda, followed by the explosives-laden Renault. To facilitate the group's escape, Khaled 'Ali placed a sticker of the Virgin Mary and a picture of Jesus on the windshield. To the same end, the two conscripts wore their military uniforms in order to reach the McDonald's parking lot unnoticed. Ali worried that his beard might attract attention, so he waited further away, under the bridge of the main Dora intersection.

They parked the Renault between the restaurant and the Almaza brewery walls. At 4 pm, al-Ka'keh set the charges to detonate 45 minutes later. Muhammad Taha entered the restaurant, followed by the two conscripts. They sat down and pretended to eat while al-Ka'keh placed a 400-gram charge of TNT—set to detonate 35 minutes later—in a bathroom trashcan. The ten-minute difference was deemed necessary so that the car bomb would detonate after the paramedics, police, and firefighters arrived on scene and hopefully ignite the brewery's fuel tanks, maximizing the carnage.

Motive and Reason to Act

The protagonists viewed the destruction of American fast-food chains as a proportionate response to American policy in the Middle East. In the Syrian-Lebanese context of the early 2000s, one had only to listen to the radio, watch television, or read a militant newspaper to be aware of the mechanisms and logic behind this language game. Following Israel's withdrawal from southern Lebanon in May 2000, an official ideology of Resistance conflating American and Israeli actions characterized the atmosphere of celebration of the *muqawim*'s (resistance fighter's) military feats. In such a climate, violence "against American interests" was an obvious choice for Islamist militants.

As a result, Sunni jihadi were spared the trouble of providing justifications for their actions. The *muqawim*'s semiotic system, tied into the national and regional state system, was partially responsible for this. However, unlike Hezbollah in southern Lebanon, radical Sunnis did not enjoy any recognized territorial area of action within this system. As a result, they risked that local powers, including Syria, Hezbollah, and Lebanese institutions, might accuse them of terrorism. Of course, in their own view, their actions bore the divine seal of jihad, and were justified as an enactment of the Muslim masses' anger. This double standard fuelled radical Sunni groups' resentment of Shi'ite Islam and its offshoots, but at the time their resentment did not result in any action against Hezbollah.

To illuminate the group's behavior, we may draw on the vengeful impulse that the German philosopher Peter Sloterdijk described in his book, *Rage and Time*.[24] Images of post–Cold War conflicts on al-Jazeera television, along with Hezbollah's heroic narrative, fueled their rage. If Muslim civilians fell victim to the embargo against Iraq, to repression in the Palestinian Territories, to wars and massacres in the Balkans, and to the American offensive in Afghanistan, then other Muslim civilians must react, since "vengeance is born of rage taking shape as a project."[25] This international dimension increased the intensity of militant commitment: Muhammad al-Ka'keh was sensitive to the fate of Muslims in Chechnya, Bosnia, and Palestine. Live TV footage facilitated this mode of politicization by activating an emotional response. The group members' identified themselves first and foremost as Muslims, and not as Lebanese, so images of Muslim victims, whatever their location, provoked strong indignation. But a critical requirement for exacting revenge was that the Muslim victim had been injured by a non-Muslim power. In Darfur, for instance, where Muslims were attacking Muslims, the conflict was construed by the jihadis as a pretext for Western intrusion in the umma's internal affairs.

Because the group never publicly took credit for their actions, this "vocabulary of motive" emerged *ex post*, during the investigation. It was not explicitly articulated during the events themselves.[26] This strategy of silence, identical to the stance adopted by the perpetrators of the September 11, 2001 attacks, was designed to minimize the gap between the protagonists and the abstract

---

[24] See Peter Sloterdijk, *Rage and Time* (New York: Columbia University Press, 2010).

[25] Ibid., 89.

[26] A distinction between "motive" and "reason" has been theorized by Charles Wright Mills in "Situated Action and Vocabularies of Motive," *American Sociological Review* 4 (1940), 670–80. Motive does not have causal status; it is a label given to an action.

"umma" they claimed to represent. In the view of its authors, the event did not need to be explained. They were acting on behalf of a victimized umma, whose subservient leaders and defeats at the hands of Western powers were lamented in mosques every Friday.

The human environment facilitated the successive initiatives of Muhammad al-Ka'keh and Khaled 'Ali. Neighborhood life offered many opportunities for interaction. Refusing to do a favor for a friend, or even an acquaintance, led to crippling moral censure in communities where everyone knew everyone else. In this particular case, the slow pace of the group's formation greatly facilitated the reciprocity of exchanges—either of services or objects—and the building of trust. This clearly demonstrates "the power of the situation" in a context where neighborhood preachers readily brandished believers' faith the better to lambast the state for neglecting its religious duties, either internationally or toward its own society.

Sources highlight two crucial elements: the significance of the local environment, and the influence of international news. All of the group's members were from Tripoli. Even though Ahmad al-'Attar was quickly marginalized, he supplied a preconstituted solidarity network based on his web of acquaintances throughout the mosques of the city's historic district. This allowed the network to begin drawing strength from an informal, fluid, and local ecosystem that operated in a densely populated urban environment in which neighborhoods provided both security against external threats and protection for the most politicized individuals.

The group also relied on local memories of the Sir al-Dinniyeh confrontation. As noted above, the incident presented opportunities for new encounters and federated various sources of support (for instance, Muhammad al-Ka'keh came to pray in the old city's mosques after meeting Ahmad al-'Attar). The group discarded its original humanitarian objective of aiding the families of the Sir al-Dinniyeh detainees in favor of a military objective: striking material or human targets to liberate Islamists arrested after the Dinniyeh clashes. The January 2000 crisis—the first confrontation in Lebanon between Sunni jihadi militants and an Arab army—affected the attitudes of all concerned: after Sir al-Dinniyeh, the Lebanese state became an enemy. Jihadism was no longer only a commitment to defend the umma's frontiers. It had become a domestic struggle.

CHAPTER 3

⇥⇤

The Anti-Syrian Movement
Rebuilding a Political Scene

Former Prime Minister Rafiq al-Hariri's assassination on February 14, 2005, sparked both international pressure and local pro-sovereignty protests, forcing Syrian troops from Lebanon in April. This series of events profoundly transformed Sunni Islamism in North Lebanon.[1] For the first time, the Future Movement (Rafiq al-Hariri's political party) could extend its political influence to the north of the country, a move that was not possible under the Syrian occupation. Salafi sheikhs with much to gain from the Syrian forces' scheduled departure also threw their support behind the Future Movement. They hoped in particular to benefit electorally from public reaction to the assassination of the main political representative of Sunni Islam in the Levant. In appreciation for this support, the new anti-Syrian majority voted to give amnesty to the Islamist detainees of the Sir al-Dinniyeh clashes. Through these deals and reciprocations, the Salafi notables became recognized as special intermediaries between the new power and their militant flock.

---

[1] For a detailed account of the 2005–2010 period, see Michael Young, *The Ghosts of Martyrs Square: An Eyewitness Account of Lebanon's Life Struggle* (New York: Simon and Schuster, 2010).

For Sunni political Islam, engaged in anti-Syrian activism since 2005, "community patriotism" (as Maxime Rodinson put it) was an essential catalyst for mobilization. Primarily, it was a response to accusations of complicity with the West stemming from the existence of Hezbollah-linked Sunni factions.[2] Soon after assuming power, Sa'ad al-Hariri became the target of two contradictory accusations. Their incompatibility was of little importance, as they were aimed at different audiences. The first came from Sunni Islamists close to Hezbollah who opposed the new government's decision to release Samir Ja'ja, the Christian Lebanese Forces' former commander-in-chief, after eleven years in jail. Citing his presumed role in the July 1, 1987 assassination of Prime Minister Rashid Karami, Islamists questioned why some assassins should be subject to international justice, while others were freed. In the same vein, they cited Rafiq al-Hariri's financial contributions to the restoration of churches as grounds to question his family's Islamic legitimacy.

The pro-Syrian secularist Syrian Social Nationalist Party (SSNP), along with Michel Aoun's movement, put forward a second set of accusations. Contrary to the Sunni Islamists, they accused the Hariris of aspiring to "islamize" Lebanon by building mosques and funding religious networks. They traced this to an influx of Saudi money, which they also deemed responsible for corrupting the political system. But despite their contradictory claims, both currents agreed that an increasingly assertive Sunni political identity increased the risk of sectarian conflict in Lebanon, akin to what had been unfolding in Iraq since 2004.

For the leaders of the new governmental majority, the challenge in the north was to harness long-restrained anti-Syrian sentiment without yielding power to Islamists. Indeed, the latter's own religious and militant support bases' overzealous behavior constantly threatened the anti-Syrian coalition's interdenominational coherence. Because of Islamist movements' strength across the Arab world, Sunni political elites were not in the same position as other Lebanese elites vis-à-vis extremists within their own ranks. The latter had been able to use their communities' most radical elements as pressure to bolster their bargaining position at the national level. In

---

[2] Maxime Rodinson, "Qu'est-ce qu'une communauté religieuse libanaise?" in *L'Islam: politique et croyance* (Paris: Fayard, 1992), 154–76.

contrast, Sunni elites faced Islamist bases radically hostile to both the Lebanese interdenominational system and its official representatives.

Thus the Future Movement had to satisfy three imperatives. First, it had to carefully assume a political identity that was both Sunni and compatible with its commitments to pro-independence Christian factions. Second, it had to defend the principle of independent Sunni decision-making without exposing itself to accusations of sectarianism. Finally, in order to institutionalize the "charisma" of the foundational March 14, 2005 protests, it had to build an organizational structure in North Lebanon rapidly and from scratch, despite the party's complete lack of experience in this field. The time was ripe to revive the image of a city fighting Syrian influence in Lebanon. Whereas the resistance fighter's image was anchored in Hezbollah's highly popular nearly quarter-century guerrilla campaign in southern Lebanon, the combatant's identity unavoidably rekindled memories of past conflicts with the Syrian regime. Since, by definition, the combatant (*muqatil*) had challenged the internal and regional status quo extant for about twenty years, those who claimed independence from Syria in 2005 were immediately accused of fuelling a new Lebanese civil war.

The disconnect between the local combatant and the resistance fighter opened the representatives of the new 2005 governmental majority to charges of manipulating the denominational fabric of the country in an attempt to destroy the Resistance. Yet the latter, despite its mystical aura, was also a roughly twenty-year-old politico-military order whose mere existence perpetuated defensiveness and fear in the other communities of the region. In other words, the Resistance perpetuated the very sectarianism it accused the new governmental majority of provoking. It operated like communist ideology during the Cold War: working in the outside world as a rhetoric of emancipation and the rejection of global and regional hegemony, while operating domestically to legitimize authoritarian structures and practices.[3]

[3] This context often makes the various actors' discourses misleading and inconsistent with their strategic or domestic interests. Hezbollah has certainly displayed its Islamo-nationalist ideology, but it has barely been able to dissimulate its other goals, connected to the expansion of revolutionary Shi'ite Islam through the struggle against Israel. At the same time, the Syrian regime has claimed to represent an Arab defense against Israeli ambitions, but the wealth that the military class in Lebanon acquired also, more prosaically, neutralized the army's political aspirations.

Searching out the "truth" about Prime Minister Rafiq al-Hariri's assassination was not a goal that many people were ready to die for. But in the opposite camp, many were ready to die for Hezbollah's cause, built on enduring religious and ideological grounds. Thus, the Future Movement had to accept the populist and sectarian emotions unleashed by the events of March 14 and take responsibility for the Sunni community's mobilizing myths. However, they also had to build a sturdy organizational structure to facilitate oversight of the community's broad coalition, just in case any one actor went overboard.

As a sign of the North's importance, a Hariri family member directly administered this structure. Nader al-Hariri was the cousin of Sa'ad al-Hariri and the son of Bahiya, Rafiq al-Hariri's sister. Nader, whose legitimacy came from his connection with the dynasty's heir, Sa'ad, managed the local balance of power and resolved political and financial disputes. In spring 2005, he was forced to choose between the multiple parties offering to instrumentalize the late Hariri's memory in order to launch political careers in the upcoming parliamentary elections.

However, the task of managing the North was not left entirely to Nader al-Hariri. In the spring of 2005, the new Interior Security Forces' director Achraf Rifi and his deputy, Colonel Wissam al-Hassan, purged the ISF of pro-Syrian officers. Other security bodies—general security and army intelligence—escaped the purge and remained close to either Syria or Hezbollah. The United States and France favored this change as promoting Lebanese governance devoid of "regional influence" (i.e., Syrian or Iranian/pro-Hezbollah) and capable of properly investigating Rafiq al-Hariri's murder. Colonel Wissam al-Hassan, a key figure in the reorganized ISF and the administration of North Lebanon, was the former head of Rafiq al-Hariri's personal security detail. In the North, the issue of security was directly linked to that of obedience. By radically modifying the population's relationship with the state's security apparatus, the new governmental majority hoped to regain the allegiance of the many groups and individuals who had suffered from arbitrary arrests, incarceration, and abuse over the previous twenty years of Syrian dominance.

The reformed ISF's strategic value was based on at least two elements. One was its ability to fully participate in the international investigation of Rafiq al-Hariri's assassination. The other was its ability to gather intelligence about the whole of the country's political and religious personnel and, therefore, to wield power over them. Personnel files stored in the ISF archives were a precise tool for selecting those who were to enjoy the support of the new government, and to deter those likely to become its opponents.

The Saudi authorities hoped to construct in Lebanon a denominational line of defense against growing Iranian influence in the region. Their presence also allowed them to monitor their own nationals who might be linked to al-Qaeda. Special channels of communication with ISF leaders allowed Prince Muqrin bin Abd al-Aziz (then head of the Saudi intelligence services) to gain knowledge of the situation on the ground and use that to distribute Saudi largesse.

Salafi Sheikhs Offering Their Services

The Salafi sheikhs were among the first to request an audience to determine areas of mutual interest with the Hariris. Sheikh Da'i al-Islam al-Shahhal, the most typical representative of this group, emphasized the causal links between some youngsters' jihadi callings (illustrated by the dramatic events of the McDonald's network bombings less than two years earlier) and the Interior Ministry's decision to close his own religious institution in 1996. According to the sheikh, by specifically targeting centers of religious instruction, the Syrians had deliberately deprived young Lebanese Muslims of the religious structures required to teach a "true" reading of Islamic texts. Isolated from religious authority and constantly victimized by the police, these youth were attracted to a deviant conception of jihad. He asserted that only the established representatives of Salafism could curb this phenomenon and derail actions detrimental to the Sunni community and Islam. Salafi sheikhs mediated between the working-class public, which they knew through the majority of their students in Salafi centers and through contacts with various representatives of authority, including leaders of the city (zu'ama'), the army's intelligence services (2nd bureau), the Interior Security Forces, and the Syrian intelligence services. In exchange for a promise to control their field efficiently and to support the new parliamentary majority, the sheikhs sought recognition of their status as notables and, therefore, an end to their own difficulties with the police and the judicial system.

Sheikh Da'i al-Islam al-Shahhal's explanation of these events warrants especially close analysis, as it makes abundantly clear how important it is that political scientists and historians critically assess how actors explain their own histories. One must try to reconstitute an actor's concerns, as they were at a particular time in his past, before evaluating his subsequent narrative about those concerns. In the Tripolitan sheikh's case, he partially appropriated the anti-Salafi frameworks of the Syrian regime in order to better convince his audience. Specifically, he made use of Syrians' portrayal of themselves to Western embassies as a barrier against the Salafi threat. According to this propaganda, if Syria retreated from Lebanon, nothing would be able to hold back Salafism's spread among the Lebanese Sunni population. In line with this Syrian narrative, Da'i al-Islam described his personal history of persecution during the Syrian era, one punctuated by multiple intrusions by the Lebanese and Syrian security forces. In 2008, during a public appearance in Riyadh on the set of the Saudi satellite television channel al-Majd, he detailed "the Syrians' reactions of exasperation with the increase in signs of piety in North Lebanon, such as men's long beards and women's wearing the *khimâr* (full veil)."[4]

The sheikh's fifteen-year retrospective omits other realities less useful for his purposes. Indeed, in many respects, the period in question was a sort of golden age for Salafism in North Lebanon. Most "Salafi" religious institutions opened and flourished in the 1990s. In 1990, for example, Da'i al-Islam al-Shahhal established a religious association—the Association for Islamic Guidance and Charity (Jama'iyyat al-Hidaya wal-Ihsan al-Islamiyya)—which ran a center for religious teaching with the same name (Ma'had al-Hidaya

---

[4] Da'i al-Islam al-Shahhal was a guest on the program "One Hour of Dialogue," broadcast on November 2, 2008 (4 Dhou-l-Qa'ada, 1429 AH) by the Al-Majd Saudi satellite TV channel, on the topic "Sunnis in Lebanon, between Alliances and Divisions." The episode is available on YouTube, http://www.youtube.com/watch?v=8y1zbvycv9q (accessed January 2010). Times have changed since anthropologist John Gulick could state in the middle of the sixties, "Judging from the large number of women in Tripoli who are not veiled at all, there must be many Muslim women and men who do not consider such expression improper." John Gulick, *Tripoli: A Modern Arab City* (Cambridge: Harvard University Press, 1967).

wal-Ihsan). Syrian intelligence services considered the association's rhetoric fairly harmless, as it was largely directed against the regional policy of the United States and its Arab allies. While he was studying at the University of Medina (he graduated in 1984), Da'i al-Islam befriended several sheikhs who became the main voices of protest in the kingdom over the following decade, among them Safar al-Hawali, Nasir al-'Umar, and, especially, Salman al-'Awda. Under their influence, he adopted the principle of the "comprehension of reality" (*fiqh al-waqi'*), according to which believers are required to attempt to understand the political questions and contexts that confront the umma. This attitude posed a challenge to the principle of blind obedience to those who wield political authority (*wali al-amr*)—a core principle of Wahhabi doctrine. In the 1990s and 2000s, Da'i al-Islam saw himself as a dissident in the deterritorialized Salafi field. In 1996, a rumor had it that the decision to shut down his center stemmed from the Saudi embassy's complaint following the center's radio broadcast (another privilege of that period) of *khutbas* (sermons) by dissident Saudi sheikhs. The Interior Ministry's stated reason for the decision at the time—that the center was "instigating sectarian hatred"—was a mere pretext, so this rumor would have it. For the Lebanese regime, Salafism also had the precious advantage that it distanced Sunnis from politics during the period from the late 1990s to the early 2000s. Sheikh Da'i and other directors of Islamic institutes repeatedly told their young audiences that the very nature of elections in Lebanon made them unlawful in religious terms.

Salafism's usefulness extended beyond Lebanon's borders as well. The fall of Saddam Hussein's regime, in April 2003, provided prominent Salafi sheikhs an opportunity to channel some of the poor youths' resentment by inviting them—with the tacit approval of the Syrian intelligence services—to go fight in Iraq against the American occupation. Thus, Salafis reestablished their religious credibility among those determined to confront the "enemies of the umma," while at the same time averting a new wave of arrests in North Lebanon, a natural consequence of renewed local terrorist attacks.

Any interpretation of the Salafi students' bitter criticism of most of the directors of Tripoli's Salafi centers after their spring 2005 political shifts must take into account this local religious environment.

Particularly, many adherents did not understand why elections that had previously been pronounced contrary to *shari'a* were now suddenly acceptable.[5] This political reclassification (some would say "justification") furthered the fragmentation already typical of the Salafi scene, given its potentially unlimited number of controversial issues and the schismatic multiplication of Salafi trends of thought. Sheikh Da'i al-Islam's entry into the arena of institutional politics certainly did not curb this natural tendency within Salafism; rather, it provoked further internal debates and opposing stances within the increasingly fragmented movement.

Building a Political Machine

The Future Movement's unstructured political and ideological framework and the difficulty of transforming an electoral machine into a political one compelled its leaders to cooperate with these religious actors. The movement undertook this cooperation in order to break Syrian control over most of the local Islamist movements and to resituate Salafi militant potential within a Sunni communitarian framework, rather than leaving it free to serve broader-based regional causes. But in order to prevent this integration from provoking the community, it was essential to incorporate the representatives of the Salafi current into as broad a structure as possible so as to dilute their influence. Hariri family members seemed well aware of the risks of this strategy. As Nader al-Hariri himself admitted, "For some of them, if there is no strong leadership, we do not know how they might act. Without political supervision, they play their own game . . . our true adversary within the Sunni community is not Miqati or Hoss, it is Osama bin Laden."[6]

[5] See Sahar al-Atrache, "Des salafismes à Tripoli-Liban: usages et instrumentalisations identitaires" (Master's thesis in political science, Saint Joseph University, Beirut, 2007), 38; Tine Gade, "Return to Tripoli: Battle over Minds and Meaning amongst Sunni Ideologues within the Islamist Field in Tripoli, Lebanon" (Master's thesis, Institut d'Études Politiques de Paris, 2008).

[6] Interview with Nader al-Hariri, Beirut, September 2009. Of course, these words were spoken more than a year after the infamous May 7, 2008 attack, when Hezbollah militants broke a taboo by using their weapons against other Lebanese citizens and, in just a few hours' fighting, destroyed the Future Movement's offices in Beirut.

The best way to control these new allies was to quickly build a security and intelligence infrastructure sufficiently powerful to discourage dissent by anyone within the nascent "Northern Alliance." Besides opening offices in Tripoli and the main cities of the North, the Future Movement set up lightly armed security forces, the "regiments of Tripoli" (Afwaj Trablus), with support from the Secure Plus security firm. They also established a training camp in the Barqawil district of Akkar. By the end of 2006, the "regiments" of northern Lebanon were about 4,800-strong.[7] Inside Tripoli, the units boasted 500 paid volunteers in Tabbaneh, 280 in Qubbeh, 170 in al-Mina, and 160 in the Abu Samra neighborhood.

Arming the units posed several challenges. In principle, it would seem difficult to reconcile the legalist aspirations of a pro-independence movement—calling for Hezbollah's disarmament, or at least for the coordination of its activities with an integrated, nationwide military command—with the militaristic aspirations of part of its working-class Sunni support base in Beirut and Tripoli. This support base could not conceive of remaining militarily impotent against pro-Syrian militias, such as the SSNP in Beirut and the North, against the Democratic Arab Party in the North, or against the Alawite militia of Rif'at Eid in the Tripoli neighborhood of Jabal Mohsen. If they retreated to their legalist position, the Future Movement would automatically lose an essential part of its internal legitimacy. But at the same time, the pressure from a political base to obtain weapons might well feed a vicious rivalry between different groups over the distribution of weapons.

A more prosaic difficulty was the danger that recipients of weapons might resell part of their stock to other protagonists. Even worse, in the event of poor center-periphery coordination, local security chiefs might be tempted to decide for themselves what quantity of arms should be allocated to whom, based on their own personal leanings.

Compounding these problems was the Future Movement's inability to find qualified and skilled individuals to populate their units. They first entrusted administration of the Afwaj to a retired Lebanese army general; then, after 2008, to a colonel on extended leave from his regiment. They even appointed retired civil servants

[7] Interview with former heads of the Afwaj of Tripoli, summer 2008.

as heads of the Afwaj's various branches. Finally, they also relied on former members of the Palestinian Fatah's anti-Syrian networks, which had been active in the 1980s, to help with some of the political work.

Components of the Denominational Dynamic

An Unabashed *Muqatil*: "Sheikh" Kana'an Naji

After several years of exile, Kana'an Naji discreetly made his way back to Tripoli in the early 2000s. His reemergence on the local political scene held considerable significance, because his name was a reminder of the period when the Tawhid Movement still eluded Syrian or Iranian control. He was the only founder of the movement still alive, having escaped assassination and imprisonment by the Syrians. Also, unlike Hashem Minqara or Samir al-Hassan, whom Bashar al-Assad had freed in 2000 after about ten years of incarceration, Kana'an had never been co-opted by the Syrian authorities. His return to Tripoli was reminiscent of the mid-1980s, when Tawhid fighters had fought alongside the city's inhabitants to repel Syrian military offensives. His presence had a more subversive side as well: during the same period Kana'an Naji had been among those in charge of supporting the Syrian Muslim Brotherhood against Hafez al-Assad's regime, as part of a broad coalition that included the PLO, Saudi Arabia, and Saddam Hussein's Iraq.[8]

"Sheikh" Kana'an was born in 1956, in Tripoli, into a family of wealthy landowners. His father's family owned land extending from the outskirts of the Abu Samra neighborhood to the al-Koura region, and his grandfather was the *qa'imaqam* (the imperial authority's representative in charge of the area, with executive powers) of this same region during the Ottoman period. Young Kana'an spent his adolescence in a quasi-insurrectional political atmosphere. As in the other main coastal towns, part of the population of Tripoli lived in tune with the "Palestinian revolution," in an atmosphere of high tension and frequent run-ins with the army.

In November 1976, when Kana'an Naji was twenty years old, he witnessed the first occupation of Tripoli by the Syrian army,

[8] Interview with the former secretary general of the Syrian Muslim Brotherhood, Adnan Sa'ad al-Din, Amman, July 2008.

deployed under the auspices of the Arab Deterrent Force. The effervescent atmosphere of partisan fervor instantly vanished, and all political parties were banned except the SSNP. Thanks to the diplomatic efforts of Khalil 'Akkawi, Syrian troops did not enter and occupy Bab al-Tabbaneh, but several units camped in front of the neighborhood's entrances.[9] Kana'an reportedly became pious during this period, after one of his brothers (Adnan) participated in Juhayman al-'Utaybi's November 20, 1979 takeover of Mecca's Grand Mosque. Kana'an then went into hiding, joining Jund Allah (the Army of God), where, thanks to his organizational talents, he rapidly became the right-hand man of its founder, Sheikh Fawaz Hussein Agha. Trained for covert operations by Palestinian Fatah operatives, Kana'an Najistood out for his military qualities and his predilection for intelligence work. In the fall of 1982, after several weeks of negotiations, he agreed to join the Islamic Unification Movement (Harakat al-Tawhid al-Islamiyya). The latter federated three local political organizations under Sheikh Sayyid Sha'ban's leadership: the Arab Lebanon Movement (Harakat Lubnan al-'Arabi), the Popular Resistance (al-Muqawama al-Sha'biyya) under the leadership of Khalil 'Akkawi (Abu 'Arabi), and Jund Allah.

Palestinian pressure explained the creation of this new political bloc in North Lebanon. Yasser Arafat had requested that the University of al-Azhar's Mission in Tripoli set up an Islamist line of defense against the Syrian regime. Several Egyptian sheikhs close to the Muslim Brotherhood had also promoted the creation of the Tawhid Movement, on behalf of the PLO leadership. However, neighborhood chiefs united in this movement could not relate to Sha'ban's increasing adherence to Iranian revolutionary values. Khalil 'Akkawi withdrew from the bloc in April 1984, as did Kana'an Naji, who had by now become the leader of the Army of God.

According to Sheikh Naji's retrospective account of this period, the means to establish an "Islamic public order" had not been worked out ahead of time. In fact, the effort was not equal to the perils of exercising power.[10] He described Tawhid being drawn into a series of conflicts against its will, first against gangs in Qubbeh, and then

---

[9] Ibid., 185.

[10] On September 14, 2007, in a very rare public interview for the "Dialogue with a Leader" show on Dawn Radio (*Idha'at al-Fajr*), Kana'an Naji was questioned on both his role within Tawhid and on more recent events, a few days after the fall of Nahr al-Bared

against all of the city's secular organizations. Some of these were hostile to Syria, such as Faruq al-Muqaddem's October 24 Movement, and Abd al-Majid al-Rafi'i's Iraqi Ba'ath Party, while others were pro-Syrian, such as the Syrian Ba'ath Party and the Communist Party. The "battle of Tripoli" pitted Tawhid against the Syrian army from September 14 to October 6, 1985. Epic accounts of the battle indicated that Tawhid's defeat was more political than military:

> Because of the situation at the time, Tripoli's fall was political. It would be very useful to learn some lessons from this defeat. Today is the 10th of September 2007, nearly 22 years have passed since the night before the 14th of September, and I am certain that if Tripoli had been united politically, we would have defeated them. . . . You could see it in their eyes at the time . . . after twenty-one days, they would have given anything for a ceasefire. The fundamental difference between them and us, the *fundamental* one, was that they were stronger than us on the political level. They defeated us politically, with obvious meddling from Iran inside the city. . . . So Tripoli fell politically before falling militarily. . . . The proof of this is that when they entered the city, we were still there. They did not defeat us militarily [repeated twice]. And thank God the city was not defeated militarily, for they would have done far worse to Tripoli than what they did to Hama . . . far worse."[11]

Negotiations between revolutionary Iran and Syrian leaders allowed Sheikh Sha'ban and his organization to survive, on the condition that they cooperate with the Syrian regime or suffer a new wave of repression. Circumstances seem to have transformed the sheikh from a *muqatil* into a Sunni *muqawim*. On another level, this position afforded him the guarantees he needed to spread the most closed-minded sociocultural concepts, demonstrating that the figure of the resistance fighter (*muqawim*) was entirely compatible with the more insidious figure of the entrepreneur (*muqawil*) of anger when it came to symbolic issues. Other less flexible and less opportunistic historic leaders of the Tawhid Movement were captured or assassinated; some, like Kana'an Naji, managed to flee.

---

camp. Sheikh Naji's complete interview can be found on the Jund Allah website, http://www.al-jond.com (accessed August 14, 2008).

[11] Ibid., 185.

After the Syrian army's return to Tripoli, Kana'an Naji managed to return to the mountain villages of Dinniyeh, where he established cells, preparing for the possibility that he might be forced to flee the city. After the assassination of Khalil 'Akkawi by the Syrians on February 9, 1986, Naji traveled to the Christian regions by bus, disguised as a mechanic to pass through Syrian checkpoints, and then moved on to Sidon. According to the terms of a security agreement between the Lebanese Forces and Fatah, the former was to grant political asylum and freedom of movement to Muslim military leaders involved in the struggle against the Syrian army. Thanks to this clause, Kana'an Naji was able to help former Tawhid members fleeing Syrian repression, working from an eastern suburb of Beirut where he had settled.

According to Kana'an Naji, the Syrians had one goal behind these actions: disarming Sunnis in order to prevent them from building a political leadership in Lebanon that could threaten the Syrian regime. Once again, possession of weapons turned out to be the decisive criterion by which to evaluate various Lebanese communities' respective degrees of vulnerability:

> Look at [the inhabitants of] Zghorta, did they lose their weapons? In Ba'al Mohsen, did they lose their weapons? Walid Jumblatt, did he lose his weapons? The only ones who lost their weapons are the Sunnis. Which is precisely the opposite of what happened to the Shi'ite community, whose weapons stock has increased, and which has taken all of Lebanon's weapons for its own use. The only ones whose weapons were confiscated are the Sunnis, no one else! We are the only ones who need arms, because they were taken from us. Hafez al-Assad said: "In Tripoli, do not even let the Sunnis have a kitchen knife or a hunting rifle."

Kana'an Naji directly referred to a strong form of political Sunnism, combining both denominational identity and independent decision-making. If this had taken the shape of Sunni Islamist radicalism, it would have cut its ties with the political legitimacy of Lebanese institutions. If it had allied itself with Syria and Hezbollah, it would have been allowed to act within the institutional framework, but would have lost all political autonomy. Thus, only an independent political leadership could appropriately embody Sunni political Islam inside Lebanon. Such reasoning was just as valid in Tripoli as it was in Damascus, and it contained a subversive aspect that explains why Kana'an Naji, to this day, is regarded as the Syrian regime's existential enemy in North Lebanon. According to Naji, Rafiq al-Hariri was assassinated in February 2005 because he was becoming a catalyst for political Sunnism in both Lebanon and Syria.

Beyond the external difficulties of wielding power, it is interesting to analyze as well the kinds of lessons the sheikh deduced from the "Islamic emirate" experience in Tripoli:

> We became involved in messy dealings. . . . We shouldn't have gotten involved in these sorts of issues. . . . People would come to us and say "so-and-so insulted so-and-so. . . . Do something!" Someone says to you: "You must intervene. . . ." So you send over a youth to deal with the problem . . . but sometimes he would mess up . . . act dictatorial. The lesson we must learn is that Muslims mustn't get involved in these kinds of issues, issues of the actual forces on the ground. . . . The most delicate and dangerous thing is justice. It takes ten years of study to become a judge. And even with ten years of study, it's still difficult. The toughest job is dispensing justice to people. And all of a sudden someone who can barely write shows up and wants to mete out justice! . . . Because he represents *de facto* power! This is what happened in Tripoli, exactly as it happened in the rest of Lebanon. Tripoli was no different. Power corrupts.[12]

Thus did Kana'an Naji recall the sordid realities of wielding power in militia circles—without any religious sugarcoating. His public assertion of the incompatibility, in principle, of Islam with power-wielding militias was not only an exercise in public self-criticism (rather rare in post-war Lebanon), but also a message to Islamists temporarily linked to the March 14 Group, who might still have had hopes of pursuing this illusion. At the same time, he was trying to reassure anyone concerned about a possible resurgence of the Islamic Unification Movement (whose intolerance of others was far

[12] Ibid.

from forgotten)[13] in Tripoli. He reaffirmed the role he had claimed for himself within the Sunni component of the March 14 Group: that of providing local endorsement to Sa'ad al-Hariri by voluntarily lending the latter his credibility, his knowledge of the field, and his military expertise.

"Sheikh" Kana'an was able to mobilize several hundred armed partisans in just a few hours, and he was very close to ISF leaders. He was probably also in charge of ascertaining the political loyalty of his partners in the Independent Islamic Meeting (al-Liqa' al-Islami al-Mustaqill). Khaled al-Daher, a former parliamentarian of the Lebanese Muslim Brotherhood (al-Jama'a al-Islamiyya), and Zakariya al-Masri, a Salafi sheikh from Tripoli, had forged this loose tripartite alliance in late 2006. Elected to parliament in 1996, al-Daher had left the Muslim Brotherhood after a Syrian veto barred him from running again in 2000. A former member of the Lebanese Muslim Brotherhood, al-Masri had been a co-founder of the Islamist party's militia, the "Jihad Combatants" (al-mujahidun), during the first few months of the civil war. In the early 1980s, he had studied at the al-Imam Muhammad bin Sa'ud University in Riyadh. Despite the Muslim Brotherhood's domination of that establishment's faculty, Zakariya became a Salafi during his stay in Saudi Arabia. Upon his return to Lebanon, he taught in several Islamic institutes—al-Jinan University in Tripoli and the Imam al-Awza'i Institute in Beirut—and created his own teaching center in the working-class neighborhood of Qubbeh—the Hamza Center for Allegiance, Scientific Research, and Islamic Action (Markaz Hamza lil-Wala' wa al-Bahth al-'Ilmi wa al-'Amal al-Islami). A rapid examination of Sheikh al-Masri's anti-Shi'ite diatribes illustrates the internal rationale of his viewpoint, connecting theology, geopolitics, and the local situation.

RELIGIOUS CRITICISM AGAINST HEZBOLLAH

To Sheikh al-Masri, Tripoli was the emblematic Sunni city in *Bilad al-Sham*. Yet enemies of Sunni Islam—all offshoots of the Shi'ite branch of Islam—surrounded it, to the point where the city "could fall under the Nusayri Shi'ite domination from the North and un-

---

[13] Soon after the first retreat of the Syrian army in July 1983, the IUM (Tawhid) closed the offices of the Iraqi Ba'ath party, then destroyed those of the October 24 Movement, forcing its members to find refuge in Christian regions.

der the domination of Twelver Shi'ites from the South."[14] Syria's war on Tripoli from 1986 to 1987 was part of this strategy, under a "framework of efforts by Syria and Iran to suppress the slightest sign of Sunni strength in Lebanon, in favor of the Shi'ites."[15]

In another pamphlet, published using a pseudonym, al-Masri accused Hezbollah of exploiting "Resistance against Israel" in favor of Shi'ite Islam and Iran's regional interests.[16] According to the pamphlet's author, Hezbollah's leaders used the ideal of jihad to strengthen the Shi'ite presence in the Levant and control centers of power in Lebanon. Even the core values of Islam had been led astray, the author claimed. Hezbollah's leaders evoked a false jihad because they insisted on two conditions: the return of the Hidden Imam (no other could legitimately declare jihad), and the theory of *wilayat al-faqih*, restricting the applicability of defensive jihad to cases determined by the Supreme Guide of the Iranian Revolution.[17] Further, the Shi'ite militia was a contributor to anti-Arab and anti-Sunni violence, as evidenced by the fact that several of Hezbollah's military leaders reportedly participated in the Iran-Iraq war (1980–1988), the group's role in the 1996 Khobar attacks in Saudi Arabia, and its crackdown on the 1999 Intifada of Sunni Students in Ahwaz, the capital of the Arab-majority province of Khuzestan in Iran.[18]

The institutional and political deadlock Hezbollah caused in late 2006—one year after the March 14 coalition's electoral success—and the sit-in protests and occupation of Beirut's city center near the prime minister's headquarters gave the Salafi movement an opportunity to assert itself as a popular counterweight to the Shi'ite organization. The Future Movement decided to let this sectarian deterrent develop in order to discourage Hezbollah from using its

[14] See Zakariya al-Masri's book, which was distributed for free in Islamist circles in North Lebanon: *Lifting the Silk Curtains: On the Extremism of Leaders from the Shi'ite Faction* [izhat al-sata'ir al-mukhmila. 'an ghulat al-qada al-mansubin ila al-fiqra al-shi'iya] (Tripoli: Hamza Center for Allegiance, Scientific Research, and Islamic Action, 1st ed., 2007 /1428; 2nd ed., 2008/1429), 223. For a further exploration of Sheikh al-Masri's ideology, see Robert G. Rabil, "The Activist (Haraki) Salafi Ideology of Sheikh Zakariyya Abd al-Razaq al-Masri," 109–123, in *Salafism in Lebanon* (see chapter 1, note 22).

[15] Al-Masri, *Lifting the Silk Curtains*.

[16] See Ali Sadiq, *What Do You Know about Hezbollah?* [madha ta'rif 'an Hizbullah] (np: 2006/1427).

[17] Ibid., 97.

[18] Ibid., 85.

weapons against Fu'ad Siniora's administration. Confronted with the dangers of "Safavid" Iran, the various currents within the Salafi movement agreed at that time to adopt a common position of denominational mobilization.

NEUTRALIZING THE *MUQAWIM*

Ahmed al-Ayyubi—another prominent name in the anti-Syrian struggle—also returned to work for Sa'ad al-Hariri. He was originally from the al-Koura region and a former member of Fatah, having worked directly under Arafat since he joined the pro-Palestinian struggle in the mid-1970s. Ideologically, he was hostile toward all forms of political Islam, to the point of defining himself as a secularist. He, too, had sought refuge in Sidon after participating in the defense of Tripoli from 1985 to 1986. Close to Kana'an Naji, al-Ayyubi operated between Sidon and the Christian regions held by the Lebanese Forces. During General Aoun's war of liberation in 1989, he coordinated military action against Syrian checkpoints with the Lebanese army, all the while acting also as a mediator between Aoun and Selim al-Hoss, the other prime minister at the time. The Syrians captured him near Sidon in 1991, incarcerated him for a year and a half, and then released him. Due to his thorough knowledge of the local terrain, his memory of allegiances and debts owed by one faction to another in the wake of past conflicts, his close ties with the inhabitants of Qubbeh (where he had lived) and with those of Bab al-Tabbaneh (with whom he had fought), and, finally, to his fundamental rejection of all forms of political Islam, al-Ayyubi was one of the Hariri family's most precious sources of information until his death in June 2010.

Memory of the past is a considerable resource in Arab politics, for new circumstances can reactivate old solidarities. In the fall of 1986, Ahmad al-Ayyubi was one of those fighting to prevent the Syrian army from regaining a foothold in West Beirut in hopes of allowing Fatah's return to the capital. During that time, he met Kamal Madhat, a young representative of Yasser Arafat. Twenty years later, they crossed paths again in Beirut, right after the Syrian troops' departure in April 2005. Madhat was there as Mahmud Abbas's special envoy. Abbas, President of the Palestinian Authority, wished to take advantage of the weakening Syrian presence in Lebanon to reaffirm his control over Fatah in Lebanon, notwithstanding the movement's divisions in Palestine. He shared several concerns with the new Lebanese government. In particular, Abbas aimed to prevent the Syrian-linked Palestinians from destabilizing Lebanon and to commence disarming the camps, ahead of the implementation of Security Council resolution 1559. He particularly hoped to use the resolution to dismantle the military bases maintained on Lebanese territory by pro-Syrian Palestinian organizations—Fatah al-Intifada and PFLP-GC. Madhat conceived of his role as that of a "guardian of the Palestinian public order," according to the view that saw the new Lebanese governmental majority and the Fatah leadership on the same side of the regional divide.[19] The circumstances had changed since 1986, but for Ahmad al-Ayyubi and Kamal Madhat the goal remained the same: to assert independence from the hegemonic ambitions of the *muqawim*, who had succeeded in exerting a strong influence in the Palestinian camps and in Lebanese Sunni militant circles, especially thanks to Hezbollah.

By the end of 2006, Ahmad al-Ayyubi had given proof of his political skill. He had provoked a schism within the Islamic Action Front (Jabhat al-'Amal al-Islami), the structure set up in 2005 by one of Syria's loyal allies, Sheikh Fathi Yakan, to coordinate the efforts of all pro-Syrian Islamist groups in the face of local and regional shifts. Al-Ayyubi poached Sheikh Sayf al-Din al-Hussami from the Islamic Action Front to join a newly formed mirror group with an almost-identical name: the Islamic Action Front–Emergency Committee. More than one hundred members of Fathi Yakan's front reportedly defected and joined the new group.[20] Soon thereafter, al-Ayyubi discreetly orchestrated a press conference in which Sheikh al-Hussami made revelations about Hezbollah's policy toward the Sunni community.

According to the sheikh, immediately after the thirty-three-day war between Israel and Hezbollah during the summer of 2006, the leaders of the Islamic Action Front started organizing military training sessions in the Beqaa Valley for young Sunnis from Tripoli. Convoys of about ten recruits each left Tripoli heading for the southern

---

[19] Interview with Kamal Madhat, Beirut, summer 2007. As a Fatah intelligence officer, Kamal Madhat was convinced of Syria's involvement in the emergence of Fatah al-Islam in Nahr al-Bared.

[20] Interview with Sheikh Sayf al-Din al-Hussami, Tripoli, October 2009.

suburbs of Beirut, and then proceeded east to the camps, near the valley villages of Janta and al-Nabi-Shit. During a ten-day training program, the youths learned urban warfare and the use of RPG rocket launchers and assault rifles such as the Kalashnikov. Some even learned how to make and handle explosives.

The training had a political and religious dimension as well. Sunni Sheikh Amir Ra'ad allegedly oversaw religious propaganda and instruction. He was a former Tawhid member, whom the Guardians of the Iranian Revolution (Pasdaran) had trained during the 1980s in Sheikh Abdallah's Baalbek barracks. He was also one of the founding members of the Islamic Action Front. After morning prayers, Sheikh Ra'ad preached to the recruits about how the prophet Muhammad, "before going to fight the Jews, purified his house by fighting the Quraysh." The logical conclusion to be drawn from this sermon was obvious: "Today, we must purify our homeland from the influence of domestic Jewish and American agents." In other words, the preacher explained, "the Future Movement was a secular current that did not represent the Sunnis and was allied with the West." Mahmud al-Budan, known as Abu al-Hassan, who was also trained by the Pasdaran in the 1980s, was allegedly in charge of supervising the camps' operations, and of managing the Tawhid/Hashem al-Minqara military organization, as well as its ties with Hezbollah.[21]

Alongside these subversive operations, Ahmad al-Ayyubi instigated a campaign calling for the public commemoration of the December 19, 1986, Bab al-Tabbaneh massacre.[22] Launched two years after the Syrian forces' departure and broadcast by the Future Movement's TV channel, this campaign broke the taboo on remembrance and lifted the burden of silence and fear. In December 2007, for the first time, Kana'an Naji's followers put up posters all over Tripoli bearing a few simple words without any partisan or religious labels: "Twenty-one years after the crime. December 19, 1986. Remembrance of the Tabbaneh massacre." The sacralization

[21] Since 2000, there have been two branches of the Tawhid Movement, both pro-Syrian: one led by Hisham Minqara, one of the group's original leaders, and the other by Bilal Sha'ban, the son of Sayyid Sha'ban.

[22] See Ahmad al-Ayyubi's article, "The Tabbane Massacre: Toward International Indictment of the Syrian Regime," on a Syrian opposition website. The author calls for the trial of Syrian leaders and an exact evaluation of the number of martyrs and wounded. www.rabeadamascus.com (accessed March 10, 2010).

of past suffering at Syrian hands became the foundation for the combatant's local legitimacy, whereas Sunni organizations associated with Hezbollah or the Syrian regime were rejected as alien entities.

Public recollection of Tripoli's heroic yet traumatic memories—through places, events, and people—served to restore continuity between the past and the present through the use of emotion. This linked those who had experienced that past with those who were currently mourning Hariri's recent assassination. Partisans of the former prime minister became the sole bearers of this heritage, while those former Tawhid combatants who had been freed in 2000 and co-opted by the Syrians were excluded.

This is exactly what the Syrian regime had recently tried to avoid. Upon becoming president in 2000, Bashar al-Assad had released some former Tawhid combatants, including Samir al-Hassan and Hashem Minqara. This move was calculated to help his friend, the Tripolitan Sunni billionaire Najib Miqati, gain votes in the city's populous working-class neighborhood of Bab al-Tabbaneh. The Syrian regime hoped this might lead to a break with the mafia-like behavior of its organic representatives, whose composition was too obviously sectarian (the Akkar Christians for the SSNP and the Alawites of Ba'al Mohsen's Arab Democratic party). This strategy, similar in spirit to the British colonial practice of indirect rule, also transformed the militant identity of its beneficiaries. By crossing back into Lebanon, these former combatants agreed to become partisans of the *muqawama* (Resistance) and to make the Syrian presence more acceptable. Thanks to these men, Syria benefited from a control mechanism all the more effective as it was derived from those who had fought the Syrian regime in the past and knew the sources of potential threats better than anyone else.

When Ahmed al-Ayyubi used the Tabbaneh massacres to call upon those "hiding behind the façade of Islamic activism" to stop restricting the use of the word "martyr" to those who had died for the "Islamic Resistance borne by Hezbollah," he was specifically referring to those former Tawhid members who had undergone this metamorphosis and joined the Syrian side.[23]

---

[23] "What will Fathi Yakan, president of the Islamic Action Front, President Umar Karami, Sheikh Bilal Sha'ban, Sheikh Hashem Minqara, Sheikh Mustafa Meles all say of the

For those who had weathered the hardships of the 1980s, the Future Movement filled a political void by offering the possibility of a new militant engagement, freed of the liabilities attached to the Islamist label. One could be secular without belonging to organizations traditionally linked to the Syrian regime apparatus (the SSNP, the Ba'ath party). People who rejected both Islamism and the Syrian regime came to place their trust in the Future Movement. As a member of the "regiments of Tripoli" in the al-Mina neighborhood, "Marwan" had enrolled in the Tawhid Movement at the age of thirteen. In 1984, he underwent military training in the Pasdaran-supervised Abdallah barracks of Baalbek. Two years later, still a teenager, he took part in the December 1986 Tawhid operations to regain a foothold in the Bab al-Tabbaneh neighborhood. There, Arab Democratic Party militiamen surrounded Marwan, and he witnessed the execution of some of his comrades. Militiamen brought Marwan to the Alawite militia's "al-Deir" interrogation center in the Jabal Mohsen district, then transferred him to the "American" (*Amrikan*) interrogation center that the Syrian intelligence services managed. There, he was tortured for several days. Later, he was again tortured in the prison of 'Anjar (the Syrian intelligence headquarters for the Beqaa Valley). After a roughly twenty-day stay in 'Anjar, he was imprisoned in the Palestine Branch (*fara' filastin*), one of the most feared of Syrian military intelligence (Shu'bat al-Mukhabarat al-'Askariyya) detention facilities, located in the Syrian capital, near the University of Damascus's humanities and science faculty.[24] There the torture sessions grew more complex ("always at night, after 1 am"), with exotic names such as "the flying carpet" or the "German chair" that scarcely concealed their horrific nature. For many months, he remained in an unlit, one-square-meter cell where guards served his food on the floor and changed his waste bucket once every ten days.

---

victims of the Tabbaneh massacre? Will they erase the word 'martyrs' as the Syrians did?" Ibid.

[24] Branch 235, known as the Palestine Branch, is one of the Syrian Department of Military Intelligence's ten branches. For a detailed description of the repressive role of the Assad intelligence system in Syria, see Human Rights Watch, *Torture Archipelago: Arbitrary Arrests, Torture and Enforced Disappearances in Syria's Underground Prisons since March 2011*, http://www.hrs.org/sites/default/files/reports/syria0712webwcover_0.pdf.

After one year of captivity, the Syrians returned Marwan to Lebanon by way of the same interrogation and torture centers he had passed through on arriving. A few hours after his release, he left Tripoli for East Beirut (then controlled by the Christian Lebanese Forces militia). He carried out missions between East Beirut and Tripoli for the February 9 Movement. Then, the entry of Syrian troops into East Beirut in October 1990 forced him to seek refuge in a Tawhid safe house in the Palestinian camp of Miye-Miye near Sidon. During this period, he distanced himself from the "Islamist sheikhs who had ruined his childhood" and whom he accused of selling out religion for personal gain. In 1992 the Syrians made a proposal to Marwan:

> We were gathered in 'Anjar center. Ghazi Kana'an and Sheikh Sayyid Sha'ban were waiting for us. Ghazi Kana'an said to us, word for word: "We are of the same flesh! We were hard on you because we wanted to educate you. We must put this behind us." We were forced to sign a document promising we would never oppose Syria again. Soon after I was summoned to the *al-Amrikan* Syrian intelligence center. They wanted to recruit me as an informant. I refused. Ten days later I was fired from my job in a local company.[25]

The return to action of some of the fighters who had paid such a heavy price for their past commitment to the Tawhid Movement or to Yasser Arafat's Fatah raised a core question. Could the Future Movement play a comparable role to that exercised by these two organizations? To endure and possess a strong political identity, the combatant figure of the *muqatil* had to satisfy at least two conditions. First, he must already enjoy a high level of Arab national legitimacy. The experience of struggle against the Israeli army usually satisfied this requirement. Second, the regional and international environment must aid his cause. International support was indispensable for the *muqatil* if he was to assert his autonomy from the hegemonic Resistance (of Iran and Syria) and thus to strengthen his position in view of peace negotiations with the Israeli government.

[25] Interview with Marwan, Tripoli, July 2009.

In the Palestinian case, the *muqatil*'s aura had been on the wane since the late 1990s. This was not for lack of historically constituted, tried-and-tested legitimating beliefs. Rather, it was because of the international system's gradually diminishing interest in a fair resolution of the Israeli-Palestinian conflict. Using the "intifada" label for the Lebanese pro-independence March 14 Movement—as the journalist and historian Samir Kassir wished—was a way of attributing a dual source of legitimacy to it, both Arab and international, identical to the legitimacy claimed for the Palestinian cause since the 1980s. Thus, the reactivation of pro-Palestinian and anti-Syrian networks was a response to the need to reclaim this heritage in order to fight the Syrian regime and its allies on the basis of Arab identity, rather than in collusion with the Bush administration's "plans" in the Middle East. Thus, in the short-term, calling upon the 1980s generation of fighters was a response to the lack of in-house organizational and technical expertise. In the long term, however, it reflected the movement's need to claim a militant identity stronger than the identity associated with the memory of Rafiq al-Hariri. This political emancipation from Syria and Hezbollah was organically linked to the Israeli-Palestinian peace process's degree of advancement. To Arab public opinion, it represented the crucial criterion that would enable conciliating Arab legitimacy, on the one hand, with international legitimacy, on the other.

In 2006, Ahmad al-Ayyubi had made an offer to Sa'ad al-Hariri to take responsibility for defending Beirut "with a contingent of 200 men."[26] His offer fell on deaf ears. Some of Hariri's advisors even rejected it outright, as if fearful of the consequences of militarizing the country's current situation. Granting al-Ayyubi a military role would also risk conjuring up an old stereotype from the civil war—that of the Palestinians of Lebanon as the "strong arm" of the Sunni community. Indeed, judging by al-Ayyubi's history of association with Yasser Arafat, he would likely have sought support within Beirut's refugee camps or from among the mixed Palestinian/Lebanese population of Tareq Jdide, which he had frequented in the 1980s.

---

[26] Interview with Ahmad al-Ayyubi, Tripoli, October 2009.

Thus, the anticipation of a pro-Syrian campaign denouncing exploitation of the Palestinian factor in Lebanese politics precluded the formation of such a political and military alliance (in the 1990s, these same forces had accused Rafiq al-Hariri of intending to settle Palestinians in Lebanon to increase its Sunni population). Had such a political and military alliance ever materialized, it would have considerably complicated Hezbollah's May 7, 2008, armed takeover of Beirut's Sunni districts.

CHAPTER 4

⊰ǝⱨⱪⱨⱪⱨⱪ⠀

The Syrian Regime Reacts

Building Up a Jihadi Network

Varying Interpretations

Fatah al-Islam proclaimed its existence from the Palestinian camp
of Nahr al-Bared on November 26, 2006. This announcement profoundly changed the political situation that had existed in North
Lebanon since the departure of Syrian troops in April 2005. From
the beginning, this jihadi group outlined a series of rather grandiose
objectives aimed at winning international, Arab, and local Lebanese
public opinion over to its cause. It would struggle against the West
and its local allies, conduct jihad for the liberation of Palestine,
and destroy all those who opposed these glorious purposes. Alongside an intense public relations campaign—featuring press conferences, communiqués, and documentary videos broadcast on jihadi
websites—members of the network also carried out more discrete,
yet equally intense diplomatic activity directed at most of the Islamist actors in the region. The group's emergence further complicated the existing political crisis that stemmed from a vacant
presidency, governmental paralysis, the Israeli offensive of summer
2006, and Hezbollah's occupation of downtown Beirut.[1] Amidst

[1] The political crisis originated on December 12, 2005, when five Shi'ite ministers, three
from Hezbollah and two from Amal, resigned in protest against the Lebanese government's

divisions within the state and rising sectarian tensions between Shi'ites and Sunnis, Fatah al-Islam's leaders strived to convince various audiences of the advantages of establishing a Sunni military force. In this vein, Fatah al-Islam partisans contested the modes of action of their Tripoli-based Islamist interlocutors in order to reorient the latter's political/religious frameworks in a direction serving Fatah al-Islam's own objectives.

Fatah al-Islam's rise was the subject of much analysis both in the Arab world and abroad. As is often the case, such scrutiny revealed more about the authors' political leanings than about the phenomenon itself. This would scarcely bear mentioning in a footnote, were it not that the commentators themselves had influenced all of the protagonists' behaviors and attitudes in one way or another.

Two contemporaneous but antagonistic narratives circulating at the time heightened the region's political divisions. To partisans of Hezbollah and Syria, Fatah al-Islam was the work of the Hariri family, backed by the Saudi secret services. Saudi Prince Bandar reportedly oversaw the project to form a Sunni militia as a counterweight to the Shi'ite Hezbollah, in preparation for a looming and seemingly unavoidable interdenominational civil war. On the other hand, the pro-independence parliamentary majority of the time (called the "March 14 Alliance")—supported by the United States and Jacques Chirac's France—saw Fatah al-Islam as yet another nuisance that the Syrian intelligence services had caused, one more manifestation of the ongoing assassination campaign against the new anti-Syrian majority, a dozen of whose leaders had already been assassinated since 2005.

Both narratives had obvious shortcomings. They were interpretations based on limited information and were unable to foresee Fatah al-Islam's long-term significance. They also disregarded the autonomy of various forms of commitments to Fatah al-Islam on the part of the actors involved. However, both did not have the

---

petition to the UN Security Council for the formation of an international tribunal to try Hariri's assassins. Following the end of pro-Syrian president Émile Lahoud's controversial mandate extension, Nabih Berri—the speaker of the National Assembly and a long-time ally of the Syrians—refused to convene the Parliament to elect a new president. Finally, in December 2006, a few months after the thirty-three-day war and the passing of UN Security Council resolution 1701, with a view to strengthening UNIFIL's military presence in South Lebanon, Hezbollah's and General Aoun's partisans occupied downtown Beirut demanding Siniora's government resign.

same impact. Western journalists who frequented the Syrian corridors of power diligently echoed the first narrative throughout Europe and the United States, incriminating the March 14 Alliance, Saudi Arabia, and possibly even the Bush administration.

Understanding the context and taking a longer-term perspective is necessary if we are to understand the presence of Fatah al-Islam in North Lebanon in the fall of 2006. Since the Syrian retreat, North Lebanon had hosted all manner of militants, both Salafi and not. To a certain extent, Sa'ad al-Hariri's support networks used and oversaw this activity, aided in their task by those trained to fight the Syrian regime by Yasser Arafat's Fatah in the 1980s. The establishment in Lebanon of a jihadi network of Syrian-Palestinian origin, whose core members had previously distinguished themselves in the anti-American jihad in Iraq, forced the distinctions between various Sunni militant actors in North Lebanon into the open. Contacts between Fatah al-Islam's leaders and representatives of the various Salafi groups dispersed throughout North Lebanon lent credence to their opponents' sweeping generalizations accusing the group of identifying with Salafism in all its forms of religious expression. Such contacts became evident in a media campaign against Sa'ad al-Hariri designed to show his allies, both in Lebanon (part of the Lebanese Christians) and abroad (the American administration), the internal contradictions within his policy. Fatah al-Islam's presence in a Palestinian environment also stood in the way of any potential disarmament process in Lebanon's Palestinian camps (as per Security Council Resolution 1559, along with the disarmament of Hezbollah). And finally, it hampered the joint efforts of Palestinian Authority president Mahmud Abbas and Lebanese Prime Minister Fu'ad Siniora to promote Fatah's control over these camps.

The March 14 Alliance's competing narrative, presenting Fatah al-Islam as a project controlled remotely, from start to finish, by the Syrian intelligence services, was also questionable. It assumed that the main protagonists had the capacity to anticipate several series of "moves" in the political game, which was practically impossible. It overlooked the internal tensions and power struggles between the multiple intelligence agencies that shaped the Syrian regime's security apparatus. And by dismissing the radical Islamists' behavior as part of a script written in Damascus, this narrative also ignored the jihadi networks' own dynamics and the actors' changing relationships with their multifaceted environment.

From Fatah to Jihadism: Shaker al-Absi's Itinerary

Several cumulative waves of militants shaped and reshaped Fatah al-Islam's network, but its original core—limited to a very few individuals—remained relatively stable. This core consisted of both Palestinian-Syrians from the Yarmouk camp (in the suburb of Damascus) and Syrian nationals converted to the jihadi cause. Almost all of them first met in the 2000s, in Saydnaya prison, about twenty miles north of Damascus.

Shaker al-Absi's remarkable personal history, in which jihadi military engagement built on an initial involvement in the Palestinian struggle, seems to have played a crucial role in bringing Islamist volunteers to Lebanese territory. His personal trajectory linked Palestinian internationalism inspired from leftist ideas—widely instrumentalized by Iraq, Syria, and Libya in the 1980s—to an Islamist jihadi internationalism still emerging in the second half of the 1990s. Al-Absi could claim a long relationship with the Jordanian Abu Mus'ab al-Zarqawi. A death sentence imposed on both by Jordanian authorities served as unimpeachable proof of his legitimacy as a jihadi. Al-Absi's position between two ideological spheres was, moreover, an ideal position from which to denounce the treachery of Arab leaders, their compromises with the West, and their lack of success in the context of the Palestinian struggle. As a former *muqatil* who had become a *mujahid*, he had professional military expertise (acquired while fighting for the Palestinian cause), whereas many young jihadis lacked technical skills equal to their religious zeal. What is more, he could rely on a new absolutist utopia to mobilize his followers, whereas his former comrades within the loyalist Fatah had great difficulty justifying the usefulness of their conversion to diplomatic realism, over ten years after the signing of the Oslo Accords.

Numerous biographies of Shaker al-Absi are available online, but since he went underground in the second half of the 1980s, a reliable chronology of certain periods of his life is missing. A Palestinian, born in the West Bank in 1950, al-Absi trained in the Jordanian Air Force before joining Yasser Arafat's Fatah. As a member of "Force 14" (the modest PLO air force) in the 1980s, he continued fighter pilot training in the Eastern Bloc countries and in Libya (he is said to have fought for Libya in Chad). In 1983 he joined the Fatah al-Intifada dissident force.[2] He had close ties to the organization's Secretary-General, Abu Khaled al-'Amleh, and was in charge of special operations in Jordan and Palestine (designated the "Occidental sector"), which he directed from Der'a, near the Jordanian-Syrian border. Part of these operations involved smuggling arms and explosives to Palestinian factions in the Occupied Territories.

His first incarceration, in Syria in the late 1980s—for reasons still unknown—marked a turning point in Shaker al-Absi's existence. In prison, he formed ties with Islamist detainees, began praying five times daily, and memorized the Qur'an. Freed in 1996, he moved to the Hajar al-Aswad neighborhood of Damascus, close to the Yarmouk camp. The near-total absence of information about him during this period strongly suggests that he went underground again. Before making a pilgrimage to Mecca in 2000, he met in Damascus with the Libyan Salem Sa'ad bin Sawid (Abu Mus'ab al-Zarqawi's representative), who told him of plans to assassinate American or Israeli diplomats in Jordan.[3] This meeting marked the beginning of his connection to the "Greater Syria" network that al-Zarqawi established from his base in Herat, in western Afghanistan. There, the Jordanian exile had become an emir (commander) of volunteers from Syria, Lebanon, Palestine, and Jordan (which together, make up the region sometimes called *Bilad al-Sham*), and had allegedly established an organization called the Jund al-Sham

[2] Fatah al-Intifada is a dissident Palestinian organization headed by former Fatah members such as Abu Musa (Colonel Sayyid al-Maragha) and Abu Khaled al-'Amleh, who both left the main movement in 1983 in protest against Yasser Arafat's political leadership. Fatah al-Intifada participated alongside the Syrian army in besieging Yasser Arafat in Tripoli, before seizing control of the refugee camps and hunting down loyalist Fatah militants. Fatah al-Intifada is organically linked to the Syrian intelligence services, just like Ahmed Jibril's PFLP.

[3] On March 16, 2007, the *New York Times* ran an article entitled "New Face of Jihad Vows Attacks." It was based on Jordanian judiciary sources, and asserted that the person directly responsible for Laurence Foley's death was the Libyan Sa'ad Salem bin Sawid. Sawid was said to have met with Abu Mus'ab al-Zarqawi and Shaker al-Absi in Syria to "finalize plans for military operations against American and Jewish interests in Jordan."

(Army of Syria) in late 1999.[4] According to Jordanian security sources, al-Zarqawi and al-Absi jointly orchestrated the assassination of an American USAID employee, Laurence Foley, in front of his home in Amman, on October 28, 2002.[5] During the murderers' trial, the public prosecutor cited a phone conversation between them and Zarqawi, in which Abu al-Ghadiya (a.k.a. Sulayman Khaled Darwish), who was close to al-Zarqawi, also took part.[6]

Thus, the foundation for Shaker al-Absi's jihadi conversion seems to have been laid in advance—in 1999—through several meetings with people close to Abu Mus'ab al-Zarqawi. As of that date, members of Jund al-Sham adjusted their conduct to take into account the complexity of the al-Zarqawi network. After the American offensive in Afghanistan (October 2001), al-Zarqawi managed to breach the Northern Alliance's encirclement of Herat. He and his men fought in Kandahar and Tora Bora. Managing to emerge unscathed from the bombings, he headed to Pakistan, then to Iran. From there, he decided to go to Iraq, which he and his companions expected would soon be at war with the United States.[7] He found refuge for a few months among the Islamist Kurds of the Ansar al-Islam group, in the Khurmal region of northern Iraq. From there, he made frequent round trips to the Iraqi capital. One veteran Iraqi jihadi who frequented the Ansar al-Islam group in Iraqi Kurdistan confirmed having met al-Absi and al-Zarqawi in 2002, in Baghdad, at the "military academy" (al-Kulliya al-'Askariyya) that the Iraqi

[4] See Fu'ad Hussein, *al-Zarqawi, al-jil al-thani li-l-qa'ida* [Zarqawi, the second generation of al-Qaeda] (Kuwait: Dar al-Khiyal, 2005), especially the transcription of Muhammad Mekawi's (a.k.a. Sayf al-'Adl) testimony, 115–42. For more on the links between Zarqawi and al-Qaida, see Jean-Pierre Filiu's *Les neuf vies d'al-Qaïda* (Paris: Fayard, 2009).

[5] The August 6, 2006 *Washington Post* mentions documents from the Jordanian State Security Court according to which, "In Syria, in the summer of 2002, Zarqawi began to train a small group of fighters to attack Western and Jewish interests in Jordan."

[6] Fu'ad Hussein, *al-Zarqawi*, 36. In September 2000, the Jordanian Security Court had already sentenced Zarqawi to fifteen years in prison for his alleged participation in a conspiracy to bomb multiple targets in the Kingdom (Mount Nebo, the Radisson hotel, the Dead Sea, etc.) on January 1, 2000. These "Millennium" attacks had been thwarted by Jordanian intelligence services.

[7] Fu'ad Hussein notes on p.138 that, "during his long journey in Iraq, a previously nonexistent trait of Zarqawi's personality appeared. He began to feel the need to exact revenge against the Americans for their crimes during the bombings in Afghanistan, which he had witnessed firsthand." However, his contacts with Shaker al-Absi, made through his Libyan go-between, indicate that his desire to attack American interests predated the trauma he suffered due to the Afghanistan bombings.

Ba'athist regime had established to train Arab *mujahidin* in hopes of stopping the imminent American invasion.[8] In March 2003, American bombings of Ansar al-Islam's positions dispersed the group. Al-Zarqawi headed for Syria. There he met Milad al-Lubnani (Milad the Lebanese, a.k.a. Hassan Muhammad al-Nab'a), whose brother had been associated with the 'Usbat al-Ansar cell that assassinated Sheikh Nizar al-Halabi in 1995.[9] According to the Lebanese military prosecutor's indictment, al-Nab'a had managed to build up a clandestine support structure for jihadis in Syria, thanks to a network of farms, apartments, and workshops made available for the manufacturing of explosives and weapons, mostly in the Iblid region. "[It was] highly organized, at both the technical level and the military level," the indictment claims, and "he (al-Nab'a) oversaw a group of operatives supervising military, intelligence, medical, information, and forgery activities."[10]

By the time Syrian military intelligence arrested him in June 2003 for planning an anti-Israeli operation from the Golan Heights, Shaker al-Absi's association with Abu Mus'ab al-Zarqawi had familiarized him with the technicalities of underground jihad. In September, a Syrian civil court sentenced al-Absi to two years and seven months' imprisonment, officially for setting up a weapons smuggling operation in Jordan in order to strike targets of strategic interest to Israel. Al-Absi later stated during a press conference that the real purpose of the operation was to transport weapons from the Golan to the Palestinian territories.[11] On April 6, 2004,

---

[8] Interview with a former Iraqi jihad volunteer, Amman, August 2008. Therefore, it is almost certain that Shaker al-Absi went to Iraq before his incarceration in Syria.

[9] Nizar al-Halabi was the head of the Association of Islamic Charitable Projects (Jama'iyyat al-Mashari' al-Islamiyya), which was known in Arabic as *al-Ahbash* (the Ethiopians), because its founder, Abdallah al-Hirari, originally came from Ethiopia. The organization spread in postwar Lebanon in working-class districts. Known for its staunch opposition to the Hanbali tradition, it commonly used *takfir* (excommunication) against Wahhabi and Salafi sheikhs. Very close to the Assad regime, it was used by Syrian intelligence as a tool to fight Sunni Islamists. Nizar al-Halabi was assassinated in Beirut on August 31, 1995, presumably by members of 'Usbat al-Ansar—three were sentenced to death and executed on March 24, 1997. Hasan Muhammad al-Nab'a was arrested on Jan. 31, 2008, by the Lebanese army.

[10] See the indictment drafted by the military tribunal's first prosecutor, reprinted by the Lebanese daily *al-Safir* on February 24, 2009.

[11] There is a record of this sentencing in the list of Syrian prisoners published in November 2005 on the Arabic website of *Syrian Human Rights Information Link* (SHRIL), http://shril-sy.info/enshril/modules/ (accessed December 16, 2009). A list of Syrian political

he was one of six Islamists sentenced to death *in absentia* by the Jordanian State Security Court after Syria had refused Jordan's extradition request.[12] It seems that al-Absi remained in prison until his June 2005 release, several months prior to the legal end of his sentence.

The Saydnaya Phase

The list of political prisoners the Free Syria (Suriya al-Hurra) association published in 2004, as well as the nearly identical list Syrian Human Rights Information Links released in 2005, shows that starting from the mid-1990s, a new generation of Islamist convicts began joining the older group of persons incarcerated for membership in the Syrian Muslim Brotherhood. Jihadism had become a fifth charge, added to the four already criminalized by the repressive Syrian regime: being a member of the Muslim Brotherhood, Kurdish organizations, or Palestinian Fatah, and advocating for human rights and democracy.

Comparing the names of Fatah al-Islam leaders with those of Syrian political prisoners (published during several public trials in Lebanon starting in 2008) shows clearly how important Saydnaya prison was for this network's formation. The prison housed hardened militants (veterans of Afghanistan or Iraq) alongside detainees whose "Wahhabi" Islamic leanings alone had raised regime suspicions. In this milieu, in 2002, Shaker al-Absi met a twenty-three-year-old Syrian named Majd al-Din al-'Abbud—later known as Abu Yazin.[13] Al-'Abbud was essentially a hostage in Saydnaya: Syrian security services were holding him and one of his brothers while

---

prisoners, including the dates and motives of their sentences, was published online by *Suriya al-Hurra* [Free Syria] on April 11, 2004, http://www.annabaa.org/nbanews/2009 (accessed December 18, 2009). The two documents contain similar information about the prisoners, but what they say about Shaker al-Absi's conviction differs. According to the SHRIL list, al-Absi was condemned "for having attempted to smuggle weapons into Jordan in order to conduct operations against Israel," whereas according to *Suriya al-Hurra*, he was planning to "strike an Israeli patrol on the Syrian border" (from the occupied Golan Heights). Al-Absi's own explanation was published by the Lebanese daily *al-Nahar* on March 16, 2007. It remains unclear why certain individuals, such as Sheikh Abd al-Salam al-Shuqayri, were sentenced by the Syrian Security Court, rather than by a civil court as was Shaker al-Absi.

[12] Sa'ad Salem bin Sawid and his driver, Yasser Freihat, were sentenced to death by the Jordanian Security Court on April 6, 2004, and hanged on March 11, 2006.

[13] For biographical information about Abu Yazin, see *al-Hayat*, June 7, 2007.

searching for another sibling.[14] Other young prisoners, among them Taha Ahmad Hajji Sulayman (a.k.a. Abu Lu'ay in Fatah al-Islam), born in Latakia in 1982, later followed al-Absi to Lebanon.

In addition to those young recruits, al-Absi also broadened his circle of acquaintances to include more experienced militants. One such was the Syrian Hani Badr al-Sankari, imprisoned mid-2002 after the Pakistani government captured him attempting to escape Afghanistan and handed him to the Syrians. Al-Sankari was of the second generation of "Arab Afghans" who had gone to Afghanistan in order to join the Taliban (the "first generation" being those who had come to help fight the Soviets in the 1980s). About thirty-five years old, he carried scars from his battles in Afghanistan, including severe burns incurred at Kandahar during the American offensive in 2001.[15] In Saydnaya, al-Absi was also reunited with members of the "Golan group," to which he seems to have already belonged. They included the Palestinian Yasser al-Shuqayri, a.k.a. Abu Salih (born in 1973 and sentenced in August 2002 for planning an anti-Israeli operation in the Golan Heights), and Syrian Muhammad 'Amer Bakri Dabbagh, a.k.a. Abu al-Sa'id al-Suri (born in Aleppo in 1978 and sentenced to two and a half years by the same court as al-Absi). The list also contained figures of religious standing from the same group, such as Abd al-Salam al-Shuqairi (imam of the Khaled bin al-Walid mosque, located near the Bab Touma neighborhood in Damascus), whom the State Security Court sentenced in August 2002 to four years in prison for plotting an operation against an Israeli patrol in the Golan Heights.[16] Finally, al-Zarqawi and al-Absi's accomplice, Abu al-Ghadiyat, was also detained in Saydnaya from January 2002 onward.

The "Saydnaya phase" was of great importance. The Syrian prison functioned as a uniquely convenient meeting place where these various individuals' paths crossed, consolidating past ties and creating new commitments. Most of those who later went to Lebanon in 2005 came from the same background: the network whose members had been arrested in August 2002, then sentenced and

[14] See the SHRIL list in note 11.

[15] See Hani al-Sankari's testimony before the permanent military tribunal, *al-Mustaqbal*, September 26, 2009.

[16] According to the same list, three other individuals were arrested and sentenced for the same reason: Ziad al-Umar, Ziad al-Ahmed, and Nayef Nimr al-Tahan.

imprisoned in Saydnaya. Likewise, the prison pooled individuals among whom Syrian intelligence services could identify new recruits, and from which they could gather information about Islamist networks.

The Exemplary Case of Firas Subhi Ghanam

On September 11, 2008, the Jund Allah (Army of God) website, which belonged to Kana'an Naji (who had close ties to the Lebanese Interior Security Forces), published lengthy excerpts from Firas Subhi Ghanam's confessions (Ghanam was a Palestinian-Syrian arrested in the Beqaa Valley in February 2006). They also posted photocopies of several pages of various Lebanese security services reports.[17] The public circulation of these reports was tied to the struggle between the competing interpretations of the Fatah al-Islam phenomenon put forth by partisans and enemies of the Syrian regime.

Under the title "Documents from Lebanese Legal and Security Organs Reveal Syrian Terrorism," the web page condemned "Islamists released from Syrian prisons" for having "transformed themselves into agents of the Syrian intelligence services," as well as for their "shift from Iraq to Lebanon in late 2005." By publishing these documents, Sheikh Kana'an sought to demonstrate the risks that would threaten anyone else who might be tempted to engage in dubious dealings with the Syrian security apparatus in hopes of continuing jihad within the Syrian framework.

Ghanam's testimony is highly valuable, for it enables us to understand the Syrian intelligence services' role in reorienting the radical Salafi networks engaged in jihad between Iraq in 2003/2004 and Lebanon in 2005. It highlights the Syrian agents' different modes of dealings with Islamists and their early detection of the "Wahhabi" threat. This in turn clarifies the role of the prison itself in the recruitment of informants into the Syrian intelligence network after

---

[17] Part of his confessions were later used by the journalist Faris Khashshan in an article published by the daily newspaper *al-Mustaqbal*—the media mouthpiece of the Future Movement. Published in the November 15, 2008, edition, the article was entitled "al-Mustaqbal publishes reliable information demonstrating the terrorist organization's involvement with the Bashar al-Assad leadership. The Syrian regime's lies are revealed by the Fatah al-Islam detainees' testimonies."

their release on parole, showing how specific terms were put in place for each prisoner. The stakes were quite high, given that the quality of this informant network would largely determine the outcome of the policy as a whole, which was based on delegated management and the manipulation of Islamism outside of Syria's borders.

Subhi Ghanam became a Salafi under Saudi influence. Born in Aleppo, Syria to a Palestinian refugee family in 1971, he spent most of his childhood in Dammam, Saudi Arabia, where his father worked as a teacher. In 1994, he returned to Syria to perform his five-year military service in the Palestinian Liberation Army (PLA), which the Syrian army managed and oversaw. In the Yarmouk camp, under the influence of another Palestinian, Ghanam immersed himself in the world of radical Salafism, with its incendiary preaching, its redefinition of "true faith," and its gatherings of new converts in the camp's apartments. His activism did not go unnoticed. He was arrested on December 10, 2002, judged by a civil court, and sent to the Saydnaya prison.[18] Several months later, he met Shaker al-Absi, who introduced himself as "a former air force colonel of the 'General Command'" (sic).[19] Ghanam was transferred to the Palestine Branch, then freed on June 2, 2005, when Bashar al-Assad issued a mass pardon. Soon after his release, he met several times with al-Absi, who informed him that he was in contact with Abu Mus'ab al-Zarqawi in Iraq and that he admired the latter very much, "even though al-Absi also told me he disagreed with al-Zarqawi on some issues, without revealing anything about the reasons for this." Al-Absi also told Ghanam that he had become head of the training camps in the Beqaa Valley, "with a view to striking Israeli and American interests in the region, from these bases in Lebanon."

Ghanam went to work in a real-estate agency. He was obliged to check in with the Palestine Branch every fifteen days (as did every former Islamist prisoner). There, ex-detainees were induced to be-

---

[18] Subhi Ghanam's name appears in the list of political prisoners published on the Arabic version of the Syrian Human Rights Information Link website.

[19] In his testimony, Subhi Ghanam several times mixed up Ahmad Jibril's PFLP-General Command with Shaker al-Absi's Fatah al-Intifada organization. However, this error bears witness to the document's veracity, especially as Ghanam's testimony remained coherent and unchanged throughout the entire judiciary process.

come informants. The frequency of interrogations and the threat of renewed detention pushed them to reproduce the same patterns of informing on others that had probably brought about their own arrests:

> Every time I went to the Palestine Branch, an interrogator would ask me questions. . . . During each of my visits, they would ask me to give them the names of Wahhabi militants, as well as other types of intelligence-related services. They would pressure me on psychologically. I remember that in August 2005, investigator Haytham asked me if I would follow his orders if I was asked to carry out a mission in Lebanon, such as killing Abu Mahjen [a jihadi hidden in Ayn al-Helweh camp near Sidon], for example, or any other person. I refused. That was when they intensified the pressure on me. The interrogator then told me that he was not happy with me and later forced me to come to his office more often, as well as to the nearby office of *al-Mintaqa* (regional) section. So I was obliged to respond to summonses from both.

In the fall of 2005, following bombings in Aleppo, the security apparatus began rounding up and imprisoning former detainees. Upon hearing that security forces had searched his home and workplace, Ghanam went into hiding. He took refuge with one of his Salafi friends; then, upon his friend's advice, he went to the residence of a man known as Abu Umar who was in charge of gathering jihadi volunteers for Iraq through a network of guesthouses. As Ghanam later discovered, this underground society in which dozens of jihadi militants moved from one house to another in the Syrian capital was a sham. In view of the high stakes involved for the regime, its intelligence agencies controlled this network even more tightly than the rest of Syrian society (the US authorities had just warned the Syrian government against sustaining flows of "terrorists" toward Iraq). Soon afterward, in December 2005, Abu Umar informed his guests that the clandestine route from Damascus to Baghdad was temporarily closed. Instead, he advised them to head west to Lebanon, newly vacated by Syrian troops. He specifically suggested Ayn al-Helweh as a stopping-off point and base for military training that would serve until the route to Iraq could be reopened.

On December 15, 2005, Subhi Ghanam agreed to go to Ayn al-Helweh. From a friend's house, he contacted a smuggler from the Qaboun district of Damascus known as Abu Ayman, whom Abu Umar had recommended. Ghanam told Abu Ayman that he was compelled to flee to Lebanon to escape the Palestine Branch of military intelligence. Abu Ayman offered to negotiate on his behalf with the head the section, one Colonel George Salloum, with whom he claimed to be well acquainted. The next day, Abu Ayman relayed the colonel's offer to Ghanam: all charges against him would be dropped if he would carry out an attack:

> I asked Abu Ayman about the details of this mission, and he told me that it would take place on February 14, 2006 during a large demonstration commemorating the first anniversary of Hariri's assassination. I would be asked to carry out an operation to destabilize the protest and provoke a panic reaction. The demonstration was to be halted by an operation that would claim lives, such as throwing a bomb on the protesters and participants. Abu Ayman then asked me to go to the Shatila district, rent an apartment there, open a telephone line and give him its number. Then once I would be settled in Shatila, men from the Syrian intelligence services would give me the necessary instructions. So I agreed.[20]

On February 10, 2006, armed with a grenade, Subhi Ghanam passed through all the checkpoints before the Syrian-Lebanese border. Accompanied by a Tunisian national, he crossed the border on foot illegally and asked the person in charge of taking the group to Beirut to drop him off in the Beqaa Valley, where his nephew worked in a hospital. After a short family visit, the Lebanese security forces arrested him.

During his trial before the Permanent Military Tribunal (al-Mahkama al-'Askariyya al-Da'ima), Ghanam claimed that he had never intended to carry out the attack. He stated that he had only pretended to accept the mission in order to leave Syria as quickly as possible via the Lebanese border, in hopes of travelling on to Iraq for the purpose of jihad—by way of a route Syrian intelligence

[20] During his trial, Syrian intelligence services colonel George Salloum's name was explicitly mentioned. See the Syrian Observatory Human Rights website, http://www.syriahr.com (accessed June 8, 2009).

did not supervise, one might add. Regardless of his sincerity, these details illustrate the relationships of deceit and calculation that existed between the security services and religious activists and, in Ghanam's case, the futility of his hope that he might free himself from this web to escape to Ayn al-Helweh. The Syrian regime acquiesced in part to the opposition's desire to wage jihad, but only so long as this took place outside Syria and in accordance with their foreign policy objectives.

Guiding Jihad: The Abu al-Qa'qa' Phenomenon

The 2005 reorientation toward Lebanon apparently came in response to a directive sent to all jihadi circles in Syria. During precisely the same period, a jihadi sheikh from Aleppo known as Abu al-Qa'qa' (whose *kunya* name refers to the heroic combatant figure al-Qa'qa' bin 'Amr bin Malik, one of the early personalities of Islam) incited the volunteers who wished to go to the Land of the Two Rivers (Iraq), to head to Lebanon instead. Iraqi al-Qaeda leaders, whom he had not consulted about this redirection, were much dismayed.

Born in 1973 in the north of Aleppo, and of Kurdish origin, Abu al-Qa'qa'(his real name was Mahmud Qul al-Aghassi) earned his title of professor at the *shari'a* college of the University of Damascus.[21] At the outset of his military service he openly defied his commanding officers by praying five times a day inside the barracks. The issue of religious practice during the standard two-and-a-half years of military service was often raised during informal discussions between students and professors at the *shari'a* college, especially at the end of certain classes. Although the college was under strict surveillance, it nonetheless enjoyed special status within the university. For instance, its walls were free of any inscriptions praising the Ba'ath party and its leaders, and its professors, many of whom had studied abroad, prided themselves on their reputation for independence from the state and its institutions.[22] As for Abu al-Qa'qa', exhibiting such religious zeal as he had shown

---

[21] See Arnaud Lenfant, "L'évolution du salafisme en Syrie au XXᵉ siècle," in Bernard Rougier, ed., *Qu'est-ce que le salafisme?* (Paris: PUF/Proche-Orient, 2008), 161–78.

[22] For more background information on the relationship between the Syrian regime and Islam, see Annabelle Böttcher, "Sunni Islam under Hafez al-Assad: Coercive and Persuasive

in his military barracks was likely to land one before a military tribunal, but the young Islamist actually escaped with a mere reprimand. Wishing to spare him, the local head of political security (Amn al-Dawla) explained that it was time to overcome the divisive memories of the 1980s, in order to unite in the face of common threats.

In 1999, Sheikh Abu al-Qa'qa' became imam of a mosque located in al-Sakhur, an impoverished Aleppo suburb in the east of the city.[23] As usual, his nomination was subject to his interrogation and approval by the security forces.[24] The sheikh's reputation rapidly spread beyond Aleppo, and his inflammatory sermons circulated throughout the Middle East on DVDs and cassettes. Al-Qa'qa' was incapable of forming a social movement on his own, and lacking internal or external ties to the Syrian Muslim Brotherhood, he played more of an advocacy role vis-à-vis jihadism. By openly expressing hatred for the West and allied regimes, he offered a rallying point for the radical circles of Aleppo, facilitated their identification by security forces, and directed popular discontent toward external targets. His growing popularity from 2002 onward also highlighted for American war planners the dangers that lurked if Syria were to join Iraq as a target of invasion. Moreover, his affiliation to the much broader Jund al-Sham network acted in his favor, since it offered the intelligence services a highly valuable capability of projecting jihad beyond Syrian borders. From his own point of view, the Aleppo sheikh was much more than their "honorable partner." He staked out areas of mutual interest with the authorities in order to expand his influence, but did not forsake his own convictions. In itself, the ability to freely use jihadi discourse to describe the regional post-9/11 environment represented a victory for Abu al-Qa'qa'. In exchange for this privilege, he had no choice but to tone down such discourse as it was potentially

Strategies in the Politics of Islam" (PhD diss., Arnold Bergsträsser Institute, Fribourg am Brisgau, 1999).

[23] In Aleppo, social segregation has long run along geographic lines: populations from rural areas are relegated to the eastern, northeastern, and southeastern parts of the city, areas where the population density is the highest. These are the very areas that the rebels have controlled since 2012. See Salwa Sakkal, "Croissance et contrôle de l'espace. L'informel et l'urbanisme, la municipalité et l'Etat," in Alep et ses territoires (see chapter 1, note 3).

[24] On the prerequisites for becoming imam of a mosque in Syria, see Böttcher, "Sunni Islam under Hafez al-Assad," 94.

subversive toward the regime's institutions. This was the price for keeping his position as the mosque's imam.

His group, Foreigners of al-Sham (*ghuraba' al-sham*) used the slogan, "The voice of truth in an era of silence." The term *ghareeb* (pl. *ghuraba'*) bears a negative connotation in Arab tribal and cultural codes. Here, however, it took on a positive connotation as a name for the small minority who remained true to their faith despite an environment forgetful of Islamic practice. A hadith recounted this inversion as "Islam started foreign and will end up foreign, so blessed be foreigners."[25]

The bodyguards protecting Al-Qaʻqaʻ perfected their knowledge of martial arts in the al-Sakhur mosque. Tall and hieratic, he appeared on the mosque's pulpit wearing a *shalwar qamis*—the term used in Urdu to designate a long vest-tunic with a closed collar, worn over loose pants. This outfit was meant as the material expression of his adoption of jihadi culture, such as it had developed and been applied in the Afghan-Pakistani crisis zone, which the young preacher had visited in 1995, shortly before the Taliban reached power. From his pulpit, Abu al-Qaʻqaʻ spoke with exceptional eloquence to express simple ideas about the umma. He lamented its humiliation at the hands of Jews and "Crusaders," its betrayal by its leaders ("Arab dogs acting under the Jews and Crusaders' influence"), and the way it was weakened by those who were Muslim in name only. The conclusion he drew was not surprising: it was because Muslims no longer believed the message of Islam and had stopped following the Prophet's example that they had ended up in such a state of powerlessness.

In his various DVDs, the camera tends to focus on worshipers of all ages gathered in the mosque. They appear to be of humble social class and fascinated by the sheikh's rhetorical pathos—some even burst into tears at the mention of the umma's hardships and its fall from past glory. In fact, the umma's status is ambivalent: it seems to come into its own in exceptional situations of crisis, persecution, and violence only, then to fall back into its debilitated state. The videos, however, present the umma as an entity that almost has a life of its own, a sort of body politic. Symbolically, the

---

[25] This hadith is attributed to the "Book of Faith" from the *Sahih Muslim* collection of hadith. Great figureheads of the Hanbali school of thought have commented on it, including Ibn Taymiyya and his student Ibn Qayyim al-Jawziyya.

notion of the umma connects the present with the past, current events with myth, history with collective memory, and the ideal world with reality. As such, it proved a source of unlimited normative material, so much so that the sheikh had little trouble finding precedents in prophetic tradition that he could use to criticize fellow Muslims. His sermons were based on a pattern of oppositions, identifications, and inversions, whereby those at the bottom of social hierarchy were lifted to the top of an eschatological hierarchy of merit and punishment. In fact, it was actually those being bombed and dying in Palestine, Chechnya, and Afghanistan who constituted the essence of the umma. They were showing their faithfulness to the heroic teachings of the first Muslims and restoring Islam's honor against the wealthy and powerful of this world, whom the West backed in return for their neglecting Islam. These inversions produced a sort of catharsis for the believers gathered in al-Sakhur mosque, freeing them from the guilt of social failure and portending their election to a superior order of religious excellence. For instance, the high point of the November 29, 2002 [9/25/1423] sermon, during the month of Ramadan, was the sheikh's repetition of the anaphora "Look around you" to denounce the disparity between the majority of Muslims' actions on the one hand, and the demands of the Islamic ideal on the other:

Look around you: the *jahiliyya* is suffocating us, illegitimate rulers governs us, abjection is everywhere, debauchery is widespread, irreverence is dominant. Look around you! Rampant permissiveness, perdition and heresy; superstition, ignorance and negligence! Look around you! Bloody conflicts between the sons of Muslims, hatred and rivalry, divisions and exclusions, neighbors pushed into exile! Look around you! Sons and daughters ungrateful to their fathers and mothers, abandoning the pillars of Islam and neglecting its rituals, indifferent to the umma's affairs. Look around you! Gaping wounds, blood gushing out like a river. Look around you! [repeated twice] Rampant impiety, the threat of idolatry, atheism is annihilating faith and doing away with it. Look around you! The caliphate is lost, *shari'a* is absent, Qur'anic prescriptions are suspended! Look around you! [repeated twice] An umma torn apart, divided territories, a land held captive, holy places held under lockdown due to the actions of the miscreants and of our "brothers"—monkeys and swine![26] Look around you! Honor is besmirched, the weak are being slaughtered, adults are killed, free men imprisoned, the voice of truth silenced, the voices of men of honor are stifled. Look around you! Satan is lurking in the hearts of homes and families! Destructive media, omnipresent *jahiliyya*, non-religious customs, non-Islamic traditions! Look around you! Imported styles, clones, the *sunna* is absent, its teachings are dead, its prescriptions frozen. Look around you! Superficial young men, Westernized young women! A generation which knows neither its identity, nor what it belongs to, and which is no longer tied to Islam except by name, inheritance and environment! Look around you! Silent minarets, dull prayers, lacking devotion and reverence! Religious fasts are undermined by all kinds of sin! People spend their days and evenings watching movies and T.V. shows, gossiping about what so-and-so said, eating out in mixed-gender restaurants. . . . Look around you! Palestine is crying out, Chechnya is drowning in blood, Afghanistan is calling for help, Kashmir is being slaughtered.

In order to exhort the umma to action, Abu al-Qaʻqaʻ claimed to be part of the mythical community of companions of the Prophet, but he carefully refrained from explicitly referring to Salafism in his sermons. The need to take into account the regime's hostility toward the various manifestations of "Wahhabism" (often associated with Salafism) lay behind this. But it could also be explained by the sheikh's desire to summon all Islamic schools of thought and orientations—even the Sufi circles of the *naqshbandiyya*, of which there were many in Aleppo, and from which he himself may have originated—to the duty of jihad.

Abu al-Qaʻqaʻ also knew how to stage himself in the manner of the Arab singers he vilified in his sermons. Thus, the Foreigners of al-Sham put together a clip, available on YouTube, in which the sheikh and his followers appear standing in al-Sakhur mosque and singing the *thuwar* (revolutionaries') chant—an ancient Palestinian song that Islamists of Hamas had adopted during the second Intifada.[27]

---

[26] This is a reference to the Jews and the Christians.
[27] The video is no longer available online.

Abu al-Qa'qa' modified the nature of the original song to accord with his own artistic and religious orientation. His version
dropped the military mood of the original poem, which had been
composed in a short meter (called *sari'*) with one final foot (*watid*)
per line, a form that had evolved from its distant ancestors, the
traditional *muwashshaha*, poems with verses sung by alternating
voices, which had been invented in Spanish Andalusia in the tenth
century. In the video, Abu al-Qa'qa', the soloist (*munshid*), appears
holding a microphone and sings the first verses *a cappella*: "The
horses of glory march inside of us / The martyrs' blood honors us /
Paradise demands men"; then the congregation surrounding him
repeats these verses in unison as helpers distribute black and white
keffiehs (Palestinian scarves) to them. The crowd calls out the cho-
rus ("*thuwar!*") while clapping in time, their hands raised high in
the air, and their enthusiasm growing as the sheikh-*mutrib* (singer)
brandishes his microphone toward the worshipers, like a singer
seeking audience participation. The same pattern is then repeated,
in the same rhythm, and the lines "Rise up, heavenly wind / Spill
out, martyrs' blood" is sung three times. Next the sheikh intro-
duces some changes to the original version. Using some of the same
rhetorical techniques he had refined in his sermons, he pronounces
a litany of symbols that call to the umma for help: "Paradise is
calling to us / Blood is calling to us / Honor is calling to us / Generosity is calling to us / The earth is calling to us." Each time the
crowd unanimously replies, "We will answer the call." The sheikh
then continues tearfully, "Who will answer, who will answer, who,
who . . . ?" He makes liberal use of vocal flourishes (*taratin*) to
highlight the misfortune of the umma which had deserted the battlefield. In his version, the affirmative nature of Hamas's warlike
hymn ("Salah al-Din, your men are with us") becomes an anxious
interrogation: "Salah al-Din, where are your men?" Abu al-Qa'qa'
substitutes the words "Qur'an" and "sword" of the original lyr-
ics with the words "Qur'an" and "army." Continuing his poetic
invention, he calls upon Bashar al-Assad (the president's likeness
then appears in the clip) to witness his troops' enthusiasm. Sung
a first time, the verse "Caravans, bring us forth so that we may
liberate Palestine" is then repeated twice, then the "government"
and the "political leadership" are called upon to move toward war.
This performance, and particularly its gradual intensification, is

reminiscent of a Sufi ceremony: the melding together of the worshipers united by enthusiasm over the idea of martyrdom at war
mirrors the incandescent fusion of the individual with God in Sufi
rituals. What we see in this video, then, is an emotional community
forming around a charismatic leader who draws his popularity in
part from his ability to infuse jihadism into deeply anchored musi-
cal and poetic traditions.

In early 2004, the Iraqi jihadi website of the Center for Services
to Mujahidin issued a warning against "Abu al-Qa'qa' the spy"
and posted a short biography of the sheikh, accusing him (seemingly incorrectly) of having been the Ba'ath party representative
in the Damascus *shari'a* faculty.[28] Abu al-Qa'qa' then retired from
the political scene for close to two years. He did not reappear in
the public eye until late 2005, and then it was as a different man.
His previously unkempt beard was well groomed, and he became
the preacher of the al-Iman mosque in the residential neighborhood of Halab al-Jadida (new Aleppo), which was built up in the
eighties. His physical metamorphosis (as well as his geographical
move from east to west) reflects the gradual transformation of the
mujahid into the *muqawim* (resistance fighter) in the Hezbollah
style. From Beirut, he was interviewed on June 30, 2006, on the
Saudi satellite television station al-Arabiyya.[29] The program, conceived in imitation of BBC's "Hard Talk," follows a format in
which guests must respond to a rapid series of tough questions. On
the set, Abu al-Qa'qa' asserted that "Foreigners of al-Sham" was
purely a media phenomenon and condemned "the blind violence
of *takfiri* groups [that label other Muslims as infidels] in Iraq and
elsewhere." Instead, he advocated "legal and organized resistance"
and rejected "murderous, sectarian militias and brigades practicing blind violence." He resorted to denial when the interviewer observed that the young insurgents who had led the assault against the
state television building in Damascus in early June had owned DVDs
of his sermons. He acknowledged his support for Bashar al-Assad's

---

[28] See the online reproduction of this warning, http://www.muslm.net/vb/ (accessed August 2010).

[29] The Saudi channel had discussed his responsibility after the tapes containing his sermons were discovered with the insurgents who had attempted to storm the Syrian national
TV station in Damascus in early June 2006. The exact transcript of his interview is available
online. http://www.muslm.net/vb/showthread.php?t=169897 (accessed September 2010).

regime and stood by this position, placing blame for the confrontations of the 1980s in Syria on the Muslim Brotherhood. On December 22, 2006, he held a conference in the al-Iman mosque's library, during which he revealed his predisposition to support the Syrian regime should the Americans invade Syria.[30] This evolution shows the kinds of directives that Sheikh Abu al-Qaʻqaʻ and others may have given to the volunteers in the "hostels" networks in Aleppo and Damascus. They were first invited to join the ranks of an "organized and legal resistance" of a kind similar to Shaker al-Absi's network within Fatah al-Intifada, so as not to fall into the "Mossad-American trap" of destructive anarchy in Iraq.

Following the effective demise of the Foreigners of al-Sham, Abu al-Qaʻqaʻ lent legitimacy to others' resistance efforts, and acted as a facilitator when it was necessary in order to satisfy the demands of Syrian policy in Lebanon, but he was no longer capable of struggling against the umma's enemies by himself. Later on, he reinvented himself as a preacher of morality, bent on defending the weakest in Syrian society. In one of his last sermons, given on July 27, 2007, he censured this system in which "people suffer because of civil servants, parliamentarians and ministers" and where "social divides are constantly increasing." He vehemently denounced "those who protect organized mafias which rob us of billions," while the poor are subject to heavy penalties for petty crimes.[31] He called upon Bashar al-Assad to remember the hopes people had invested in him when he rose to power. Despite these carefully chosen words, Abu al-Qaʻqaʻ had transgressed a taboo by criticizing the realities of life under Assad's rule—in a way that anticipated the moral bent of the 2011 Arab Spring revolt. On September 27, 2007, he was assassinated at the age of thirty-four, as he walked out of his mosque in Aleppo. It remains unclear whether his killer was a jihadi who wanted to punish "Abu al-Qaʻqaʻ the spy" or someone from the "mafias" he had vilified in his sermons.

---

[30] See the Tawba website, created after al-Aghassi's death, which presents a rather toned-down and incomplete rendition of this. http://toba-sham.com/?tag (accessed September 2010).

[31] Part of the sermon is available online. http://all4Syria.info/content/view/31920/122 (accessed August 2010).

The Regional Stakes Involved in the Reorientation of Jihadis toward Lebanon

The prisoners who met—or were reunited—in Syria's Saydnaya prison were all transferred to the Palestine Branch shortly before their liberation (Shaker al-Absi was transferred on May 1, 2005). The procedure required that before their definitive release, the intelligence service that had originally arrested them would evaluate them one last time. That service could decide to defer the prisoner's release if it saw fit. Thus, Subhi Ghanam and other prisoners were said to have been released from the Palestine Branch in June 2005, before al-Absi was.[32] However, when they were freed, organized departures to Lebanon were not yet on the table; for around six more months—until January 2006—Iraq was still the jihadis' main destination. Hence, upon his release, al-Absi resumed receiving volunteers and arranging for their transport to Iraq.

Their redirection toward Lebanon cannot be understood without taking into account the complex triangular relationship between the Syrian intelligence services, the jihad support networks in Iraq (of which Shaker al-Absi was still just one link in the chain), and the main representative of jihadism in Iraq, Abu Mus'ab al-Zarqawi (until his June 7, 2006 death), and then his successor, the Egyptian Abu Hamza al-Muhajir. Syria served as a support base for the anti-American insurrection. Large-scale hostage taking and ransoming in Iraq allowed a variety of groups to fund themselves. The money raised would be sent back to Syria to purchase weapons from the black market. Smugglers then moved the arms and munitions back into Iraq and distributed them to the different jihadi cells. Syria also served as a back-up base that jihadi leaders from the Mujahidin Advisory Council (Majlis Shura al-Mujahidin)—established in 2005, and to which al-Zarqawi's al-Qaeda in the Land of the Two Rivers belonged—could retreat to if necessary.

As Ghanam's testimony indicates, the various stages of this process were, if not controlled by the Syrian intelligence services, then at least known to them. They could arrest this or that leader for a

---

[32] Shaker al-Absi is said to have been released from the Palestine Section in mid-June, that is, about one week after Subhi Ghanam (released June 6) and about ten days before Hani al-Sankari.

time, cut off one of the network's routes, or, conversely, turn a blind eye to the financial and human circuit between the two countries. The regime's regional interests would determine what was done at any given time, as would, most directly, the state of its relationship with the United States. The most important objective for Syrian authorities was to monitor the itineraries of these different groups, so as to prevent any individuals from defecting from this semi-clandestine network. To achieve this end, its actions had to be based on highly specific and detailed knowledge of the network's channels, leaders, and internal hierarchies. Also required was a tacit arrangement by which Syrian authorities would give jihadi militants sanctuary and, in return, the militants would not attack Syrian territory. But this risky arrangement did not prevent Syrian intelligence services from intervening against the militants if they planned any operations against Europe or the United States from Syrian territory. This allowed Syria to maintain credibility vis-à-vis Western governments, and, in turn, gave them a hint of the consequences that might follow any attempt to cut Syria out of their regional and international strategies.

In the fall of 2005, certain jihadis wished to challenge this agreement. According to the Lebanese military court prosecutor's indictment, al-Zarqawi's lieutenant in Syria, the aforementioned Milad al-Lubnani (Hassan Muhammad al-Nab'a), had fiercely opposed a militant known as Abu Anis after he announced his intention to turn Syria into a land of jihad. The indictment states, "This quarrel resulted in the two groups starting to seize control of most of the resources and property available: people, weapons, houses, farms, and workshops for making explosives."[33] The judicial report corroborates the version a Salafi sheikh from the Nahr al-Bared camp had offered over a year earlier. According to him, al-Zarqawi and al-Absi supported preserving the Syrian sanctuary. In his account, only the name of al-Qaeda's emir in Syria differs:

> Shaker al-Absi considered that Syria needed to remain a place of safe passage (*ma'bar amin*). One of al-Zarqawi's envoys came to settle the issue, and chose this option. . . . Abu Jandal al-Dimashqi was al-Qaeda's emir in Syria. He wished to fight the Syrian regime. The organization was then called the

---

[33] See the military prosecutor's report, quoted in *al-Safir* (see note 10 above).

"Brigades of Unity and Jihad in Syria" (*kata'ib al-tawhid wa-l-jihad fi bilad al-sham*). The organization split into al-Absi's group and Abu Jandal's group. A Saudi al-Qaeda religious judge came. Abu Jandal al-Dimashqi was disowned. No front was opened in Syria. This must have happened in late 2005 or 2006. . . . The Saudi sheikh told them to go to Iraq or Lebanon. Shaker al-Absi created his own organization: *kata'ib al-muqawama al-islamiyya fi bilad al-sham* ("the Brigades of the Islamic Resistance in Greater Syria").[34]

While jihadi leaders did not believe the time was right to attack Syria, this was not the case when it came to Lebanon. First a base for anti-Western terrorist actions (the McDonald's network), after 2003 the country turned into a base for sending jihadi volunteers to Iraq, and then, after 2006, it became the locus where an ambitious jihadi plan took shape. Abu Hamza al-Muhajir was involved in all three of these successive stages. Prior to the arrival of the Yemeni Ibn Shahid at the Ayn al-Helweh camp (see chapter 2), Abu Hamza had also done a stint in this Palestinian refugee camp. Born in Egypt in 1969, an engineer by training, al-Muhajir spent two years (1998 and 1999) in al-Qaeda camps in Afghanistan, moving from al-Faruq, the camp "for new recruits," to the Airport camp "for advanced courses."[35] He entered Lebanon illegally via Turkey in December 2000, and may have been given hospitality by the chief of the local militia, 'Usbat al-Ansar. His stay in Ayn al-Helweh for a few months also enabled him to meet the leader of the Dinniyeh group, Ahmad al-Mikati. He allegedly took care of renting apartments in Beirut and Mount Lebanon at this time, in order to prepare the ground for terrorist operations (a tactic that would be copied by the FAI a few years later). The fall of Saddam Hussein's regime in March 2003 postponed the jihadis' terrorist agenda in Lebanon. They preferred instead to turn their efforts to channeling volunteers to Iraq from Lebanon. Al-Muhajir had in fact anticipated this move, as he was already in Baghdad when American troops entered the Iraqi capital. Having joined the leadership of al-Qaeda in the Land of the Two Rivers, he took over for Abu Anas

[34] Interview with a Salafi sheikh from Baddawi camp, August 2007.
[35] Quotes from Thomas Hegghammer, *Jihad in Saudi Arabia: Violence and Pan-Islamism since 1979* (Cambridge: Cambridge University Press, 2010), 109.

al-Shami, Zarqawi's ideologue, after al-Shami was killed in an American raid on Abu Ghraib on September 17, 2004, before becoming the leader of al-Qaeda, then "war minister" of the Islamic State in Iraq. According to testimony from the Nahr al-Bared sheikhs, "Abu Hamza al-Muhajir was in favor of Islamic State group members like Shaker al-Absi and Abu Medyan going to Lebanon, the idea being to open a front there against Israel."[36] The redirection of attention toward the east could also be discerned in statements made by Zarqawi in a video showing his face, issued on April 25, 2006, in which he reasserted that although he was fighting in Iraq, his eyes were still on al-Qods/Jerusalem. This move coincided with strong pressure from the United States administration on Syria to reinforce surveillance of its eastern border.

Importantly, this change of direction toward Lebanon began seven months before the Israeli military campaign against Lebanon in the summer of 2006. The war undoubtedly accelerated this militant migration, but it did not provoke it.

A Path to Jihad: The Fatah al-Intifada Organization

After his release, Shaker al-Absi somehow rejoined his former commander from Fatah al-Intifada, Abu Khaled al-'Amleh. Since the Syrian retreat from Lebanon in April 2005, the Fatah al-Intifada secretary-general ceaselessly exhorted militants in Syria to travel to the party's bases in Lebanon. According to Khalil Abu Yasser (the representative of Fatah al-Intifada in Lebanon), al-'Amleh put al-Absi in command of a wing of the organization known as the "western force" (al-quwwa al-gharbiyya), whose main theater of operations was the "western sector" (al-qita' al-gharbi), meaning "Palestine" in Palestinian fedayin jargon.

According to Khalil Abu Yasser, Shaker al-Absi convinced Abu Khaled al-'Amleh to place Fatah al-Intifada's Lebanese infrastructure at the disposal of jihadis who wished to launch attacks on Israel from the group's bases in Lebanon, and to provide funding via al-Absi's connections in Iraq.[37] Other sources indicate that al-'Amleh invited al-Absi—as a former leader in his organization,

---

[36] Interviews, Nahr al-Bared, August 2007.

[37] Interview with Khalil Abu Yasser, head of Fatah al-Intifada in North Lebanon, Baddawi camp, party headquarters, August 26, 2007.

now with newly acquired jihadi experience—to join forces again, this time in the Lebanese camps.[38] An exchange of services facilitated their cooperation: al-'Amleh managed administrative and organizational issues, while al-Absi committed to providing a critical mass of battle-hardened fighters with experience in Iraq, ready to die in the name of jihad. The news that a new route to Lebanon had opened using the Fatah al-Intifada facilities spread rapidly within the circles al-Absi frequented. The leader of Fatah al-Intifada in the Palestinian camp of Yarmouk in Syria also spread the word. In early 2006, Muhammad Saleh Zawawi (a.k.a. Abu Selim Taha, who later became the spokesperson of Fatah al-Islam) heard from the Palestinian-Syrian Abu Bakr al-Shar'i (a.k.a. Mahmud 'Awad Falah) that Fatah al-Intifada ran training camps for volunteers in Lebanon and intended to prepare for operations in Palestine:

> My group and I agreed to join these camps, where we were given photo identification cards as Fatah al-Intifada fighters. A Fatah al-Intifada bus transported us to the Helweh camp, where Shaker al-Absi welcomed us. With him were Abu Abdallah, Abu Ahmad (a Palestinian-Syrian), Abu al-'Abbas, Abu al-Sa'id, Abu Yazin, Abu Lu'ay—all of whom were Syrian—as well as other young men.[39]

By late January 2006, the first expeditions departed Syria for the Fatah al-Intifada training camps of Helweh (near Rashaya) and Qusaya (further north)—both very close to the Syrian border in the Lebanese Beqaa Valley. There, Jordanian-Palestinians gave recruits rudimentary military training. The available testimonies almost all indicate generalized pressure toward Lebanon, as if the objective had been for the Islamist threat to increase immediately, as soon as the Syrian withdrawal was complete.

Abu Khaled al-'Amleh's own intellectual evolution toward an increasingly religious radical stance facilitated the establishment of links between a dying Palestinian organization—known for its organic ties with Syrian intelligence services—and mobile jihadi networks in the Levant. Born in Jericho in 1938, a 1956 graduate of the

[38] This is the version given by *al-Hayat*, on May 27, 2007.

[39] The biographical details and confessions of the indicted persons from Fatah al-Islam are available online in an article published on March 12, 2009. www.youkal.net (accessed March 20, 2009).

Jordanian military college, and a member of Fatah since 1967, he left the Hashemite army to fight with the *fedayin* during the 1970 Black September conflict. He later found himself at odds with Yasser Arafat, president of the PLO, whom al-'Amleh felt was guilty of recognizing UN Security Council resolution 242 during the 1982 Israeli invasion of Lebanon. He and Colonel Abu Musa then founded the dissident organization Fatah al-Intifada. With support from the Syrian artillery, Fatah al-Intifada then besieged Arafat in the Nahr al-Bared camp of Lebanon in the fall of 1983.

In many Palestinian circles, Fatah al-Intifada was viewed as lacking autonomy, as an excrescence of the Syrian intelligence services, doing their dirty work by hunting down "Arafatist traitors" and other "deviationists" in Lebanon and Syria. Fatah al-Intifada, in their view, performed the same services as another Palestinian-Syrian duplicate, Ahmad Jibril's PFLP-GC.

Following the example of other Arab nationalist intellectuals, Abu Khaled al-'Amleh's violent revolutionary rhetoric vis-à-vis any negotiation with Israel found a new source of inspiration in radical Islamism. In the introduction to his latest book, published in 2006, al-'Amleh paid vibrant homage to various "martyred leaders," including Gamal Abd al-Nasser, Hafez al-Assad, and Ayatollah Khomeini, "who caused the downfall of one of the citadels of imperialism, took sides with Palestine and Jerusalem, called for their liberation, and stood with the disenfranchised of the world."[40] Condemnation of the United States' role in the region may have served as a retroactive justification of the connections between the author's militarist populism and the jihadi ideology Bin Laden articulated in his 1998 manifesto.[41] Thus, al-'Amleh wrote that the Second Intifada (also known as the "al-Aqsa Intifada"), which began in September 2000, had had the merit of revealing "the reality of America as a direct enemy" (*al-'aduw al-mubashir*):

> It exposed all of the trivial and vain attempts by America and the different Arab regimes to peddle a friendly image of the United States and to sell the elements of a solution to the Arab-

[40] Abu Khaled al-'Amleh, *The al-Aqsa Intifada: Introduction to a Victory Foretold* (*Intifada al-Aqsa: Muqaddima al-Nasr al-Qadim*) (Damascus: Union of Arab Writers, 2003), 6.

[41] See the transcript of the manifesto in Gilles Kepel, ed., *Al-Qaeda dans le texte* (Paris: PUF, 2005), 63–69.

Zionist conflict. Now everyone, including the regional Arab system, has realized that America is none other than a greedy imperialist enemy that wishes to seize Arab wealth, markets and natural resources. When their interests demand it, the United States does not hesitate to overthrow regimes—even those of its allies—and modify regional geography and political structures.[42]

Al-'Amleh's ideological matrix reproduced the "resistance" paradigm and rested on the need to "obstruct" (*mumana'a*) Israeli-dominated Western plots. This discourse itself was nothing new in Syria or all across the region. It combined the anti-imperialist and anti-Western lexicons, offering a rhetorical framework for convergence between Islamists and Arab nationalists. However, the author crossed a line when he labeled the United States a "direct enemy"—a line that even Hamas has refused to cross to this day. Without basing his discourse on a religious corpus, al-'Amleh joined Bin Laden in accusing America of being a reproduction of the Zionist entity on a global scale, engaged in an enterprise aimed at the dispossession of the entire Muslim umma, similar to the goal that Israel had accomplished against Palestine.

Acclimatizing to the Camps of Lebanon

The Fatah al-Intifada military camps in the Beqaa Valley were just the first step, and from February 2006 on, the first jihadi volunteers headed to the Palestinian refugee camps of Beirut. Thanks to the identification documents al-'Amleh had given them, they were able to justify their presence there through their membership in Fatah al-Intifada, which allowed them to use the organization's infrastructure. Shaker al-Absi moved into Shatila and built a rapport with the camp's imam, all the while shuttling back and forth between Syria and Lebanon. He also contacted Abu al-Layth, who, from his base in the Ayn al-Helweh camp, oversaw the transportation of volunteers to Abu Mus'ab al-Zarqawi's group in Iraq. Other volunteers were sent to Burj al-Barajne, in the southern suburbs of Beirut controlled by Hezbollah, as well as to the Mar

---

[42] al-'Amleh, *The al-Aqsa Intifada*, 139

Elias camp.[43] Tensions surfaced when these bearded militants—
who numbered about fifty during the first few months—tried to
lecture the traditional party cadres about religion. These Fatah al-
Intifada men—self-styled custodians of the Palestinian cause for
the Syrian regime's benefit—were used to holding a radical line vis-
à-vis the PLO, which they considered guilty of yielding to American demands. Here, for the first time, they found themselves on
the defensive, confronted with the radical Islamists' new brand of
self-righteous stance, on both the political and the religious level:

> They came into the camps under the cover of the "Western
> force." We hadn't imagined that Abu Khaled al-'Amleh might
> hijack the organization away from its original mission. We had
> respect for him. We didn't think he was religious, we thought
> he was secular. He would use religious expressions in his
> speeches, but it was out of political opportunism, because it
> was the heyday of Islamism. We didn't feel at ease with him.
> Abu Khaled would say: "We need to take after Hezbollah.
> Their members don't drink, don't smoke, and pray five times
> daily." We accepted this idea. He would say he could fight Is-
> rael from within Palestine. He would say that the members of
> the "Western force" were all originally from inside Palestine.
> In Shatila, at Burj al-Barajneh, they threatened and beat those
> who were not religious in the same way they were. There
> were problems.[44]

In midsummer 2006, Shaker al-Absi asked his men to go to
the North with a view to moving into the Baddawi and Nahr al-
Bared camps (however, he made sure to retain several apartments
to serve as hostels for new recruits in the following months). Several factors explain the reasons for this initiative. Ever since the
"war of the camps" (1985–88), both the Lebanese army intelligence apparatus and Hezbollah had kept a close watch on the Beirut camps, which had long been reservoirs of support for Yasser

---

[43] This was the route followed by a former Saydnaya inmate, Yasser al-Shuqayri (see p. 90).
Having been deprived of his identification documents in the Syrian prison's Palestine Section,
he later procured fakes that allowed him to cross the Syria-Lebanon border at Masnaa. With
a Fatah al-Intifada card, he then went to the Burj al-Barajne camp, where he was welcomed by
Shaker al-Absi. See the judiciary council session transcript, al-Safir, July 24, 2009.

[44] Interview with Khalil Abu Yasser (see note 37 above).

Arafat. Moreover, the camps' openness to their Shi'ite surroundings presented a security risk, especially Shatila, which, since the end of the war, had become a poor, diverse neighborhood grouping Syrians, Kurds, and Lebanese in close proximity. While this type of human environment was useful for a small group, it could pose a threat to a growing organization. But the decisive factor in al-Absi's decision was doubtless the summer 2006 war with Israel: the intensity of the bombings increased political tensions inside Lebanon and caused general disorganization. These deteriorating conditions presumably enabled Abu Khaled al-'Amleh and al-Absi to be more ambitious, both politically and militarily. Once again, the modification of a situation's parameters opened up new opportunities for the protagonists. The transformation of northern refugee camps into training grounds for the *mujahidin* seemed to create a new militant dynamic, broader than the network of connections al-Absi had been building since the late 1990s.

From the Baddawi Incidents to the Birth of Fatah al-Islam

In fall 2006, young bachelors rented out several dozen apartments in the Baddawi camp. Because the camp's regulations only permitted married couples to rent apartments, this attracted the attention of the camp's security committee, composed of the Tahaluf (alliance) of Palestinian factions close to the Syrian regime. On November 23, members of the security committee noticed the comings and goings of several young men who seemed to be living in the same apartment. Interested in the reason for their presence, the security men attempted in vain to open dialogue with the bachelors. Soon thereafter, the security committee approached them again, this time accompanied by a delegation of twelve armed men. The young men—there were about twenty of them—were summoned for questioning, and they pretended to acquiesce, accompanying the committee's armed patrol back to the Fatah al-Intifada headquarters in the Samed center.[45] They all claimed to be "theology

---

[45] One of the main institutions of Palestinian "civil society" in Lebanon, Samed (The Palestine Martyrs Works Society) was initially set up by the PLO in 1970 to provide vocational training to "the martyrs' children," before extending its activities to all Palestinians. In Nahr al-Bared camp, what was left of Samed was a closed-down weaving shed.

students" of Palestinian background, and said that they had managed to rent the apartment thanks to a Salafi from Baddawi named Yusef Hassan Khalil (a.k.a. Abu al-Mu'tazz), who was part of the group. Suddenly, the latter threw a grenade and took cover in the Samed center, along with his armed comrades. Two hours later, Fatah al-Intifada militia had the insurgents surrounded, but they managed to escape and retreat either to Tripoli or to the Nahr al-Bared camp:

> After this, I received a call from Abu Khaled al-'Amleh. He asked me to calm things down. I was furious. Shaker al-Absi also called me, to tell me that the *shebab* (youth) were at fault in this matter, but that he had to protect them. I told him that they had to leave the camp. He insisted that they stay. I asked him: "Does religion allow them to bear arms within the camp?" After this incident, they all headed to Nahr al-Bared. Al-'Amleh had asked me for forty-eight hours for the move. Then al-Absi declared the creation of Fatah al-Islam. In the camp, there was a meeting with all the Palestinian organizations of the Democratic Front. I asked them to expel this group. They refused. The only ones who agreed were the people from Yasser Arafat's Fatah.[46]

The Baddawi incidents precipitated the creation of Fatah al-Islam in Nahr al-Bared camp. It is difficult to determine whether the members of the network already had the intention of creating a new Palestinian jihadi group, or if circumstances essentially forced them to do so. In the Baddawi camp, as in Nahr al-Bared, the apartments had been rented according to their proximity to the different Palestinian centers, perhaps indicating Shaker al-Absi's intention to seize control of all Palestinian camps in the North. It is possible that the network had interpreted the behavior of the Baddawi Fatah al-Intifada cadres as a sign that the Syrian security services no longer supported them. In that case, contrary to what they had been told in Damascus and in the Beqaa Valley, the pro-Syrian Tahaluf organizations would not provide the security guarantees necessary for the continuation of their activities. Therefore, the plan for a slow, clandestine accumulation of men and equipment in the sanctuary of the

---

[46] Interview with Khalil Abu Yasser (see note 37 above).

Palestinian camps was no longer realistic. The Hamas representative in North Lebanon, Sheikh Muhammad al-Hajj, argued against the premeditation theory, claiming instead that their actions were precipitated by circumstance. He stated:

They did not wish to proclaim the existence of Fatah al-Islam. They wished to take advantage of the Fatah al-Intifada infrastructures. After the Baddawi incidents, they felt abandoned by Fatah al-Intifada. Abu Khaled al-'Amleh ordered them to go back to Nahr al-Bared. They were not ready to organize themselves; they were in a state of turmoil and confusion (halat irtibak). There was a leader—Shaker al-Absi—but no command council (majlis qiyadi).[47]

However, publicizing the network's existence did not cause it to emerge entirely from underground.

Seizing Nahr al-Bared

To explain how easily a small group of (initially) just a few dozen men took virtually complete control of the second largest Palestinian refugee camp in Lebanon (with over 30,000 inhabitants), it is necessary to briefly review the situation in Nahr al-Bared in late 2006. Since 1983, the Syrian security apparatus had subcontracted political control of the camp to various Palestinian militias belonging to the Tahaluf umbrella group, such as al-Saiqa, Fatah al-Intifada, and the PFLP-GC. Such a hands-off approach to the Palestinian issue in Lebanon had several advantages for the Syrian regime. As either a facilitator or a disrupter, it would be able to play a role in the settlement of the refugee question in the event negotiations resumed. It could prevent disarmament of the camps until it obtained guarantees as to Syria's own regional status; and it could preserve a useful, monitored network of militant and military safe houses throughout Lebanese territory, serviceable for its own security agenda. This indirect and flexible form of control satisfied the requirement of adaptability to regional developments. One manifestion of this adaptability was operative throughout 2002: as the

[47] Interview with Sheikh Muhammad al-Hajj, Sidon, September 29, 2007.

American invasion of Iraq loomed, the Syrian military ceased direct surveillance of the various camp entrances.

Maintaining all of this required a constant effort to prevent loyalist Fatah from becoming the main political reference for Palestinian refugees in Lebanon. In fact, after the onset of the Second Intifada in September 2000, Fatah had managed to gradually regain part of its stature by offering scholarships and social services to the community, even though it did not manage to build up much military capacity. Since the Syrian military retreat from Lebanon in April 2005, the security committee (composed of militias from the Tahaluf grouping) was no longer able to function, due to the growing strength of alternative forces connected to Fatah and Hamas. Both had become more influential following Hamas's electoral victory in the Palestinian Territories in January 2006. Moreover, the arrival of Islamist militants, who claimed legitimacy for their presence in Nahr al-Bared in the name of the organization's own secretary-general, caused a division in the ranks of Fatah al-Intifada. This paralyzed the camp's security structures and explains the shortfall of military strength that made possible Fatah al-Islam's power grab.

During the day of November 24, 2006 (the day after the Baddawi incidents), Fatah al-Islam carried out its coup d'état in Nahr al-Bared. It seized stocks of weapons and munitions belonging to Fatah al-Intifada, as well as the most strategic positions in both the "new" and the "old" camp. The old sector of the camp (al-mukhayyam al-qadim) was about half a square kilometer and was located at the historic center of Nahr al-Bared. This area included the UNRWA school on the seaside and the offices and headquarters of the main Palestinian institutions, as well as a "vegetable market" famous across the whole of North Lebanon for offering cheap goods smuggled in from Syria. In certain areas, buildings had grown so tall that they had formed a compact mass of concrete that little daylight could penetrate. It was a maze of tiny, shaded alleys, cluttered with electric wires that ran dangerously close to water drainage channels. The "new camp" (al-mukhayyam al-jadid) was twice as large; it was the result of the geographic and demographic extension of the camp southward, eastward, and northward.

Shaker al-Absi had taken up position in three old bases that Fatah al-Intifada had itself taken after Yasser Arafat's departure in 1983: the Organization Office (Maktab al-Tanzim) located on the main street, in the center of the old camp, which had been Fatah's headquarters in the early 1970s; the Cooperative (Ta'awuniyya), in the north of the old camp; and in the new camp, the Samed center, beside the sea. The latter location was named for the clothing workshops that the PLO had set up in all refugee camps in the region in the late 1960s. Jihadis enrolled in Fatah al-Intifada had taken over the Office during the summer 2006 war, without arousing any reaction from the organization's "secular" leadership. The Cooperative building occupied a strategic location at the intersection of a north-south axis, the main street linking the two entry points to Nahr al-Bared, and the perpendicular route from the al-Mahmara village in the east, westward to the sea. The leaders of Fatah al-Islam transformed the vast commercial warehouse of the first floor into a weapons depot, but waited until February 2007 before seizing control of the Popular Committee's (al-Lajna al-Sha'biyya) office on the second floor.

At the Samed center, which had been almost entirely abandoned for several years (except for a family of squatters), al-Absi established the headquarters where he held press conferences and political meetings. Samed was also the site of various kinds of military training, ranging from urban warfare and the use of car bombs to the manufacture of explosives using acetone. Between training courses, believers-in-arms could pray at the nearby Salafi Khaled bin al-Walid mosque. Lastly, Fatah al-Islam now also controlled the al-Khan archeological site (known as the "caravanserai"), located along the seafront going toward al-'Abdeh, which was a well-established military training base for the different Palestinian factions. This explained its exposure to Israeli bombing throughout the various stages of the Lebanese war. It was also isolated from the rest of the camp (and often used by couples seeking intimacy unavailable elsewhere); new volunteers from Fatah al-Islam once again used the site as a military training grounds.

These four locations—the Office, the Cooperative, Samed, and al-Khan—gave Fatah al-Islam a strong territorial and military base from the start. Later the group tried expanding its sphere of influence southward, in hopes of controlling the camp as a whole. This caused internal tensions and armed skirmishes with loyalist Fatah, which was attempting to regain a foothold in Nahr al-Bared following its 1983 expulsion from the camp.

Fatah al-Islam did not limit itself to the four aforementioned sites for long. Its leaders had also secretly taken possession of the "Yasser Arafat bunker," located in the camp's historic old district; this was where the PLO leader had set up operations during the Syrians' November 1983 siege of Nahr al-Bared. Buried deep under thirty feet of soil, the bunker connected to several underground galleries, each with its own exit to the outside. The jihadis also moved into another, even more fortified bunker, located in the "new camp." This subterranean network had been built during the first Israeli bombings of the camp in 1972 and consolidated during the civil war; it later played a considerable role in the summer 2007 fighting.[48]

Notably, there was no massive rejection of the group upon its arrival. With the exception of the Cooperative building, Fatah al-Islam's "institutional" premises were duly and legally rented from their owners. Similarly, Fatah al-Islam leaders easily found personal housing. According to various testimonies, the newcomers endeavored to establish civil relations with the camp's inhabitants, and they showed an ostentatious degree of piety by leaving their weapons at mosque entrances before going in to pray.

The Proclamation of Fatah al-Islam

On Sunday, November 26, 2006, leaflets bearing Fatah al-Islam's manifesto appeared in the hands of the residents of Nahr al-Bared. This new actor's ideological identity had a hybrid nature, halfway between the Palestinian organizations' nationalist phraseology (Fatah al-Intifada) and the jihadi vocabulary of Sunni militants in Iraq (the Islamic State of Iraq). At its most basic level, Fatah al-Islam's

---

[48] On September 8, 1972, to exact vengeance for the assassination of Israeli athletes in Munich, the Israeli air force bombed the main Palestinian refugee camps in Syria and Lebanon, including Nahr al-Bared. The total death toll of these bombings was two hundred. On February 21, 1973, Israeli commandos were dropped by helicopter to attack the "terrorist facilities" in Nahr al-Bared and Baddawi, killing about forty Palestinians. On July 10, 1976, these two camps were shelled by the Syrian army, then allied with the Christian militias. On April 21, 1979, following a bomb attack in Tel Aviv, the Israeli air force bombed Nahr al-Bared once again. The Palestinian camps of Lebanon were systematically targeted in these "preventive operations" after each new Palestinian attack. See Henry Laurens, *La Question de Palestine*, vol. 4, *1967–1982, Le Rameau d'olivier et le fusil du combattant* (Paris: Fayard, 2011).

agenda represented a return to the roots of Palestinian revolutionary action: indeed, its leaders presented themselves as "the sons of the Palestinian Fatah national liberation movement" that Yasser Arafat founded in the late 1950s. To confront Fatah's "deviations" and "corruption," they had attempted an initial "rectification" (*tashih*) by creating Fatah al-Intifada in 1983. Despite this attempt, the "sacrifices made and the blood spilled for liberation" were in vain. Fatah al-Intifada lost its credibility when it allowed itself to be used "by such and such regime," and finally became the instrument "of an intelligence service." Rather than trusting states and political leaders, one must pledge allegiance to God alone, "because only the path of Islam guarantees victory." To infuse an old image with new meaning, one must find the way to victory "in the path to God."

This idea was part of a familiar framework in the political history of the Palestinian factions—a history marked by "betrayals" and "deviations" from an absolute "Palestinian liberation" norm. The term "rectification" expressed how official Syrian political discourse had influenced the manifesto's authors. Later, they gradually shifted toward a different, much looser framework of interpretation. Its effect was to portray Palestine as an image of the umma; the former's humiliation symbolized the latter's destiny also to suffer humiliation:

> Having entrusted our fate to God's will (*al-ittikal 'ala Allah*) and having met with the masses (*jamahir*) of our Muslim umma—who have finally understood that our enemies always act against the umma itself—we have realized it is impossible to fight against them without returning to God and devoting ourselves to Him. God is our only weapon against an enemy who possesses the most modern equipment, facilities and weapons of war. This umma agreed to shed its blood for various organizations, but they contributed to the spread of vice among the sons of the Muslim people and let them down. The [umma] will not cut corners along the path to God—for this is the way to please Almighty God, and to attain paradise in heaven and on earth. This is why we have decided to correct the course of things, to return to God Almighty, his religion and the jihad he saw fit to put at our disposal, the

same jihad waged by our Prophet Muhammad. God Almighty said: "So flee to Allah. Indeed, I [Muhammad, PBUH] am to you from Him a clear warner" [Sura 51:50, *al-Dhariyat/* "The Winds that Scatter"].[49] We proclaim from this day forth that the name of this movement (*haraka*) we represent is "Fatah al-Islam."

Fatah al-Islam asserted that "to liberate Palestine and fight the Jewish enemies and those who support them among the crusader Zionized West," required mobilizing "the whole of the Islamic umma" to "save our honor and repel the invaders' raids." By combining two different registers of meanings—that of the Palestinian struggle and that of anti-Western jihad, the latter as embodied by al-Qaeda—the manifesto's authors recoded the Palestinian issue through the Salafi-jihadi worldview. They invented new frontiers of identity that enabled them to mobilize all willing Muslims, regardless of their nationality, in defense of the symbol that was Palestine. Thus, Fatah al-Islam's leaders established their frame of reference in their very first communiqué, inaugurating a jihad against Israel and America to liberate Palestine and the whole of the umma from the influence of infidels.

Understandably, this double source of inspiration raised many questions about the true intentions of the group's promoters. How far did the network extend geographically? Did they intend to remain rooted in the camp, or to disseminate action throughout the country, or even the whole region? Would they limit their theater to "occupied Palestine," or might they expand to other areas and targets?

Studying the foundational moment of Fatah al-Islam allows us to grasp the protagonists' repertory of action. Given the group's heterogeneous make-up and goals, it is not surprising that a little bit of everything peppers their founding manifesto: God, the umma, Palestinian political history, the struggle against "the Jews and Zionist crusaders," and so on. In any case, looking at any one pre-existing social unit (such as "Palestinian refugees") would not suffice to analyze the phenomenon: the already diverse core group became ever more varied as volunteers from the Mashriq coun-

---

[49] Different translations of verse 51:50 can be found online. http://corpus.quran.com /translation.jsp?chapter=51&verse=50 (accessed April 13, 2015).

tries (Syria, Lebanon, Jordan, Iraq), the Arabian Peninsula, and the Maghreb countries gradually enlisted.

Fatah al-Islam's dynamic offers rich material for sociological analysis. The network's initial forms were reminiscent of the fluidity of the social world, as its protagonists had the ability to map out new frontiers and assign to people new ways of belonging. They also challenge those who rigidly conceptualize social phenomena, and, in the case of Lebanon, those who analyze forms of political expression through a preexisting framework of sectarian affiliation. Instead, the birth and rapid development of Fatah al-Islam demonstrates the existence of a connection between, on the one hand, the general context of political crisis—on Lebanese, Palestinian, and regional levels—and on the other, the ease with which individuals can detach themselves from institutional frameworks to invent their own spheres of political expression—often through the use of religious rhetoric alone.

The group was still being formed as the manifesto circulated. It slowly became objectively *real* as various "publics"—future recruits, the Arab and international press, Lebanese and regional political protagonists, Western embassies—each interested in this endeavor for its own reasons, recognized it. The group was constituted through language, signs, and symbols. Videos soon appeared online showing armed masked men, Kalashnikovs slung over their shoulders, absorbed in study of the Qur'an. Images filmed with mobile phones were shared online through Iraqi and transnational jihadi websites. Fatah al-Islam members recognized the potential benefits they could reap from using the media in this way, and they descended in numbers upon the many internet cafés scattered throughout Nahr al-Bared's alleyways. In order for this new actor to be recognized on the Middle Eastern political scene, it first had to produce performative acts that would leave a trace: testimonies, declarations of intent, practical actions, and so on. Similarly, the attention that Shaker al-Absi attracted through press conferences and interviews (he presented himself as the group's founder), and that the Arab and international media amplified, contributed to the group's materialization.

Initially, the jihadi spokesman exerted influence through a form of seduction, a means of exercising power that is most effective from a distance: "The fact that seduction works on curiosity, taking advantage of attitudes and values that are already present, while leaving open the possibility of rejection or indifference, is what gives it its considerable reach, yet at the same time curbs its intensity."[50] In this case, Fatah al-Islam's spokesman simply repackaged key points of the jihadi vulgate, all freely available online. In this way he reconstructed the virtual category of the jihadi combatant, or, rather, of an ideal type with which the often-young users visiting these sites could identify, even before they were invited to join a movement. Seduction rests upon choice; that is the source of its power of attraction in authoritarian systems, where politics exists within imposed limits and operates by coercive means. Hence, the seduction of the Fatah al-Islam's spokesman cannot be differentiated from that which was already expressed, virtually, on jihadi websites. The charisma of the Palestinian ex-mercenary Shaker al-Absi, the network's leader, in fact predated his emergence in this context and was not of his own making. The wide diffusion of a jihadi and resistance ideology, borrowing its human face from both the figure of the *muqawim* (the resistance fighter) and that of the *mujahid* (the jihadi fighter), constituted his charisma.

The real and virtual emergence of this character opened the door to the possibility of jihadi sympathizers taking action, since al-Absi was providing an accessible meeting place and promising that volunteers would receive military training before they were sent to one of the jihad's fronts. Thus, the websites constructed the figure of the *mujahid* and provided the framework for "jihadi subjectivity." What happened here was nothing less than the creation of a new political orientation, a new kind of "inner life" learned online thanks to the virtual corpus of songs, poems, biographies, images of Western soldiers torn to pieces by bombs in Iraq or Afghanistan, and theological texts penned by the movement's leading intellectuals. As a counterpoint to local media, which was highly controlled at the political level, jihadi "information" fashioned clandestine personalities who could participate openly in discussion forums. In these virtual democratic spaces, Internet users could converse with jihadi actors in question-and-answer sessions that covered issues on which their opinions were of no interest to the authorities.

---

[50] John Allen, *Lost Geographies of Power* (London: Blackwell, 2003), 103.

The nationalist referent, as constructed by the PLO during the 1960s and 1970s, was no longer a consensus factor for broad sectors of the Palestinian population dispersed across Lebanon's camps, especially after the Israeli invasion of 1982. As Durkheim noted in *The Elementary Forms of Religious Life*, as soon as a community is no longer carried by a "shared name"—in this case, the "Palestinian people" as the PLO defined it—it ceases to exist as such. The name is the *totemic symbol* that provides a group with its unity and its political identity.[51] This essential role that politics played—creating unity by fashioning a political identity through the assignment of a single name to scattered individuals—was no longer functional in the case of Palestinian refugees in Lebanon, who had become a fragmented population, divided on countless levels.

The Exploitation of Palestinian Divisions

After Fatah al-Islam announced their creation, the Palestinian Authority's representative in Lebanon, Abbas Zaki, invited the leaders of all Palestinian organizations—even the pro-Syrian Tahaluf—to a meeting on the "Palestinian embassy" premises in Beirut, with the aim of defining a common position vis-à-vis the new jihadi group. At the meeting, the factions formed a delegation to visit Nahr al-Bared and meet with the leaders of Fatah al-Islam. Abu Tahan—one of the oldest Fatah political prisoners in Syria, who had been imprisoned in Saydnaya for twenty-two years—led the delegation, and representatives from Hamas, the PFLP, the PFLP-GC, the DFLP, and Fatah accompanied him. Fatah al-Islam's core leaders explained to the delegation that they had established a jihadi organization (*tanzim jihadi*) in order to fight Israel. For them, compromising with the PLO leadership or participating in any Palestinian Authority initiative was out of the question.

To the Fatah representative in North Lebanon, Hajj Rif'at Shan a'at, "it was clear they (Fatah al-Islam) had decided to consolidate

---

[51] See Emile Durkheim, *The Elementary Forms of the Religious Life*, Joseph Ward Swain, trans. (London: George Allen and Unwin Ltd, 1915/1947), 233: "The unity of the group is visible, therefore, only in the collective name borne by all the members, and in the equally collective emblem reproducing the object designated by this name. A clan is essentially a reunion of individuals who bear the same and rally around the same sign. Take away the name and the sign which materializes it and the clan is no longer representable."

their presence in Nahr al-Bared, as a first stage, before expanding their influence throughout the rest of the region."[52] After this meeting, only Fatah seemed determined to drive the intruders out of the camp and send them back to wherever they had come from. The other Palestinian factions preferred to play for time and momentarily ignore the group in hopes of avoiding a new inter-Palestinian conflict months after Hamas's takeover in Gaza. Hajj Rif'at recalled that "the other organizations believed it might be possible to reach a compromise with this group and eventually assimilate it, since it had an Islamic orientation."[53] In fact, the paramount concern of the other factions was that if they expelled this new jihadi group, Fatah might exploit the situation to reestablish its control over Nahr al-Bared, marginalizing them and sparking clashes. Hence, Hamas representatives tried to push for a political solution, rather than any military initiative.

These efforts at prioritizing negotiation gave Fatah al-Islam the time it needed to consolidate its armed presence in the camp, making any operation against it more costly. Moreover, the Lebanese army had to approve, in advance, any Fatah initiative against Fatah al-Islam, meaning it would have to agree to Fatah's rearming in North Lebanon. In early 2007, this option seemed out of the question, both because of expected reactions inside Lebanon (due to the memory of how the country's civil war had begun), and because of the regional implications of Fatah's return to North Lebanon after Syria and its allies had expelled the group. The Lebanese army's commander-in-chief at the time, Michel Sulayman, found the prospect of facing these consequences unacceptable, especially since he had to adopt very cautious strategies in domestic politics in order to present himself to the public as a consensus candidate in the upcoming presidential election.

As for the leaders of Fatah al-Islam, they understood the potential benefits of exploiting Palestinian divisions. Thus, Shaker al-Absi and his deputy, Abu Medyan, agreed to establish political relations with all Palestinian factions except Fatah, which they considered an "atheist" organization. They used no such term to

---

[52] See Rif'at Shana'at's account, *The Nahr al-Bared Camp: From Destruction to the Obstinacy of Reconstruction* [*Mukhayyam Nahr al-Bared: min al-Damar ila-l-Israr 'ala al-'Amar*] (Tripoli: Bureau for the Study and Follow-up of the Nahr al-Bared crisis, 2008), 17.

[53] Ibid.,17.

describe the pro-Syrian factions whose "leftist" or "secularist" orientations were, in fact, far more pronounced. In his meetings with the camp's sheikhs, al-Absi asserted that before fighting Israel, it would be necessary to "reform the refugee camps in Lebanon so they satisfied the requirements of *shari'a*" and that all those who fight "under the flag of Islam" were his allies. Palestinian and Lebanese Islamists in the region viewed this language favorably, as evidenced by Rif'at Shana'at's words:

> A large number of Palestinian and Lebanese religious figures from many different currents entered the camp of Nahr al-Bared to talk with the Fatah al-Islam people and familiarize themselves with their ideas. Initially, they showed no hostility. To the contrary, some of those who got to know their orientations showed signs of relief. It did not even occur to these religious figures to publicly express the least bit of apprehension about Fatah al-Islam's presence, or to oppose their daily practices, which were intended to increase tensions within the camp. Fatah al-Islam benefited from this positive attitude to a great extent: it reinforced the idea that they were accepted by Islamist actors, that all the doubts and questions raised about them by the PLO had been unfounded, and that it was merely a smear campaign orchestrated by Fatah.[54]

---

[54] Ibid.

CHAPTER 5

Jihad and Resistance in North Lebanon

THE HISTORY OF FATAH AL-ISLAM

The Normative Power of Salafi Islam

As the Lebanese civil war was drawing to a close, various Salafi groups began incorporating the country's Palestinian camps into their religious networks. That they were so quickly successful bears witness to the failure of the PLO's political socialization tools within the camp. Several factors explain this dynamic. First, Salafism offered a new intellectual horizon to its partisans, allowing those who had not personally experienced the Palestinian nationalist struggle to look beyond their geographical, legal, and political restrictions as "Palestinian refugees" in Lebanon. Salafism offered a new religious identity and new possibilities for action severed from a Palestinian cause that had lacked a military outlet since the late 1980s.

Several dozen young Palestinian students from the Nahr al-Bared camp watched the Lebanese civil war end while at the Islamic University of Medina. At the time, the Saudi Kingdom was beginning to experience a wave of religious and political activism, initiated by groups that, despite their many differences, all identified themselves as Salafi. Upon their return to Lebanon in the early

1990s, these University of Medina graduates leveraged their Arabian contacts to obtain funding to build mosques, establish Islamic institutes, and spread a new version of Islam. These ties and the resources they provided vaulted the young Palestinians to positions of importance in their communities and allowed them to avoid traditional routes of social advancement via involvement with various Palestinian nationalist factions, all of which were becoming increasingly discredited in the eyes of the local population.

Starting in the early 1990s, this new generation of sheikhs offered some of the camps' youth the possibility of bypassing the camps' crumbing education system. Within these Salafi religious institutes, students began to define themselves as a religious elite-in-the-making through participation in debates between various strains of Salafism. In so doing, they assumed a Salafi identity that allowed them to over-emphasize the value of religious knowledge. This gave them the sense of belonging to a religious elite, which enabled them to disregard local social and political hierarchies devoid of religious legitimacy.

Theologically speaking, their dogmatics were in line with the tenets of Wahhabism—centered on the cult of divine unity—which rendered them hostile to the Sufi orders that had once flourished in the camps. Yet on the political level, they had nothing in common with the Saudi religious establishment loyal to the royal family. Salafis within the camps openly opposed the Western political order and its various military and cultural manifestations in the region. At the same time, they accused the Muslim Brotherhood of reproducing the hierarchies found in the profane world by vesting too much importance in the political stakes at issue in elections.

Thus, Salafism succeeded in the Palestinian environment because it offered believers a valuable resource. It gave them a new identity, dissociated from a past of defeat, humiliation, and exclusion. Within this new identification, any religious or political influence linked to history and the collective memory was scrutinized and selectively filtered though religious references. Most important, Salafi militants deconstructed the foundations of extant political authority by arguing that it lacked Islamic values. As a substitute they emphasized the necessity to obey norms taken directly from the foundations of religion.

The institutional weakness of the refugee camp allowed factional disputes to fester and prevented any legitimate authority from coalescing. Salafi activists exploited this weakness by introducing a form of regulation based on the internalization of discursive norms derived from imitation of the Prophet and his first companions. The refugees' inability to assert their views during the Oslo negotiations, for example, was no longer of any significance whatsoever; their main priority now ought to be distancing themselves from the ongoing, low-intensity conflict between the Syrian regime's allies in Lebanon and Yasser Arafat's Fatah. Theirs was a more intimate, more essential, and less risky enterprise: that of believers reclaiming their faith without any external oversight. The discord inherent in the dominant, impious political order was akin to the despicable art of *kalam* (philosophical speculation on the nature of God and his "attributes") in the history of Islamic doctrines. It fueled controversy and severed true believers from the roots of their religion.

The Role of the Salafi Preachers

In order to analyze Salafi preachers' role in legitimizing Fatah al-Islam, I interviewed the relevant actors who were on the scene during the fighting in and after the fall of Nahr al-Bared camp in September of 2007. Naturally, this raises a methodological issue: protagonists were inclined to reshape their testimonies in retrospect, in order to protect themselves—politically and legally—from their enemies' accusations of complicity and collusion. Moreover, our discussions could not be free of the constraints imposed by current political conditions, in particular by the extreme tension between the contemporary Lebanese government—backed by the United States and Saudi Arabia—and Hezbollah—backed by Iran and Syria.

Yet instead of hampering analysis, these difficulties provided insights into the various actors' successive efforts at self-justification. Because they were on the defensive, the camp's most prominent sheikhs wrote a testimonial entitled "Fatah al-Islam and the Battle of Nahr al-Bared," detailing their relationships with members of Fatah al-Islam. It was essentially an argument in their own defense and a response to their critics.[1] The stakes were high: discussions about reconstructing Nahr al-Bared were ongoing, and all parties involved hoped to regain their antebellum positions with their attendant material benefits.

The testimonial revealed new information, but, more significantly, it brings to the fore the ambiguous, complex, and controversial relationships between different categories of actors—who all claimed to be Salafi but disagreed over core principles, such as the status of jihad and the role of violence. Thus, the text sheds light on the way in which the heated debates within the field of transnational Salafism affected Lebanon-based sheikhs, and on how they, in turn, reacted to militant jihadis' incursions into their own human and geographic territory.

Fatah cadres made the most serious accusations against the camp's Salafi sheikhs. And these accusations carried a certain weight because they were made two months after fighting had begun, precisely at the time when the sheikhs adopted an anti-Syrian/anti-Hezbollah stance, in the process aligning themselves with Fatah and the Palestinian Authority:

> The camp's Salafi sheikhs defended Fatah al-Islam. . . . They exploited the mosques as platforms from which to improve the group's image in the eyes of the camp's residents. They used to meet with Fatah al-Islam every Thursday night to discuss topics for the next day's sermon. They wished to normalize the group's presence. They would say that Fatah was a secular movement made up of *kuffar*! [infidels]. . . . This influenced the camp's residents. Those sheikhs were in constant contact with Fatah al-Islam. They rented apartments and houses within the camp to the group. We had asked them not to do so, because each rented house was then made into a military stronghold—with eight to ten militants in each apartment![2]

[1] See *Fatah al-Islam and the Battle of Nahr al-Bared* [*Fatah al-Islam wa-ma'rakat Nahr al-Bared*], by the "Council of preachers of camp Nahr al-Bared's mosques," Tripoli, 2007. This long text (over 590 pages) was written by Sheikh Muḥammad ʿAbd al-Ghani and included many quotations from the press.

[2] Interview with a high-ranking Fatah leader, Baddawi camp, August 28, 2007.

Fatah cadres blamed the Salafi preachers for having normalized Fatah al-Islam's presence in the camp, in the name of nondiscrimination between believers. Accustomed to condemning Muslim heads of state for defending their own interests at the expense of the umma, the Salafi sheikhs refused to consider the Fatah al-Islam militants as "strangers" (*ghuraba'*).[3] In Sheikh 'Abd al-Ghani's view, Fatah al-Islam was popular when it first appeared in the camp because "people were looking for an alternative to the secular movements" and the group raised "the standard of Islam, at a time when all other currents had failed."[4] The Islamic morality of Fatah al-Islam's partisans played in their favor, for it contrasted with the "deviant" behavior of the dominant political factions, and this in a human environment where the temptation to mix morals and politics was particularly strong.

The Salafi sheikhs repeatedly reaffirmed their resolve to keep an equal distance from all political protagonists. Local Fatah representatives, who saw themselves as the main organization within the PLO, perceived this as proof of the sheikhs' disloyalty to the Palestinian political heritage. In fact, as we noted earlier, Salafi preachers had been rejecting this national and cultural heritage for over a decade. To them, and to the entire Islamist movement, it was the secular nature of PLO member organizations that had caused their failure. No political future could be built on a foundation of serious religious transgression: the recognition of Israel through the 1993 Oslo accords. To the Salafi sheikhs, the term "secularism" (*'ilmaniyya*) itself was an insult. They saw no connection between the existence of a security vacuum that, according to them, was "one of the main reasons Fatah al-Islam was able to assert its authority and influence in the camp," and their own efforts to undermine any "secular" authority in the camp since the early 1990s (in hopes of establishing their own religious legitimacy).

Moreover, the local sheikhs minimized or relegated to the private sphere any practical assistance that certain camp residents provided to Fatah al-Islam. According to them, renting houses to Fatah al-Islam militants was not a display of solidarity, because "the houses

---

[3] The Hamas representative in Nahr al-Bared noticed the same thing: "The Salafi sheikhs would tell us, 'Don't accuse them of being strangers. You too, you are strangers!'" Interview with Abu Suhayb, Baddawi camp, September 2009.

[4] *Fatah al-Islam and the Battle of Nahr al-Bared*, 105.

that were rented were not military centers, they were places of residence. There were very few houses; it was not a mass phenomenon, many families lived in [the movement's] military centers."[5] The sheikhs made no mention of the fact that those homes could easily be transformed into fortresses, even though this had already occurred when they wrote their testimony. They also deftly elided distinctions between renting buildings inside the camp from owners who knew the uses to which they would be put, and clean-shaven Islamist tenants, taking pains to conceal their ideological affiliation, renting from landlords outside the camps.[6]

Fatah leaders also blamed the sheikhs for having "explained" the camp to the leaders of Fatah al-Islam. The insider knowledge thus gained, comparable to an unprecedented form of "Islamist Orientalism," allegedly allowed the jihadis to rally more support inside the camps. Specifically, anthropological knowledge of Nahr al-Bared's underlying dynamics allowed Fatah al-Islam to better integrate into its social networks and to exploit antagonisms between tribes and families, so as to satisfy the thirst for revenge of this or that clan. Moreover, the Salafi sheikhs were said to have personally legitimized Fatah al-Islam's presence in the camp: Sheikh Ahmad al-Mithqal (the imam of Khaled bin al-Walid mosque, located close to the Samed center) reportedly designated Shaker al-Absi as the "new emir."

In addition, the sheikhs seized opportunities that the camp's deteriorating security situation provided to promote themselves as indispensable mediators between all parties. They formalized this tactic by creating a new body called the Council of Preachers of the Nahr al-Bared Mosques (Majlis Khutaba' Masajid Nahr al-Bared). They hoped that this council would soon become the most trusted representative body for the camp's inhabitants, in contrast to the Palestinian political factions, weakened and discredited by internal rifts. In the broader context of rivalries between the Salafi movement and the Muslim Brotherhood, the sheikhs also tried to undermine the influence of Hamas and its "League of Ulemas of Palestine."

[5] Ibid., 90–92.
[6] "And do we blame those who rented apartments outside the camp to Fatah al-Islam, in Mitayn Street or in the Abu Samra neighborhood of Tripoli, in Ashrafiye or in Beqaa, or in any other region of Lebanon?" Ibid., 91.

On March 19, 2007, the camp was in a state of military alert. A sniper had targeted Shaker al-Absi as he prepared for sunset (*maghrib*) prayer at the Samed center. Return fire from Fatah al-Islam injured two Fatah al-Intifada partisans suspected of having carried out the initial attack. That same evening, during the mediation session that the Council of Preachers organized in the Khaled bin al-Walid mosque, a member of Fatah severely injured a Fatah al-Islam operative named Abu Muhammad al-Maqdisi. After heated discussion, the sheikhs managed to convince the Fatah al-Islam leaders not to seek revenge. They also dissuaded Shaker al-Absi from agreeing to Qasim 'Azzam Nahar's (a.k.a. Shahin Shahin) insistent requests that he be allowed to force his way across a Lebanese military roadblock to get his wounded Fatah al-Islam comrade access to medical care (the man died of his wounds the next day).[7] On March 21, Fatah al-Islam published a leaflet titled "Letter to the People of Truth" (*Risala ila ahl al-haqq*). In the document, the organization announced that it accepted the settlement proposed by the Council of Preachers, and called on the camp's refugees to attend the deceased man's funeral. They also sought to calm inhabitants' fears of an ongoing feud by asserting: "He, who loves the Prophet of God and cherishes this love in his heart, cannot think—for a single second—of spilling the blood of innocents, because then Muhammad would be his enemy on the day of Resurrection."

These words struck a chord with the inhabitants: since the end of the civil war, the only "martyrs" from Nahr al-Bared had been those killed in gunfights between factions. The day before Fatah al-Islam published the leaflet, the group circulated Abu Muhammad al-Maqdisi's obituary, in which they underlined the claim that he had "participated in numerous battles in Palestine" and had been a fighter for the Palestinian cause whose only goal was to "return to Palestine to train members of Fatah al-Islam in this blessed land," but that the "hands of treachery had stopped him."[8] Their

[7] According to those who met him in Nahr al-Bared, he was one of the most dangerous individuals in Fatah al-Islam. He headed the "security committee" (al-Lajna al-Amniyya). He is said to have been killed in August 2007 during aerial bombings by a Lebanese army helicopter.

[8] Dated March 20, 2007, the Fatah al-Islam "information bureau" leaflet briefly evokes the memory of a "military cadre exceptionally gifted in military sciences, which is one of the reasons he was killed in such a traitorous way." The text continues: "This hero, born

description of his death—he was killed as he was about to return home for *iftar* (the breaking of the Ramadan fast)—highlighted the strength of his faith. God willing, he would finally break his fast "in the gardens of paradise." Although they did not retaliate against Fatah, Fatah al-Islam fighters did take advantage of the general commotion to seize control of the top floor of the Cooperative building, where the Popular Committee was traditionally based. There, they reportedly removed portraits of Syrian President Bashar al-Assad and Hezbollah Secretary-General Hassan Nasrallah from the premises, leaving only photos of "martyrs" of the Palestinian cause, from Abu Jihad to Sheikh Ahmad Yasin.

PLO leaders saw the large crowd at Abu Muhammad's funeral, and the presence of leading figures of the Council of Preachers at the front of a procession of armed Fatah al-Islam men in military uniform, as a referendum in favor of Fatah al-Islam. Three weeks later, in Khaled bin al-Walid mosque, the sheikhs organized a meeting of "Forgiveness, Reconciliation, and Indulgence" (*liqa' al-'afu wa-l-musalaha wa-l-musamaha*) between Shaker al-Absi and representatives of those accused of murdering Abu Muhammad. By these actions—and with the laudable motive of preventing bloodshed—the Salafi sheikhs also spared Fatah al-Islam the consequences of a revenge that would have alienated the group from many people in the camp. Various indicators, such as the number of participants and the food provided for Fatah al-Islam leaders at the funeral during the first three days of mourning, showed that a significant section of the refugee population sympathized with the movement. In fact, Fatah al-Islam seemed to be taking on the population's aspirations, aspirations that the self-appointed spokespersons of Palestinian activism had long since abandoned.

Inevitably, these encounters between the sheikhs and Fatah al-Islam created a form of complicity. "At the time, nobody wanted loyalist Fatah domination over Nahr al-Bared," a Hamas leader argued. "Moreover, there were many Salafis within Fatah al-Islam, whose leaders welcomed any opportunity to underline that fact."[9] The sheikhs remained silent when Shaker al-Absi and one of his

---

in Gaza in 1985, participated in numerous battles in Palestine. He studied chemistry. He turned down a scholarship to study medicine in Germany because of his decision to get involved with the mujahidin."

[9] Interview with a Hamas leader, Tripoli, July 25, 2008.

most trusted deputies, the Syrian Ibrahim Umar 'Abd al-Wahhab (a.k.a. Abu Medyan), compared the leaders of the March 14 Alliance to "American agents" in their hearing. This silence denoted neither approval nor disapproval, but rather conveyed the idea that it was inappropriate for sheikhs of their stature to publicly defend leaders discredited by the "civic" (or "secular") nature of their political engagement. They also had to keep in mind that Fatah al-Islam partisans came to pray in their mosques, which were not immune from takeovers similar to those that had occurred elsewhere.

By contrast, the sheikhs did not shy away from conflict over those religious issues that threatened their legitimacy. They refused to follow the members of Fatah al-Islam's "legal committee" (al-Lajna al-Shar'iyya) who wished to apply to their political enemies the penalties prescribed by Islamic legal jurisprudence for highway robbery or rebellion (*hadd al-haraba*). According to this line of reasoning, Fatah al-Islam's enemies should be treated as highway robbers and rebels and as such be subject to the death penalty.[10] Fatah al-Islam's legal committee distributed a leaflet at mosque exits with a title borrowed from one of Ibn Taymiyya's treatises—*The Sword Drawn against Those Who Insult the Lord, the Religion, or the Prophet*—to remind people that no Muslim who insulted God and his Prophet could be forgiven for their sin.[11] However, aware of how invoking divine unity at every turn ratcheted up tensions, the Council of Preachers now, in its own way, rediscovered the autonomy of politics from religion by deciding to ban "recourse to Islamic arbitration for every incident."[12] When Salafi Sheikh Hay-

[10] In his influential work on Ibn Taymiyya, Henri Laoust recalled, "The *muharib* [rebel/bandit] who has committed murder, deserves death, a sentence which is one of 'God's punishments,' of which the burden of execution rests on the imam. The muharib's fate is not in the hands of the victim's heirs, unlike the case of murder in private law. In fact, such a bandit causes general damage to the whole of the community." H. Laoust, *Essai sur les doctrines sociales et politiques d'Ibn Taimîya (661/1262-728/1328)* (Cairo: IFAO [Institut français d'archéologie orientale press], 1939), 385.

[11] *Al-sarim al-maslul 'ala sab al-rabb aw al-din aw al-rasul.* The leaflet ends with the following threats: "Know that our goal is to combat the Jews and all those who support them within the Zionist-Crusader West. Let no one stand between us and them; do not be the first to defend them. May he who imagines he is harming our movement beware: God has incited us to follow his path through sheer passion for martyrdom, we love death on God's path more than we love life. So return to your religion."

[12] *Fatah al-Islam and the Battle of Nahr al-Bared*, 118.

tham al-Sa'id stood at the pulpit of al-Sahaba (the Companions') mosque to warn people against attacking army roadblocks because the guards stationed there were "our brothers from neighboring Islamic villages," Fatah al-Islam spokesman Abu Selim Taha challenged him "to review his Islam and his faith."[13] The Salafi sheikhs were also surprised by their interlocutors' religious innovations:

They used a new expression to speak of the Prophet. They would say: "the Prophet of mercy and the sword" (rasul al-rahma wa-l-sayf). This is an invention. We would never add "and the sword."[14]

A council member also spoke at great length with a certain Abu al-Harith. His real name was Abdallah Mubarak Thamar al-Dusri, and he was a twenty-three-year-old former fiqh (Islamic jurisprudence) student from al-Imam University in Riyadh.[15] The bill of indictment read: "He had been for some time at the head of Fatah al-Islam's 'legal committee' in charge of expounding religious arguments to justify the group's decisions" (a position normally held by Abu Bakr al-Shar'i). In that role, al-Harith had claimed that Lebanon belonged to the dar al-kufr (the "land of unbelief"). His main contact person within the Council of Preachers said afterward that he refused to endorse al-Harith's position.[16]

The issue was not merely theoretical: by including Lebanon in dar al-kufr, Fatah al-Islam religiously legitimized (from their point of view) the bank robberies that were their chief source of funds.[17] The Council of Preachers' president, Sheikh 'Abd al-Ghani, had noticed Fatah al-Islam's tendency to brand Arab regimes and

[13] Ibid., 115.

[14] Interview with Sheikh Muhammad 'Abd al-Ghani, Baddawi camp, July 27, 2008.

[15] According to the terms of the indictment, Abu al-Harith entered Lebanon at the al-Masn'a Syrian-Lebanese border crossing on October 15, 2006. He was killed on September 2, 2007 in Nahr al-Bared. His death was confirmed by his father's DNA.

[16] Interview with one of the members of the Council, Tripoli, July 25, 2008.

[17] In the fall of 2006, the jihadis robbed two banks in less than a month, getting away with a considerable sum both times: the Crédit Libanais bank in the 'Abdeh district north of Nahr al-Bared on October 18, and the al-Jamal bank of Ghaziye on November 10. Operations of this kind continued in 2007: another Crédit Libanais branch in Tripoli, on al-Azmeh street, was held up on February 23, 2007, as well as the Western Union office in the Christian village of Zghorta on April 7, 2007, and the Banque Méditerranée in Amyun on May 19, 2007. After that, the Lebanese Internal Security Forces (ISF) stormed an apartment Fatah al-Islam partisans rented in Tripoli.

"secular" political organizations as apostate institutions. 'Abd al-Ghani later stated that when he had asked Fatah al-Islam leaders whether his own father, who had been a "preacher in the camp for almost 40 years," could be considered an apostate if he decided to join an Arab-nationalist or Palestinian party, they told him that such family ties did not rule out a person's being considered an infidel.[18]

In so far as it is possible to reconstruct its content, the intellectual relationship between a young Salafi sheikh brought up in Nahr al-Bared camp and Abu al-Harith, Fatah al-Islam's main theologian from Saudi Arabia, provides interesting elements about the former's understanding of the current debates dividing the Salafi religious spectrum. Asked about his view of the spectrum of trends in the Salafi field, the Palestinian sheikh drew a multiple-entry table.[19] On the right side of the table, he placed the category "official Salafism" (referring to Sheikh al-Madkhali and some of the Saudi Wahhabi institutions). In the center, he placed the word *takfir* (the act of labeling someone an apostate), which he used to qualify the most radical, extreme movements—both excommunicatory and jihadi—of which Zarqawi was the main figurehead. Finally, the left-hand column heading was "total Salafism" (*al-salafiyya al-shumuliyya*), which the sheikh defined as "religion, state, and way of life." He subdivided the latter into two varieties of "total Salafism": one "violent" and the other "peaceful." The "violent" subcategory shared some of the *takfiri* current's positions: the urgency of jihad against occupying forces and the importance of struggle against official state institutions (e.g., leaders, the army). However, it set conditions for excommunicating believers that were far more restrictive than in the case of the *takfir* (implying that al-Qaeda was part of the violent strain of "total Salafism"). As for the "peaceful" category, it contained three further subdivisions: the sheikh classified some "peaceful Salafis" as "close to governments," others as "critical of governments but accepted by the population" (such was

---

[18] Testimony by Sheikh 'Abd al-Ghani during an interview with the al-'Arabiya satellite television channel, June 20, 2007.

[19] Interview with a sheikh from the Council of Preachers, Baddawi camp, August 27, 2007.

"the case of Saudi sheikhs Salman al-'Awda and Safar al-Hawali"), and others as "very critical of leaders."

Within this array of Salafi variations—which was clearly influenced by internal Saudi debates—the council's Salafi sheikh in charge of relations with Abu al-Harith placed himself in the "total Salafism" category, but refused to reveal any more about his positions on particular issues. He seemed to be situated within a Salafi triangle, each side of which was defined in terms of how members related to institutionalized powers. They corresponded to the three orientations under his umbrella of "total Salafism": its "violent expression," its "peaceful expression" (both critical and populist), and, finally, its "ultra-critical expression." The violent expression corresponded to the position held by Bin Laden, the peaceful to the Saudi Sahwa movement of the 1990s, and the ultra-critical to Sheikh Abdallah bin Jibrin's position (d. 2009). The latter was the most radical of Saudi clerics with whom the sheikh readily associated.[20] Over the course of his conversations with Abu al-Harith, it is likely that the council's sheikh carried on an internal conversation, weighing within himself his own opinions and reconfiguring his sentiments on disputed points. His positions were necessarily provisional, shifting with changes in local conditions, international events, and his own quest for survival. This was all the more true as the three expressions of "total Salafism," although they all highlighted the fundamental importance of jihad, differed markedly on the conditions necessary for its proclamation, the framework for its use, and its place among the most basic tenets of the faith.

Although they did not agree on everything, the sheikh and Abu al-Harith understood each other easily because they relied on the same frame of reference, used the same brand of rhetoric, and drew their ideas from the same intellectual sources. Their closeness, due to immersion in the Salafi universe—acquired in part through

[20] Born in 1932, Abdallah bin Jibrin came from a traditional Wahhabi background. Despite having the attributes (tribal and geographical origin, formal qualifications) that usually led to influential positions within the Wahhabi establishment, he did not receive the institutional recognition to which he felt entitled. His affiliation with the Sahwa protest movement in the early 1990s brought a degree of proper Wahhabi legitimacy to this movement comprised of younger activists, well versed in the issues of international politics and strongly influenced by the Muslim Brotherhood. For more on Sheikh bin Jibrin, see Lacroix, *Awakening Islam* (see chapter 1, note 23), 169–70.

consulting the most famous Salafi sheikhs' websites and constantly participating in online forums on current events—explains why the Salafi sheikh from Nahr al-Bared felt closer to a recent Saudi *fiqh* graduate than to the political leaders in the very camp where he lived.

Fatah al-Islam's Internal Organization

Fatah al-Islam was a quasi-bureaucratic organization structured around multiple committees. There was an "administrative committee" (*al-lajna al-idariyya*), a "security committee" (*al-lajna al-amniyya*), a "military committee" (*al-lajna al-'askariyya*), a "coordination committee" (*lajnat al-tansiq*), an "information committee" (*al-lajna al-'ilamiyya*), and a "legal committee" (*al-lajna al-shar'iyya*) in charge of religious issues.

One member of the security committee was Taha Ahmad Sulayman (a.k.a. Abu Lu'ay). Shaker al-Absi recruited this young Syrian, born in 1982 in Latakia, in the Saydnaya prison and put him in charge of gathering information about the political, charitable, and religious institutions in all of Lebanon's Palestinian camps. As for Shahin Shahin, he was a member of both the security committee and the military committee. As a Palestinian from Syria, he had served in Abu Nidal's terrorist organization (the Fatah-Revolutionary Council splinter group) for twelve years. In 1992, the Palestinian police chief of Ayn al-Helweh, Munir al-Muqdah, incarcerated him for two months during a period when the Fatah-Revolutionary Council was conducting an assassination campaign in Lebanon against loyalist Fatah cadres. Later, Shahin Shahin became a jihadi, traveling to Iraq at some point after 2003.

Shaker al-Absi made Shihab Khudr al-Qadur (a.k.a. Abu Hurayra), a Lebanese national, head of the military committee. Born in 1971, originally from the village of Mishmish in the Akkar region of North Lebanon, Abu Hurayra spent his childhood in the Ghurba district of Tripoli, where his studies were interrupted at the end of middle school.[21] One night in December of 1986, at the

---

[21] Abu Hurayra's biographical information is taken from three written sources: the August 8, 2007 edition of *al-Hayat*, the August 31, 2007 edition of *al-Akhbar*, and an August 8, 2007 article from the *Sana* Islamic information agency. I obtained additional information from residents of Bab al-Tabbaneh and Nahr al-Bared, who wished to remain anonymous.

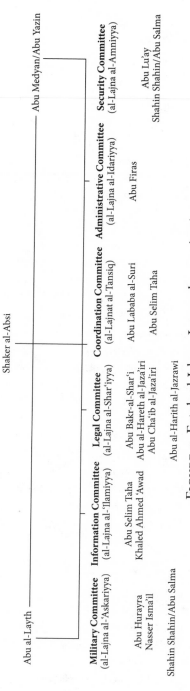

FIGURE 1. Fatah al-Islam: Internal organization

age of fifteen, he cut the electric cable supplying the Syrian military post that controlled access to the Bab al-Tabbaneh neighborhood near the Abu ʿAli River. This heroic act allowed around one hundred Tawhid combatants who had been hiding out in Bab al-Tabbaneh to escape under cover of darkness. Later that month, the Syrian intelligence services captured and imprisoned him for three years in the Tadmur prison in Syria. Freed on October 31, 1989, he returned to Lebanon, to the Ayn al-Helweh Palestinian refugee camp, where his comrades of the Tawhid group had also sought refuge. It was around this time that he met and was influenced by Palestinian sheikh Hisham Shraydi, founder of the jihadi ʿUsbat al-Ansar cell. After the war, he spent several months frequenting the Daʿi al-Islam al-Shahhal's al-Hidaya wa-l-Ihsan religious institute. In 1992, Syrian intelligence services arrested him once again as he travelled between Ayn al-Helweh and the mosques of Bab al-Tabbaneh. Later, in Saydnaya prison in Syria, he continued his religious training. Upon his release in 1996, he moved to Ayn al-Helweh for fear of being detained again in Tripoli. There, he married a Palestinian woman and earned a modest living by selling coffee in the Taʿamir neighborhood, on the outskirts of the camp. During this period he became a member of ʿUsbat al-Ansar. After the Dinniyeh incidents in December 1999 and January 2000, the judiciary council sentenced him in absentia for his alleged participation in Bassam al-Kanj's jihadi network.

In 2003, Abu Hurayra went to Iraq to join Zarqawi's group, reportedly returning to Lebanon in 2005. In Ayn al-Helweh, he became one of the figureheads of Jund al-Sham, the Levantine militant network that Zarqawi and Shaker al-Absi had led since the mid-1990s. In September 2006, with about forty volunteers, he joined the group that later came to be known as Fatah al-Islam.[22] At this point, Abu Hurayra was a considerable asset for al-Absi: the anti-Syrian past of this recruit mostly allayed suspicion about the Fatah al-Islam leader's loyalties. Moreover, Abu Hurayra's daring act of 1986 in Bab al-Tabbaneh was far from forgotten in that neighborhood, and his reputation as a jihadi hothead held potential appeal for the radical circles of East Tripoli.

---

[22] This information is from the August 8, 2007 edition of *al-Hayat*.

The Palestinian Nasser Isma'il, born in the camp in 1961, one of the main arms dealers of the camp, was a member of the military committee, and in charge of supplying it with weapons. A PFLP-GC leader also allegedly granted Fatah al-Islam access to several arms depots in the camp.

Khaled Ahmad 'Awad led the information committee. A Palestinian born in Hama, Syria, in 1981, he was a former militant in Ahmad Jibril's PFLP-GC. One of his cousins on his father's side was none other than Abu Muhammad Shahrur, a jihadi "emir" living in Ayn al-Helweh.[23]

Leadership of the legal committee was entrusted to the young Saudi graduate Abu al-Harith (see above). The legal committee also set up a religious library in the Samed center, equipped with computers with Internet access, and its members offered classes about Islam to the camp's children.

Two subgroups existed within Fatah al-Islam: a main group consisting of members from the Levant (Palestinians from Syria and Lebanon, Lebanese, and Syrians) and a secondary group of militants from the Gulf—including at least fifty young Saudis. Very little public information exists about them. It seems they were about twenty-five years old on average, lacked previous experience of military jihadi activities, and were not members of al-Qaeda in the Arabian Peninsula.[24] Those who were detained at Beirut airport in early

---

[23] According to an article published by the Saudi daily *al-Sharq al-Awsat* on November 20, 2008, Abu Muhammad Shahrur (his real name is Abd al-Rahman Muhammad 'Awad) was said to have left Fatah in the early 1990s to become a bodyguard for "Sheikh" Hisham Shraydi, founder of the jihadi 'Usbat al-Ansar group in Ayn al-Helweh. After a series of attacks and bombings in Sidon and in the camp itself, he was sentenced in absentia by a Lebanese court. In 2003, he is said to have slipped out of the camp disguised as a woman and gone to Iraq to pledge allegiance to Zarqawi. He is believed to have returned to Ayn al-Helweh after Zarqawi's death in 2006 in order to form an al-Qaeda cell there. He allegedly plotted the terrorist attacks that marked the first days of the battle of Nahr al-Bared: an explosion in the ABC mall parking lot in the Christian neighborhood of Ashrafiye on the night of May 20 (one person was killed); a bomb placed under a car at the Verdun mall, in the predominantly Sunni western side of the city, on May 21 (one person was killed); and another attack of the same type on May 23 in Aley, a Druze-majority city. His name was also mentioned in connection with the June 26, 2007 car bomb attack that claimed the lives of six Spanish soldiers from the UNIFIL contingent.

[24] Of the fifty-one Saudis mentioned among the accused, more than forty had been born between 1983 and 1988, and were aged nineteen to twenty-four at the time (see the April 5, 2008 edition of the Saudi daily *al-Watan*). For more on jihadism in Saudi Arabia, see Thomas Hegghammer, *Jihad in Saudi Arabia* (see chapter 4, note 35).

2007 on their way back from the camp stated that they had come to Lebanon because contacts promised them it was a way into Iraq; yet several weeks after their arrival, they were yet to see any sign that this promise would be fulfilled. Only those who had committed to carrying out a suicide attack as soon as they arrived in Iraq were allowed to leave the camp. Martyrdom operations were an undesirable prospect to most of the young Saudis, who had been socialized in a country where the vast majority of ulemas considered this a capital sin. Segregated from the rest of the group and housed in separate apartments, these Saudi volunteers and their compatriots had decided to leave Nahr al-Bared, despite strong pressure on them to stay.[25]

The Connection with al-Qaeda:
A Contentious Relationship

Fatah al-Islam's leaders came from a Syrian-Iraqi jihadi universe in which Abu Mus'ab al-Zarqawi was a signal authority. This network existed in parallel to al-Qaeda's network, without being part of it. In Shaker al-Absi's view, acquiring the "al-Qaeda franchise" would increase Fatah al-Islam's regional prestige. In other words, such recognition would end speculation that Syria was sponsoring the group to further its own regional interests. This suspicion had been undermining his group's credibility and causing potential new recruits to hesitate about joining the group.

Before granting Fatah al-Islam this recognition, the historic leaders of al-Qaeda investigated the group. They had several Lebanese contacts at their disposal for this task, concentrated in the Beqaa region and, closer to Nahr al-Bared, in Tripoli. According to the military tribunal prosecutor's indictment, in 2005 al-Qaeda-Central chose Tripolitan sheikh Nabil Rahim as their representative in Lebanon, tasking him to coordinate at all times with al-Qaeda in the Arabian Peninsula and al-Qaeda in the Land of the Two Rivers (i.e., Iraq).[26] Born in 1971, Sheikh Rahim had attended Salafi sheikh

---

[25] Interview by Hazem al-Amin, for *al-Hayat* daily, August 2007.

[26] For more on Sheikh Nabil Rahim's role, see the text of the examining magistrate's indictment for the permanent military court, which was made public on November 15, 2009. The Lebanese daily *al-Akhbar* ran a biography of Sheikh Nabil Rahim in its January 11, 2008 edition.

Da'i al-Islam al-Shahhal's courses at the latter's al-Hidaya wa-l-Ihsan institute. Soon after the 1996 decree closing this institute, he became director of the Dar al-Hadith (House of Hadith) center in the Abu Samra district of Tripoli. In February 2005, following Rafiq al-Hariri's assassination, he was incarcerated for about two weeks in the Defense Ministry. After his release, he ignored all subsequent court summons and went to Saudi Arabia for an undetermined period. From there he organized transportation networks moving jihadi recruits from North Lebanon to Iraq. During the month of Ramadan in 2006, he met with al-Qaeda leaders in Mecca, while performing the *'umra* (lesser pilgrimage). This was his chance to collect funds for the group he had patiently been forming in Tripoli. At this time, one of his close friends, Sheikh Bassam Hammud (a.k.a. Abu Bakr), owner of a shop selling recordings of Islamic chants in Abu Samra, was detained in Saudi Arabia for belonging to al-Qaeda. Sheikh Rahim, however, managed to escape the kingdom.

In early 2007, Sheikh Rahim received an al-Qaeda emissary, Saudi sheikh Abdallah al-Bishi, in Lebanon. On this occasion, al-Bishi inquired about Fatah al-Islam, in order to determine whether the group met the criteria for the international terrorist organization's seal of approval. According to the Saudi *al-Watan* newspaper, Abdallah al-Bishi, born in Riyadh in 1976, had taught Islamic studies in the Saudi town of Rafha, close to the Iraqi border.[27] In July 2006, he allegedly left Saudi Arabia for Iran, at the request of two al-Qaeda members, to teach young Sunni Kurds in the city of Sanandaj, the capital of Iranian Kurdistan.[28] In Iran he met with his compatriot Talha al-Sa'udi (Abd al-Rahman al-Yahya) who left for Lebanon in December of 2006. Hosted there by Sheikh Rahim, Talha al-Sa'udi called Sheikh al-Bishi in Iran and suggested he come join him in Tripoli. The latter agreed, arrived at Beirut's international airport in January 2007, and travelled to Sheikh Rahim's home in Tripoli. From there, al-Bishi went to Nahr al-Bared to

[27] The article from *al-Watan* is available on the Saudi online forum *ankawa*, http://www.ankawa.com/forum (accessed January 19, 2009).

[28] Not "Sanadraj" as was written in the *al-Watan* article, which also contains other typos: the name of one of the Saudi recruiters for Fatah al-Islam, Abu Ritaj, was misspelled "Abu Rishaj."

meet the main leaders of Fatah al-Islam, a meeting that took place in Shaker al-Absi's office in the Samed center.

During his roughly two-week stay al-Bishi taught Islamic studies courses in the Samed center and the Cooperative. He listened to the young Saudi volunteers' grievances about being confined in the camp—their main complaint being that despite contributing several thousands of dollars, they were not actually allowed to go fight in Iraq as promised. Sheikh al-Bishi believed these young men ought to be free to return home if they so desired. No religious obstacle should prevent them from doing so. This opinion angered Shaker al-Absi and his deputy, Abu Medyan. If the volunteers were to depart, it could weaken their organization. They needed Saudi nationals to show that they had the credentials to attract more Wahabbi-bred young Saudis. Moreover, if Fatah al-Islam deserters were arrested, they might provide the Lebanese and Saudi security forces with valuable information about the group—a concern that later proved justified.

Sheikh al-Bishi saw too many shortcomings in Fatah al-Islam, even beyond the situation of the young Saudi volunteers. Religiously, the sheikh found the leaders' Islamic credentials unconvincing. There seemed to be no good reason why the leaders' refusal to deal with Fatah was not extended to all of the Palestinian factions, all being equally guilty of impiety in the sheikh's opinion. He also seemed to oppose the practice of robbing banks—the source of most Fatah al-Islam funds. In a more practical vein, the group's open existence in a camp in North Lebanon and the sketchy backgrounds of the leaders raised the possibility that one or several of the region's intelligence services might have infiltrated the organization.

The end result was that the Saudi sheikh's "jihadi audit" did not produce the results Fatah al-Islam leaders had hoped for. They expressed their disappointment to him and later, more or less under threat from the most radical members of the group, al-Bishi had no choice but to flee the camp as quickly as possible.

From Tripoli, another al-Qaeda leader, the Syrian Hani Bakr al-Sankari (a.k.a. Abu Elias), offered to send the Sheikh al-Bishi to the al-Anbar province in Iraq to train young jihadi volunteers. Sending a sheikh hostile to the unbridled use of *takfir* was most likely an attempt to rectify Zarqawi's anti-Shi'a practices in Iraq, and possibly related to Ayman al-Zawahiri's attempts to reestablish control over the network. On February 13, 2007, Lebanese security forces arrested the two men at the 'Abudiyya border checkpoint as they were attempting to enter Syria, just a few hours after the explosion of two buses in the town of 'Ayn 'Alaq.

Establishing closer ties with al-Qaeda also required that a respected *'alim* (scholar of Islamic law) within the jihadi community get involved. To this end, Shaker al-Absi contacted the Jordanian-Palestinian Abu Muhammad al-Maqdisi (Muhammad al-Barqawi), who had been Zarqawi's prison companion when they were incarcerated in Jordan from 1995 to 1999. Al-Maqdisi had been under house arrest from 2005 to 2008.[29]

The categories that Sheikh Maqdisi used to structure his ideas frequently appeared in Fatah al-Islam's communiqués. To him, rigorous divine unity (*tawhid*) meant that believers would refuse to acknowledge and follow rules other than those emanating from God alone. In a pamphlet entitled "Declaration to the Knights of Righteousness," distributed in Nahr al-Bared on March 28, 2007, Fatah al-Islam reminded camp residents that the principle of divine unity entailed the rejection of "corrupt tyrants" (*al-tughat al-mufsidin*). Hence, true believers should disobey their political leaders because the norms of government in modern states are not inspired by divine texts. In fact, the leaders of Fatah al-Islam identified with the idea al-Maqdisi developed in his book *The Abrahamic Community* (*millet Ibrahim*), that *any* participation in state institutions was tantamount to apostasy. Thus, they did not hesitate to deride secular Arab leaders with the insulting term *zanadiq*, whose semantic field extends from "heretics" to "drunken libertines." Moreover, al-Absi the activist and al-Maqdisi the intellectual had both distanced themselves from Zarqawi's descent into anti-Shi'ite sectarianism, despite the history they shared with him as militants and detainees.

Al-Maqdisi's obsession with releasing believers from the hold of positive law in every field also legitimized the jihadi groups' practice of committing common-law crimes (theft, hostage-taking, etc.). This explains why Fatah al-Islam's leaders began robbing banks the very moment they arrived in Lebanon. Yet far from earning

[29] For more on this important Jihadi ideologue, see Joas Wagemakers, *A Quietist Jihadi: The Ideology and Influence of Abu Muhammad al-Maqdisi* (Cambridge: Cambridge University Press, 2012).

Abu Muhammad al-Maqdisi's support, this practice met with his censure. In a letter to Shaker al-Absi, al-Maqdisi questioned the relationship between means and ends in Fatah al-Islam's practices:

> Do not expect me to encourage our brothers to resort to pillage! Are such actions logically part of the path of jihad? . . . Did they pledge allegiance to us for that purpose? They pledged allegiance to us on the basis that we were al-Qaeda, and I have been asked time and time again, "Where are the resources, the equipment, the weapons?" And when I told them to be patient, that we were preparing for all that, they answered: "Did we not pledge an oath to al-Qaeda?" Where is the equipment, indeed? Only the few volunteers who are unable to leave the camp are convinced that robberies are authorized [by religion]. The others want to kill and fight. . . . Please answer me clearly . . . either we continue working together, or we will provide you with fraternal support.[30]

Sheikh al-Maqdisi's questions are typical of the mixture of interest and wariness that characterized responses to Fatah al-Islam by other famous jihadi figureheads able to grant religious legitimacy. His doubts reflected his refusal to become an involuntary role model for a group without real recognition that was locked into a cycle of common-law criminality, at a time when he was endeavoring to improve his image in Arab public opinion.

The 'Ayn 'Alaq Bombings

On February 13, 2007, the day before a demonstration planned in commemoration of Rafiq al-Hariri's assassination, two buses exploded in the area of 'Ayn 'Alaq, in the mountainous Christian-majority region of Metn, near Bikfaya, killing three and injuring twenty-three. As soon as the bombings hit the news, Shaker al-Absi appeared in Lebanese media to deny any involvement by his group in the event, just as he had done following Minister Pierre

---

[30] It is impossible to ascertain whether this was written freely or under duress. See Simon Haddad, "Fatah al-Islam in Lebanon: Anatomy of a Terrorist Organization," *Studies in Conflict and Terrorism* 33 (2010), 548–69. Haddad, however, wrongly attributes this letter to the Fatah al-Islam activist killed at Nahr al-Bared who had the same *kunya* name as the Palestinian-Jordanian jihadi sheikh (discussed earlier).

Gemayel's assassination on November 21, 2006. However, his denial did not include any condemnation of the terrorist act itself. During private conversations in the camp, when asked to publicly condemn this sort of action, al-Absi would remark, "We have fought against them and they fought us," speaking of the attack as if it were a new episode in an endless civil war between Muslims and Christians. To him, Palestinian collective memory in Lebanon served to fuel use of the sectarian referent, while he assimilated national Palestinianism to a kind of idolatry.[31] Accustomed to deliberate ambiguity in his public declarations, al-Absi obviously could not speak out squarely against the bombing since he knew that a wing of Fatah al-Islam based outside Nahr al-Bared, whose core members were Syrians and Palestinians from Syria, had carried out the attack. By the time Fatah al-Islam announced themselves, this external wing had already rented several apartments in various areas of "Christian-majority Lebanon": the Qurnet Shehwan village in Metn, the eastern suburbs of Beirut, such as Dora and Antelias, the Armenian neighborhood of Burj Hammoud, and the Ashrafiyye neighborhood of Beirut.

One of the 'Ayn 'Alaq bombers, a twenty-three-year-old Syrian, Mustafa Ibrahim Siyyu, had stayed in the Burj al-Barajne and Shatila camps before receiving the order to join Abu Yazin's Fatah al-Islam cell in Qurnet Shehwan, in late November 2006. In early February 2007, he met with Shaker al-Absi at the Samed center of Nahr al-Bared and agreed to take part in a secret operation in exchange for five hundred dollars. Al-Absi told him nothing else and sent him to ask a man named Umar al-Hajji for further directives. In his testimony before the Judicial Council, Siyyu tried to downplay his involvement in the bombing.[32] He said that he had initially refused to plant a bomb in Riyad al-Sulh Square in Beirut, where Hezbollah and the Aounist movement were staging a sit-in protest against the Siniora government. Later, during a meeting in Dora, Umar al-Hajji gave Siyyu several bags and told him to bring them to Bikfaya. In the Dora apartment, one of the bags came open and, seeing the contents, Siyyu asked al-Hajji why he was to transport "putty, paste, and colored strips." He testified that

---

[31] Interview with the Hamas representative in Nahr al-Bared, September 2009.

[32] For operational details of the 'Ayn 'Alaq bombing, see the transcript of the hearings published in the May 22, 2005 edition of *Al-Safir*.

he had only understood the literal meaning of the answer: "It is a message which will become political when placed in two buses going from Bikfaya to Beirut."[33]

The next morning al-Hajji asked Siyyu to take one of the bags and board the Bikfaya-Beirut bus. Once he had done so, al-Hajji called him and ordered him to get off the bus but to leave the bags on board. Just before leaving the bus, Siyyu said, he had asked two women sitting in front of him to move to seats closer to the front, perhaps wishing them to move away from the mortal harm he was about to inflict. According to Siyyu, Abu Yazin (described as the operation's mastermind, from whom Umar al-Hajji took instructions) detonated the bomb against his will. Siyyu told the tribunal that he learned of the bombing from the radio on his way to Dora. He claimed he was "furious he had been tricked into carrying the bomb," and that he then decided to gradually dissociate himself from the group. He also stated that Abu Yazin had threatened him several times, and that his younger brother was being held hostage in Nahr al-Bared at the time. He attributed his failure to turn himself in to the police after leaving the camp to his fear of retaliation, because Abu Yazin "knew his whole family" in Syria. Two days before Siyyu's arrest on March 8, 2007, Abu Yazin had ordered him to take photographs of the Jordanian, Saudi, Russian, and British embassies. According to Siyyu, Umar al-Hajji himself placed the explosives on the second bus.

The specifics of the 'Ayn 'Alaq bombing give evidence of a division of labor within Fatah al-Islam, in particular of the existence of a secret group charged with "special operations." Mustafa Siyyu described an extremely compartmentalized jihadi network: "The members of Fatah al-Islam knew nothing of what the leaders were planning, until they led us to disaster." The core of the secret group consisted of Palestinians from Syria such as Abu Medyan, including former Saydnaya inmates such as Abu Yazin and Yasir al-Shuqayri, as well as other Syrian nationals such as Umar al-Hajji. Only a few newcomers had knowledge of the details of the operation. Shaker al-Absi imposed a particular meaning—a "frame"—upon various situations, concealing their true nature, the "fringe,"

[33] Ibid.

from the vast majority of his men.[34] The young Saudis who were deceived into coming to Nahr al-Bared by the promise they would be sent to fight in Iraq were also victims of this tactic.[35]

As a whole, the secret group was keen on preserving its underground nature—in the camp, several militants still wore keffiehs over their faces. But within this clandestine structure, there existed an even more secretive "backstage" where most of the real political work was done. The latter presented a stark contrast to the Fatah al-Islam's public performances. There they courted the footlights, taking pains to call attention to themselves via press conferences or during the welcoming of new recruits at the Samed center.[36]

As indicated previously, internal discussions about potential targets for a terrorist attack preceded the 'Ayn 'Alaq operation. Fatah al-Islam had considered attacking the sit-in that Hezbollah and its allies organized in front of government buildings on Riyad al-Sulh square, various political and religious figures (including the Maronite patriarch), a *husayniyya* (Shi'ite place of worship) in a Shi'ite neighborhood, foreign tourists, the UNIFIL premises in Beirut, and the Phoenicia Hotel (which had been reconnoitered several times). As the editorialist Hazem Saghiyyeh noted, attacking an upscale hotel in the region would expose as a falsehood the Lebanese state's pretense, vis-à-vis the outside world, that it was the embodiment of modernity, for in fact it was failing to produce modernity for its own society. Such an attack would also highlight the gap between "hotel people" and "street people," which the state was failing to bridge.[37] Finally, for Lebanon in particular, it would revive memories of the first weeks of the civil war, when the destruction of chic hotels boded ill for the state's ultimate survival. It would most

[34] See Erving Goffman, *Frame Analysis: An Essay on the Organization of Experience* (Boston: Northeastern University Press, 1986 [1974]), 83: "Those who engineer the deception can be called the operatives, fabricators, deceivers. Those intendedly taken in can be said to be contained—contained in a construction or fabrication."

[35] Only the belief in an objective social reality, on an ontological level, can allow us to appreciate the existence of a fabrication, since it is necessarily contingent on there being differences between protagonists' points of view. Based on these differences, those who are aware of the true status of an activity manipulate those who are not aware of it.

[36] Erving Goffman, *The Presentation of Self in Everyday Life* (New York: Anchor Books, 1959).

[37] See Hazem Saghiyyeh, *Al-'arab bayn al-hajar wa-l-duhrra* [The Arabs between the rock and the atom] (Beirut: al-Saqi, 1992), 165–68.

definitively have turned the Phoenicia's seaside location—close to where Rafiq al-Hariri had been assassinated—into the grave of Oriental, Arab, and Mediterranean aspirations.

The variety of themes discussed reflected the internal dissension within the network. The target finally chosen had both sectarian and political significance. As one of the instigators later explained, the aim in deciding to attack the two buses was to terrorize the March 14 anti-Assad Movement. This "message" would arrive the day before planned demonstrations in downtown Beirut to commemorate the assassination of Rafiq al-Hariri. The climate was very tense in Lebanon at the time, punctuated since 2004 by an assassination campaign targeting political figures specifically hostile to Syria and Hezbollah. One of Shaker al-Absi's most trusted deputies, Abu Medyan, reportedly refused the option of bombing Riyad al-Sulh square, where Hezbollah sympathizers were staging a sit-in against the government.[38] Compared to Pierre Gemayel's assassination three months prior (Fatah al-Islam was a prime suspect), the double bombing of 'Ayn 'Alaq can be read as the expression of a different, more implicit signal directed at the Syrian intelligence services following the crisis within Fatah al-Islam generated in November of 2006.

By considering a diversity of targets consonant with their militant identity, but always choosing to strike at the same side, Fatah al-Islam's leaders were adapting jihadi identity to regional political demands. It is unclear which theory best explains this—anticipation of their former jailers' (the Syrian intelligence services') wishes? Following their instructions to the letter for fear of reprisals? In either case, Shaker al-Absi and his men were still negotiating with

---

[38] The March 23, 2007 edition of *al-Hayat* cites sources within the "Lebanese security services." These are most likely leaks from the "intelligence section" of the ISF. These sources' information was based on confessions of suspects arrested in the wake of the 'Ayn 'Alaq bombings, according to whom Abu Medyan had ruled out the idea of planting a bomb in Riyad al-Sulh Square in the heart of Beirut, "to prevent any misunderstandings as to the nature of the target." Preliminary discussions indicated that the instigators had a clear understanding of the site's symbolic dimension. Thus, Abu Medyan opted for a bombing at Bikfaya, which he called a "political target" because the village was the birthplace of the Gemayel dynasty, emblematic of "political Maronitism"—rather than Brumana, a holiday destination for Arab tourists, considered a mere "touristic target." Abu Medyan was killed in the early stages of the fighting at Nahr al-Bared, on May 20, 2007.

the Syrian regime from afar at the time of the bombing, even though they had declared themselves free of any state-related constraints. In fact, their actions on the ground showed them unable to extricate themselves from the regional Realpolitik. This regional context provides a framework for analyzing their actions that is at least as important as the jihadi beliefs so loudly proclaimed in the media.

The 'Ayn 'Alaq bombing carried certain risks. News of the attacks troubled the Fatah al-Islam volunteers of Nahr al-Bared, driving some to question the group's true orientation. They did not understand the connection between the jihadi leaders' public commitments and operations against civilians. Fatah al-Islam's volunteers (particularly the young Saudis) viewed attacks on civilians as contrary to Islamic rulings. Doctrinal quarrels ensued that had various parties reminding others of certain rules governing what was or was not "Islamic" in their behavior. The bank robberies were equally controversial. Carried out nationwide, they involved considerable sums and, as we have noted, provided most of Fatah al-Islam's funding. The legal committee approved the tactic, but even this was contested, especially following Sheikh Abdallah al-Bishi's controversial visit and his disapproval of the practice.

Against a background of robberies and attacks on Lebanese civilians, and absent any military initiatives in Iraq or Palestine, Fatah al-Islam's partisans increasingly began to question their relationship with the organization. By the end of February 2007, Shaker al-Absi was forced to organize a meeting with about sixty militants to try to restore his credibility. He managed to generate some enthusiasm by announcing that Fatah al-Islam was now bound by an oath to al-Qaeda in Iraq, the latter organization having finally accepted his allegiance.

In the jihadi world, the procedure for acknowledging allegiance is comparable in form to the Catholic Church's procedure for registering miracles. The request for recognition does not come from the center, but from the periphery. The main authority takes its time in awarding its recognition, as it is aware that it might jeopardize its own symbolic credibility by too hastily recognizing groups later found to be unsuitable. Once a secondary group obtains recognition of its allegiance, it gains considerable prestige, which spares it the considerable time and effort that it would normally expend in explaining and justifying its actions. In the case of Fatah al-Islam, however, Shaker al-Absi was simply lying. Al-Qaeda in Iraq had not recognized the group's *bay'a* (oath of allegiance). In fact, he had only sent a letter to his Syrian son-in-law, Muhammad Ahmad Tayura (a.k.a. Abu al-Laith), to be delivered to Abu Hamza al-Muhajir, al-Qaeda leader in Iraq. Al-Absi's letter explained his group's jihadi nature and reiterated his insistent request for recognition. The fact that he never received such recognition leaves room for conjecture. Abu Hamza al-Muhajir was apparently in favor of sending a jihadi contingent to Lebanon, and so perhaps hesitated to accept Shaker al-Absi's oath of allegiance publicly, so as not to further strain relations with al-Qaeda-Central. It will be remembered that the organization did not look favorably on Fatah al-Islam in the wake of Sheikh al-Bishi's audit.

Fatah al-Islam's Relationship with the Sunni Sheikhs of Tripoli

On the one hand, the March 14 Alliance exploited the initial phase of the network's formation to highlight the Syrian regime's implication in the group's birth. On the other, supporters of Iran and Syria used Fatah al-Islam's consolidation phase to carry out a media counteroffensive. They attempted to put the Future Movement in an awkward position vis-à-vis its Western allies by making it appear responsible for transforming Fatah al-Islam into a Sunni, anti-Shi'ite militia. Contacts between Shaker al-Absi and several Sunni religious figures fueled these rumors. Though transcripts of what was said and negotiated during these meetings are unavailable, a plausible account of the process and its dynamics can be found by crosschecking various sources, including interviews with witnesses or protagonists and newspaper articles.

According to several witnesses, Shaker al-Absi publicly expressed satisfaction at having so rapidly forged sound ties with all of the Islamic figureheads in Tripoli. On one level, this diplomatic effort aimed to anchor the group in the Sunni religious environment and legitimize it, as a means of protection in the event of trouble with Lebanese security forces. To this end, al-Absi had only to pull the same rhetorical strings as he pulled inside the camp with his own partisans: exploit his interlocutors' expectations, instrumentalize regional tensions, play for time, and keep his intentions vague.

When he met local representatives of the opposition March 8 Alliance, he cast himself as a resistance fighter exclusively motivated by the desire to thwart "American-Zionist" plans for the region and to oppose implementation of UN Security Council Resolution 1559. His history of fighting—relayed in the Arab press—helped make his commitment seem more sincere. In each of these statements he carefully distinguished between collaborator Shi'ites (in Iraq) and resistant Shi'ites (in Lebanon), a distinction conceived to calm fears of an Iraqi-style sectarian conflict occurring in Lebanon. When he met with sheikhs from the opposite end of the political spectrum, he strongly emphasized the defense of Sunnis in Lebanon, and promised that Fatah al-Islam would never undertake any action likely to have negative repercussions on the community's collective future in Lebanon.[39] In such company, he would call Hezbollah "Hizb al-Lat" (meaning "Party of al-Lat," the pre-Islamic Meccan pagan goddess, referencing an iconoclastic designation used privately in Salafi circles). For instance, al-Absi allegedly pledged to refrain from using military action against UNIFIL forces in South Lebanon. As soon as rumors of this promise began to circulate, they apparently prompted heated discussions with the group's other leaders.[40]

There was a second, even more crucial dimension to Shaker al-Absi's diplomatic efforts. In his view there was no way, ultimately, to separate ends and means. The most pressing priority was to accumulate the means of military action as quickly as possible in order to legitimize Fatah al-Islam in the eyes of the Tripoli's Islamist and Salafi sheikhs. In Abu Samra, home to most of the Islamist organizations, Fatah al-Islam was seen as a *de facto* force

[39] See Da'i al-Islam al-Shahhal's account of his two encounters with Shaker al-Absi, according to which al-Absi "seemed receptive to his advice" to "not rush things, to not take any military or security initiatives in Lebanon, because this might harm the Sunni community in particular," in *al-Hayat*, May 22, 2007.

[40] See Hazem al-Amin's article in the May 24, 2007 edition of *al-Hayat*: "One of the Salafi sheikhs mentions that 'there were several discussions with the group' which resulted in them 'giving up their plans to strike the UNIFIL forces.' [The Salafi sheikhs were] in favor of jihad in Iraq, but [did] not consider that fighting UNIFIL was appropriate at the time."

whose mere presence could upset the local balance of power. Thus, when Fatah al-Islam began to exhibit its military strength through action, religious actors were forced to deal constructively with the group, as its coercive capacity made the consequences of dismissing it potentially serious.

To build strong ties with the most respected sheikhs of Tripoli, Shaker al-Absi used a successful past experience as a model: his coexistence with religious figures in Nahr al-Bared. Despite serious doctrinal disagreements, he had used near-daily contacts to induce them to ally with his group. Though the Nahr al-Bared Salafi sheikhs wished to maintain relative autonomy so as to be able to continue negotiating with all parties, some of the young men attending Islamic studies classes at the home of one sheikh gave into the temptation and joined Fatah al-Islam. As the sheikh himself put it, "I used to give classes to about fifteen youths in my home, and ten of them left to join Fatah al-Islam. I could not convince them to stay. They declined to take the path of Salafi preaching (al-da'wa al-salafiyya)."[41]

Reproducing this experience on the scale of the city of Tripoli offered Fatah al-Islam an opportunity to sow discord between its enemies and destroy the two-year-old anti-Syrian alliance uniting the different civil and religious components of the Sunni community. To this end, al-Absi used the Salafi frame of reference to break the "community patriotism" of the sheikhs of Tripoli and force them to resituate themselves on the exclusive and abstract terrain of "defending Islam." Of course, this maneuver had been easier to carry out in Nahr al-Bared with Palestinian sheikhs lacking a national referent than it would be with their Lebanese counterparts tied to both a confessional sphere and a state sphere. In Weberian terms, Fatah al-Islam leaders sought to induce Sunni religious representatives to trade their ethics of responsibility for the ethics of conviction, in order to extract them from the communitarian framework in which they had been operating since Rafiq al-Hariri's assassination in February 2005. Needless to say, abandoning this framework meant modifying their relationship with the Future Movement. The sheikhs' qualified support and constructive criticism would evolve to outright hostility toward these secular political leaders who were

---

[41] Interview with Sheikh Muhammad 'Abd al-Ghani (see note 14).

usurping the sheikhs' natural role as political representatives of Sunni Islam in Lebanon.

The differences between the two parties were not so much about the content of their religious beliefs as about the relevance of the respective systems of rules that each party applied to a situation. At that moment, the Salafi sheikhs of Tripoli followed a confessional framework as the only norm in evaluating behavior in dealing with Hezbollah and its regional allies. Therefore, they had to convince Fatah al-Islam that its own rules were inappropriate because they were outdated, in hopes of preventing the group from weakening the Lebanese Sunni community. The jihadi group from Nahr al-Bared was following the same approach, but from the opposite direction: they hoped to persuade the sheikhs to backtrack mentally until they hit the pre-2005 period. At that time, the sheikhs had willingly identified with a religious rhetoric through which supranational initiatives reaching beyond Lebanon's borders could be justified. Daʿi al-Islam had espoused the principle of supporting jihad abroad—in Chechnya at the end of the 1990s and in Iraq after 2003. Sheikh Zakaria al-Masri had unequivocally condemned loyalist Fatah's behavior following the 1993 Oslo accords. In the classes he offered in his center, al-Masri had then taught his students that resorting to jihad—the "umma's fortress"—was necessary to thwart obstacles to the preaching of Islam (his understanding of it).[42]

Shaker al-Absi and his followers endeavored to exploit the "thirty-three-day war" of 2006 by moving the struggle against the "Zionist-crusader" West to the top of the Islamist agenda. Their two-sided militant identity was oriented toward the image of "resistance" on the one hand, and, on the other hand, toward defending Sunnis across the region—not the Lebanese Sunni community in its denominational sense—through jihad. The Sunnis' Hezbollah

---

[42] "If someone prevents religious preaching (daʿwa) from reaching people, he becomes an oppressor of these people he is depriving of access to the daʿwa. In these conditions, you are legitimately authorized to use force, to be a jihad fighter on the path of God. . . . God says: jihad on the path of God is a fortress that protects the umma against its enemies. Without jihad, our society would be easily dissolved in other societies. Abandoning jihad is abandoning the fortress that protects the umma, rendering it vulnerable to thieves and enemies. Abandoning jihad means the enemy can invade us inside our home." Cassette tape from a lecture by Sheikh Zakariyya al-Masri, Markaz al-Hamza (Sheikh al-Masri's institution), Tripoli, 2000.

allies would logically relate to the former theme, and the Salafi sheikhs of Tripoli could not be indifferent to the importance of the latter. After what Fatah al-Islam had achieved with Nahr el-Bared's Salafi sheikhs, the next step was to win over the Tripoli sheikhs and promote a Sunni-wide jihadi discourse that would upset the old rules of Sunni politics within the community. To eliminate any distinctions between Fatah al-Islam and true Salafism, it was necessary to reorganize the Salafi ideological categories, most critically the need to obey the current holder of political power. This required destroying any kind of cooperation between Salafi sheikhs and the Future Movement.

These are the motives that seem to have guided Fatah al-Islam's religious and political diplomacy from beginning to end, far more than some *ex ante* plan to establish an Islamic emirate. Fatah al-Islam leaders presumably evoked the prospect of such a plan—a common idea among Islamist circles in the North and an enticing one for enthusiastic young men—as a potential last-resort to rally local support in the event of an army attack against Nahr al-Bared camp. Should this happen, numerous military initiatives in Tripoli would trigger an Islamic insurgency against the Lebanese state and its impious army. Setting up terrorist infrastructure to this end involved renting apartments in Tripoli and using farms in the Akkar mountains. The latter locations were used as hideouts or chemical labs, and were put at the group's disposal by local Lebanese sympathizers, some of whom had previously been arrested during the Dinniyeh clashes (December 1999/January 2000) or at the time of the bomb attacks on American-franchised businesses (see chapter 1).

In retrospect, it is surprising that Fatah al-Islam did not strike at Shi'ite targets in Lebanon, such as a Shi'ite place of worship or the tents of the March 8 Alliance's sit-in on Riyad al-Sulh square. In terms of recruitment and propaganda, Fatah al-Islam might have benefited from any anti-Sunni reprisals that would have ensued. Such events would have made jihadi discourse much more relevant in Sunni Islamist circles. Moreover, Hezbollah would have attributed such attacks to the Future Movement, which the opposition press apparatus already accused, virtually every day, of creating a sectarian climate favorable to such deeds, or even of secretly supporting Fatah al-Islam.

There are several possible explanations of why Fatah al-Islam never went beyond internal discussions when it came to such acts. First, Shaker al-Absi's jihadi thought focused first and foremost on fighting the West and its Arab allies in the region. Reproducing Zarqawi's anti-Shi'ite policy in a Lebanese context would have lost him of any hope of the group's recognition by an "al-Qaeda Central" wary of alienating Iran, which at the time was hosting some of their cadres.

Second, Nahr al-Bared constituted a political and military sanctuary. It was in the interests of both Fatah al-Islam and Hezbollah to prevent the implementation of UN Resolution 1559 disarming factions and militias, and to keep the Lebanese state from reestablishing control over the refugee camps. Just a few days before its May 20, 2007, clashes with the army, Fatah al-Islam was still insisting on the importance of preventing "the confiscation of Palestinian arms, under the pretext of wanting to put them at the state's service." The group was under growing pressure from Fatah within the camp and from the army outside.[43] Therefore, there was no reason for them to risk turning Hezbollah from a passive ally into an active enemy on this issue.

Furthermore, Fatah al-Islam had not yet finished consolidating its hold over Nahr al-Bared. It still needed support from factions close to Hezbollah, such as the PFLP-GC—from which it had already received some of their own weapons—in order to eliminate Fatah's residual presence in the camp. Finally, the core Syrian-Palestinians within the group (Shaker al-Absi and his closest deputies, Abu Medyan and Abu Yazin) were unwilling to transgress the double taboo (confessional and political) of turning on Lebanese Shi'ites. Indeed, such a hazardous undertaking would have put Syria's leaders in a difficult position, given their increasing political and psychological subjugation to Iran.

---

[43] "As we wish to preserve the Muslims' interests and honor, we ask them to be vigilant and look out for plots against us and our cause, such as the seizing of Palestinian arms under the pretext of wanting to put them at the service of the state, or the occupation of land (*tawtin*) through the abolition of Muslims' right [to live] on the land the Prophet's companions watered with their own blood." Extract from the final Fatah al-Islam communiqué distributed in Nahr al-Bared, dated May 11, 2007.

Contextualizing the Army's Decision to
Strike Fatah al-Islam

On May 20, 2007, the ISF raided an apartment located on Mi-tayn Street in a residential neighborhood of Tripoli. Fatah al-Islam retaliated by attacking several Lebanese army positions around Nahr al-Bared. Rumors of about twenty soldiers' throats being cut in their sleep at the al-Mahmara military post provoked the army to immediately shell the camp. On September 4, nearly three months later, the fighting finally ended in the near-total destruction of Nahr al-Bared.

To the ISF leadership, which was close to Sa'ad al-Hariri, Fatah al-Islam was not (or was no longer) salvageable. Several Tripoli-tan sheikhs and figures such as Kana'an Naji had attempted to mediate between the ISF and Fatah al-Islam, but their efforts had produced no tangible results. In fact, the ISF intelligence unit made strategic use of these contacts to collect information and infiltrate the group. In this triangular negotiation, the Tripolitan sheikhs were likely trying to convince the ISF leadership to grant them enough time to modify the Fatah al-Islam network's internal equilibrium and transform it into a Sunni deterrent force against Hezbollah. ISF promises of immunity in exchange for details on the Syrian intel-ligence services' role in forming the network may have encouraged such efforts. But the head of ISF's Information Branch, Wissam al-Hassan, was well aware of the Tripolitan sheikhs' own agenda. In their dealings with the ISF, the sheikhs tried to reconcile respect for public order with a defense of the Sunni community. In their deal-ings with Fatah al-Islam, they presented themselves as seeking the best way to protect Sunni Islam in the region—while in fact trying to increase their negotiating power in Sunni politics to the detri-ment of the Future Movement.

This game might have continued had the ISF leadership not re-ceived intelligence that Fatah al-Islam was planning more bombings after the 'Ayn 'Alaq attack. In addition, the continuing negotia-tions exposed the March 14 Alliance to continued criticism in the opposition press (which conveniently ignored the occurrence of just as many secret meetings between Shaker al-Absi and figures from its own ranks).

The March 14, 2007, 'Ayn 'Alaq bombings had convinced Wissam al-Hassan that Fatah al-Islam was a terrorist group. He had also become certain of Syria's involvement in planting the group in Palestinian refugee camps. Finally, he was worried about the growing fascination of Islamist militants from North Lebanon (and the whole of the Middle East) with the existence of an open-air training camp.

Faced with these factors and with the impossibility of getting Fatah al-Islam to repent, both politics and public security made it increasingly urgent to end Fatah al-Islam's activities. On May 20, 2007, following yet another bank robbery in a suburb of Tripoli, Lebanese security forces raided the apartment on Mitayn Street that Fatah al-Islam used to conceal weapons and explosives. This raid led to the decisive confrontation between Fatah al-Islam and the army. After three months of fighting and over four hundred dead, the camp fell to the armed forces in early September 2007.

The War of Nahr al-Bared

Fatah al-Islam made up for its numerical inferiority (it had no more than four hundred fighters at best, which left it outnumbered 10 to 1) by thoroughly exploiting the camp's geography. Its combat tactics show that its leaders had devoted considerable efforts to military engineering since November 2006. The group also utilized fully the knowledge of urban warfare that some members had acquired in Iraq. They managed as well to turn the army leadership's tactical decisions to their advantage. Paradoxically, two weeks' worth of heavy shelling actually improved the camp's natural defenses. Collapsed buildings formed compact ruins that favored the highly mobile jihadi combatants and hindered the progress of the army's soldiers and armored vehicles. In the month of June, paratrooper commando units managed to advance north of the area known as the "new camp" and capture the Samed center training ground without facing any real resistance. Still, Fatah al-Islam's internal lines of organization remained intact. Well aware of their military inferiority, the jihadis had decided to abandon the new camp since it was much larger and more exposed, and hence more difficult to defend than other areas. Their territorial losses were quite literally superficial, as underground tunnels allowed them to move with relative ease between various points in the old and new camps. Thus, the camp's topography—which only the jihadis had completely mastered—gave them the advantage by forcing the Lebanese army to fight on unfamiliar terrain not of their choosing.

Determined to maximize military casualties, Fatah al-Islam devised urban harassment tactics based on circulating between the old camp, which served as a refuge, and the new camp, now defined as an enemy zone, and easily accessible through the underground tunnels. Shaker al-Absi's improvised officers assigned symbolic code names to its various "platoons," corresponding to their base locations—the Salah al-Din group for the al-Khan area, the Izz al-Din al-Qassam *katibat* (battalion) for the Cooperative area, and so on. Thanks to these tactical plans, Fatah al-Islam's men were able to attack the new camp with "swarming" maneuvers learned from urban warfare in Iraq: small units of two to four fighters would move between adjacent buildings in predetermined zones by piercing holes through the walls, thus avoiding detection by the army out in the open streets. By freeing themselves from conventional positioning, they often found themselves behind army soldiers disoriented by such an evasive enemy. And thanks to night-vision goggles, which the army did not have, Fatah al-Islam's combatants sapped the soldiers' morale by regaining positions at night that they had lost during the previous day. The insurgents made up for their numerical inferiority by mastering the element of surprise.

Attacked from the rear, the Lebanese soldiers became potential targets for ultra-mobile attackers specializing in booby-traps, ambushes, and (with considerable success) sniping. Fatah al-Islam snipers borrowed tactics that the Soviets used during the siege of Stalingrad in 1942. Waiting in a camouflaged position, protected and concealed by several walls pierced in a gradually broadening angle, their snipers could target moving soldiers from adjacent buildings without risking counter-fire. True to Clausewitz's observation that "behind every surprise, there is always a certain degree of ruse," Fatah al-Islam riddled the new camp with homemade bombs triggered by timers, remote controls, or pressure-detonators. These were hidden inside the most harmless objects—furniture, television sets, doors, refrigerators—and scattered at random throughout the camp's apartments and houses.[44] Explosive charges concealed inside walls were detonated remotely as army infantry units advanced. Cadavers and animals were used as well; soldiers' accounts of the battle mention stray dogs strapped with explosives being sent toward their lines. During the final days of fighting, Fatah al-Islam combatants, closely-shaven and wearing army uniforms, executed very close-quarter attacks. Others were able to escape using the same stratagem.

Fatah al-Islam's weapons came from stocks that Palestinian organizations had accumulated during the Lebanese civil war, and that Fatah al-Intifada and the PFLP-GC had appropriated after 1983. A quick overview of the group's arsenal illustrates the remarkable degree of continuity between the post–World War II partisan wars and the conflicts of the late 2000s. The progressive myths of the revolutionary generation had certainly disappeared, but the poor man's armory—a vestige of that earlier period—remained almost identical to what it had been as long as fifty years ago: RPG-7 rocket launchers, SPG-9 recoilless anti-tank canons, AK-47 assault rifles, M16s, 82mm mortars, and Simonovs. The Islamist snipers used Dragunov semi-automatic precision rifles (first used in 1963 by the Soviet Union). Except for the night vision goggles they had obtained from Iraq, Fatah al-Islam's arms and equipment were actually quite obsolete—contrary to a persistent rumor suggesting that the group had purchased state-of-the-art weaponry.

The jihadi network's implantation in this distinctive space, in which legal institutions had no authority to intervene, had finally given working-class people drawn to jihadi revolt a rallying point beyond the influence of the Tripoli sheikhs. The latter had not anticipated these conditions and were no longer able to accomplish the mission given to them since Hariri's assassination: directing Sunni militants' zeal against Hezbollah only, and, in broader terms, orienting Salafism's potential for conflict against Shi'ite Islam.

This mission became even more difficult after the "thirty-three-day war" of 2006, during which the Israeli army attempted to destroy Hezbollah's military capabilities in South Lebanon, as well as its political and media facilities in the southern suburbs of Beirut.

44 Ibid., 151.

Hezbollah's resilience in the face of these attacks, however, considerably increased its popularity among Arab and Muslim publics. The Qatari television station al-Jazeera amplified Hezbollah's popularity by labeling the war the "fifth Israeli-Arab conflict." A fear of being eclipsed by Shi'ite Hezbollah forced the Sunni jihadi militants to assert their existence—at least verbally—on the frontline of the anti-Zionist struggle. One example was Ayman al-Zawahiri's numerous attempts to inject himself and al-Qaeda into the narrative of an Israeli-Hezbollah war.

The Fatah al-Islam Salafis could potentially express their jihadi dimension while remaining free of the local and regional alliances that entangled Saudi Salafism. Consequently, the Tripoli sheikhs and their Saudi backers found themselves unable to control such a potentially explosive ideological resource. At this point, a group of militants from various organizational backgrounds, including some battle-hardened militants from the constellation of groups that made up al-Qaeda in Iran, freely debated Fatah al-Islam's potential. By simply being present, it attracted volunteers from the Levant and the Arabian Peninsula, some of whom even made their way to the camp after encountering the group through online forums.

Regionally, the network illustrated Sunni Islam's importance as a key battlefield in the confrontation between Syria and Saudi Arabia. By facilitating the reorientation of jihadi networks from their focus on Iraq to Lebanon through positive incentives, the Syrian regime had sown discord at the heart of the religious apparatus the Future Movement and its Saudi advisors deployed. The leaders of Fatah al-Islam had thwarted the Tripoli sheikhs' efforts to use Salafism in a sectarian direction by designating the enemy as Israel, the West, UNIFIL, and the "allies of America in Lebanon." The jihadi agenda of struggle against the West actually ended up protecting Hezbollah and its Iranian backers. Divided between the urgency of fighting a homegrown enemy (Hezbollah) and an external enemy (Israel and the United States), Sunni Islamism weakened from within. The Salafi sheikhs' unsuccessful attempts to trap Fatah al-Islam within their sectarian political agenda actually sparked a political campaign—adroitly echoed in the international press—alleging ties between the Future Movement and jihadi groups. Thus, reorienting jihadism from Iraq to Lebanon would be a winning bet for its promoters whichever way it played out. While a powerful Fatah al-Islam would have destroyed the Lebanese Sunni community from the inside, a weaker, co-opted Fatah al-Islam would have destroyed the Future Movement's political credibility from the outside.

Ideologically, Fatah al-Islam connected the Palestinian and Iraqi crises. All of these causes were collapsed into one, with a single enemy—the figure of the West as essentially hostile to Islam. With a core group of fighters hailing from Iraqi battlefields, Fatah al-Islam easily convinced young recruits—particularly Saudis—that it was necessary to stay in Nahr al-Bared for a time before they could be sent, as promised, either to Iraq or to carry out an operation "to liberate Palestine."

The Damascus Confessions

After the evening news bulletin on Thursday, November 6, 2008, Syrian state television broadcast videotaped confessions of the alleged perpetrators of the September 27, 2008, car bomb attack in Damascus. The attack was in the al-Qazaz region, near the premises of the security forces' Palestine Section—of sinister repute—on the road from Damascus to the international airport. According to official sources, twenty-seven were killed and sixty-five injured.

Under the title "The Confessions" (al-i'tirafat), the 50-minute documentary reconstructs various sequences of events that led to the bombing. Several witnesses appear in it, including Shaker al-Absi's daughter and her husband. The film is edited to give the viewer a (false) sense of objectivity: the interrogators' questions are excised so that each witness, seated before a black background, seems to speak spontaneously to an unmoving camera. One main witness connects the dots between the different testimonies, so that the film appears as a perfect reconstruction of a terrorist act, precisely as the perpetrators willed, conceived, and executed it.

From the Syrian regime—hardly known for the transparency of its institutions or political practices—such a public relations effort came as a surprise. It had several objectives. Syrian state television's staging of the account was designed to discredit the Future Movement (the main representative of the Lebanese pro-independence movement) by blaming them for funding the Fatah al-Islam members who had carried out the al-Qazaz terrorist operation. Although this media counteroffensive dated to early 2007, the television production gave it tangible content by highlighting the presumed ties between the terrorist group and the Sunni contingent of the Lebanese parliamentary majority at that time.

A second objective was to rebut American accusations that the Syrian regime was aiding jihadi networks on Iraqi soil. Through the film, the regime sought to show how terrorist groups targeted Syria, just as they targeted the United States and Europe. The film appeared a few days after the Americans had killed a jihadi courier on October 28, 2008. The man, Abu al-Ghadiya, was killed in the Syrian village of al-Sukkariyya, in the Abu Kamal region, on the main route from Syria to Iraq.

Admittedly, Damascus had already suffered several Islamist attacks, including the bombing of a UN building in April 2004 and an attack against an abandoned state television building in June 2006. But rightly or wrongly, the circumstances of these attacks raised a number of questions and doubts: they were particularly ineffective—the main targets were unscathed—and mysterious—none of the attackers survived. Moreover, no serious demands had accompanied these operations, further obscuring both their origins and purpose. Following the al-Qazaz attack, the Syrian government could at last claim the status of a "victim of terrorism," a claim that had to be taken seriously in light of the significant casualties and extensive damage.

Finally, the media coverage of the incident also served several domestic policy objectives. The bombing retroactively justified the minister of *Awqaf*'s (sing. *Waqf*, Islamic endowments) earlier reforms strengthening state control over Syria's private religious institutions. In November 2008, the minister presented to the People's Council (parliament) a bill affiliating these institutions to the *Awqaf* Ministry.[45] The bill definitively passed the following year, making institute teaching staff state employees under the ministry's

---

[45] On September 30, 2008, the minister of Awqaf decided to put private religious institutions under state control, "on the administrative, scientific, procedural, and financial levels." The text of the bill is reproduced on a Syrian parliamentarian's blog, http://www.k-alsayed.com/k-alsayed/waz/4999e3347d2b5.doc (accessed Septermber 2010, this page has since been suspended).

direct authority and giving Syria's new mufti, Sheikh Ahmad Hassun, responsibility for standardizing their religious curriculum.

In the beginning of the documentary the various interviewees recount their time at the Institute of Islamic Conquest (Ma'had al-Fath al-Islami), while the covers of classics of Wahhabi literature—fatwa collections and commentaries by famous Saudi sheikhs—appear onscreen. The effect is to designate an evil whose ideological and geographical source lies outside the borders of blameless Syria. Immediately afterward, two books by Egyptian ideologue Sayyid Imam Abd al-'Aziz al-Sharif (a.k.a. Dr. Fadel) are given pride of place on-screen, while the narrator intones: "The al-Qaeda people told us that all of Islam could be found in these two books."[46] At regular intervals, certain images are superimposed on sequences of the protagonists' testimony, connected to the theme they are evoking. For instance, when someone mentions weapons, images of explosives, machine guns, grenades, wiring, and detonators are shown to illustrate the supposed quality and variety of Fatah al-Islam's arsenal—a practice reminiscent of the Israeli army's habit of exposing weapons confiscated from its enemies. Photographs of certain figures sometimes appear on-screen as the witnesses mention them. Finally, tragic-sounding oriental music accompanies footage of the wreckage at the bombsite, as well as the faces and names of the victims.

The film essentially rests on the confessions of Abd al-Baqi Mahmud al-Hussein (a.k.a. Abu al-Walid), who is the main witness. He bookends the broadcast, opening and closing the footage. He seems very poised, speaks deliberately, and his words constitute the guiding thread of the documentary's story line, connecting an otherwise incongruous mix of disparate sequences. The subtitles state that he was "head of security of Fatah al-Islam." In reality, he only played a peripheral role, and appeared rather late in the group's history. For that matter, the Syrian TV film pays no attention to the formation of Fatah al-Islam's network in 2006, or to its subsequent evolution. Instead, it seeks primarily to incriminate the

---

[46] Al-Sharif, formerly of the Egyptian "Islamic Jihad" group, later agreed to forsake the use of violence for jihad while he was in prison in the 2000s, becoming a "reformed" ex-jihadi.

Syrian regime's political enemies of the day—the Future Movement and its Saudi backers—for their part in the al-Qazaz bombing.

Abd al-Baqi claims that al-Qaeda leaders recruited him in Syria in 2005 [4:15]; and that he traveled to Tripoli in 2007 to evade capture after the arrest of his Syrian emir, a man called Abu Saleh [7:12]. Once in Tripoli, he relates, he opened a mini-market with an associate named Abu Abd al-Rahman, who was close to the al-Qaeda representative in North Lebanon, Sheikh Nabil Rahim. Two months after the end of the battle of Nahr al-Bared, Abu Abd al-Rahman revealed that Shaker al-Absi was alive and well, in hiding in the Baddawi camp, and that he had agreed to meet Abd al-Baqi. During their second meeting, al-Absi told him he hoped al-Qaeda would help him to leave Lebanon and cross Syria on his way to Iraq. Abd al-Baqi then introduced al-Absi to a Syrian named Yasser Inad who claimed he was a member of al-Qaeda and had the necessary contacts to smuggle al-Absi out of Lebanon.

But Sheikh Rahim and Abu Abd al-Rahman's arrests forced Abd al-Baqi to seek refuge in the Baddawi camp. In February 2008, Abd al-Baqi and a small group of Nahr al-Bared survivors managed to sneak into Syria and settle into several apartments in Damascus. One, located in the Hajar al-Aswad neighborhood, had been al-Absi's residence before he was arrested [15:00]. One of al-Absi's close friends was none other than the Tripolitan sheikh Ahmad al-'Attar, who, as noted earlier, masterminded the McDonald's network. The plethora of details, names, nicknames, and places Abd al-Baqi provides works to lend credibility to the documentary's account of events, as well as that of the witnesses appearing before the regime's camera.

Yet significant omissions throughout the documentary's various accounts weaken its credibility. Though al-Absi managed to reach the Baddawi camp after fleeing through the ruins of Nahr al-Bared by night, he actually owed his rescue to the hospitality of Sheikh Hamza Qassem, who had close ties to the camp's chapter of the Palestinian Islamic Jihad organization. This, however, likely stems as much from inter-Palestinian solidarity in a time of crisis as support for al-Absi's political stances. Yet this makes it all the more difficult to explain why a volunteer who joined Fatah al-Islam in February of 2007 should mention Sheikh Hamza Qassem's name. Participants in a discussion on the "Jihadi Victory" Internet forum suggested Sheikh Hamza's al-Quds mosque to the prospective volunteer (before his enlistment) as a landmark and meeting point, before he was to join Fatah al-Islam.[47]

After the narration of events, another more reflexive sequence follows in which questioners probe Fatah al-Islam's political and financial support "during the Nahr al-Bared period." Three witnesses, tied to Shaker al-Absi by ideology and blood, appear in turn for about ten minutes, with a cumulative effect exemplifying what the scholar Kenneth Burke called "the power of endless repetition." This rhetorical process combines truthful and dubious elements, beginning with undisputed facts: bank robberies and monetary donations sent from the Middle East or Europe. Yasser Inad (al-Absi's new son-in-law) and Abd al-Baqi Mahmud al-Hussein (who considers he has become close to al-Absi since the two were acquainted during their forced stay in the Baddawi camp [16:55]) successively mention these facts.

Wafa al-Absi (Shaker al-Absi's daughter) completes this first collection of testimonies [18:15]. According to her, friendship between Abu Hurayra—a Fatah al-Islam cadre from Tripoli—and a man who was close to Da'i al-Islam al-Shahhal, whom she calls the "representative of the Salafi current in Lebanon" is evidence of "financial and material support" between "Salafi circles" and "the Fatah al-Islam organization." This theory is hardly new, but the witness's identity is supposed to lend it new credence.

Then her husband, Yasser Inad, confirms that the Future Movement had managed to "infiltrate every single one of the Islamist organizations in Lebanon, from al-Shahhal's group to the Jama'a Islamiyya" [19:29]. Inad refrains from mentioning the pro-Syrian Islamist organizations present in Lebanon, such as the Islamic Action Front (under the authority of the well-known Tripolitan sheikh Fathi Yakan [d. June 13, 2009]) or the two groups identifying themselves as part of the Tawhid Movement. As noted earlier,

---

[47] See the testimony of Fares Hamid al-Tirkawi, a Syrian computer science student in the city of Homs. He was recruited through the Jihadi Victory (al-Nusra al-Jihadiyya) Internet forum. Although he had stated that he wished to fight the Americans in Iraq, his online interlocutor advised him to join Fatah al-Islam in Lebanon to receive military training. He was to contact Sheikh Hamza Qassem in the Baddawi camp. Upon his arrival at Baddawi in February 2007, he was arrested by the camp's military committee, to whom he stated that he wished to "fight the forces of the March 14 Alliance because they collaborate with the Americans." See the September 18, 2007 edition of al-Akhbar newspaper.

these groups had regularly been in contact with Shaker al-Absi. An old Syrian regime friend, Sheikh Fathi Yakan, even interceded with the Syrian authorities to obtain the release of Saddam Dib, who later participated in several robberies for Fatah al-Islam, only to be killed in the May 2007 clashes with the army.[48] Jumping to the conclusion that direct financial support went from the Future Movement to Fatah al-Islam merely because some of the group's sympathizers had withdrawn money from the Banque Mediterranée (owned by the Hariri family, and which Wafa al-Absi assimilated to the Future Movement) seems unwarranted. It would be tantamount to arguing that Western Union is responsible for the September 11, 2001, attacks because some of the suicide bombers withdrew money there before committing their crime. In fact, Fatah al-Islam robbed one of the Banque Mediterranée's branches, in Amyoun.

These claims are presented to introduce Abd al-Baqi's final revelation. As he begins this confession the camera zooms in for a close-up, underlining the importance of the moment. Drawing on memories from his time spent in Lebanon, he is about to reveal a hoax involving Shaker al-Absi's bodyguard—Muhammad Hussein al-Khaled (Abu Ayman). According to Abd al-Baqi, Abu Ayman "never ceased repeating out loud, 'Legally speaking, what would prevent the establishment of a relationship between Fatah al-Islam and a political actor?'" [20:00]. Abd al-Baqi's doubts pushed him, he claims, to entrap Abu Ayman into finally admitting that Fatah al-Islam "served as a cover for a political party" [20:42]. Yet, he emphasizes, al-Qaeda forbids such a practice: "That question is settled once and for all." Next, Yasser Inad expresses surprise at the contradiction between Abu Ayman's oft-stated intention of returning to Lebanon and the reality of his prolonged stay in Syria, for

[48] German authorities wanted Saddam al-Hajj Dib for his suspected role in the failed bombing of two passenger trains in Germany's Coblenz station on July 31, 2006; they had already arrested his brother. The bombing was motivated by the publication of caricatures of the prophet Muhammad in the Western press, and was also meant to avenge Zarqawi's death in June 2006. However, Saddam Dib's temporary incarceration in Syria was unrelated: he had been apprehended smuggling jihadi militants between Syria and Lebanon. On December 19, 2007, the Beirut criminal court gave Youssef al-Hajj Dib an *in absentia* life sentence with forced labor. The other bomber, Jihad Hamad, was sentenced to twelve years in prison. The court lifted the charges against Saddam Dib after his death in the May 2007 clashes with the army.

unknown reasons, "especially as Shaker al-Absi had always said that our efforts must be concentrated in Lebanon."

Abd al-Baqi then reappears to confirm that he had heard, in detail, from Yasser Inad, "that the organization depended on instructions and contacts which confirmed the identity of the political actor in question, in such a way that it was obvious to Fatah al-Islam members in Ayn al-Helweh that the political actor in question was none other than the Future Movement" [21:50]. This explains how the jihadi group could move about so easily "in regions under the influence of the Future Movement."

The film explains that in June 2008 the group considered an operation in Syria, aimed at a series of potential targets such as the regime's "security centers," Western diplomats, and military vehicles. They also considered robberies to fund these operations, with targets as ambitious as the Central Bank of Syria. At least two robberies targeted jewelry stores (one of which failed). Other robberies targeted gas stations (ranked according to the confessional identity of their owners and, more mundanely, according to how busy they seemed), but were never carried out despite a great deal of preparation (the witnesses go into a rather fastidious amount of detail on this).

Of course, if the Banque Méditerranée truly funded the group, as stated many times in the film, then it is difficult to understand the need to risk armed robberies in Damascus and its suburbs. Surely it would have been far simpler to transfer or smuggle the Lebanese funds to Syria, especially since crossing the border clandestinely seems to have been a routine matter.

Abd al-Baqi Mahmud al-Hussein's testimony includes further inconsistencies. He states that since 2007 he had been convinced that an external power might be able to infiltrate and exploit Fatah al-Islam. However, even though he claims he was close with Shaker al-Absi, he never warned the leader of this danger so as to prompt him to take precautions, as per al-Qaeda's principles.

The only tangible evidence Abd al-Baqi cites of his closeness to al-Absi is that he was nominated "head of security for Fatah al-Islam" [16:55/17:20]. To say the least, he does not seem to have taken his new duties very seriously. According to Abd al-Baqi, al-Absi "disappeared" in July 2008. He considers three possible explanations for this: a trip to Iraq, a return to Lebanon, or that security forces arrested him. The last scenario is probable because, as he explains, "Since we returned to Syria, al-Absi had been under heavy surveillance. We would get news from young men we had contacts with in the areas of Dhiabiyye and Hajar al-Aswad: the security forces were conducting intense surveillance activities, as if they wished to arrest everyone, not just one or two individuals. So we thought he had been arrested with his two companions. They left one day to go to a meeting and never came back." Abd al-Baqi testifies that he was aware of the surveillance measures targeting Shaker al-Absi, but despite his responsibilities as head of security, he did not try to find al-Absi a hiding place.

The rest of his testimony is schizophrenic: Abd al-Baqi—who, recall, is speaking in a setting staged by the Syrian security forces— relates how those forces likely arrested al-Absi. If this were the case, al-Absi should be on trial in Lebanon, where several courts had accused him of crimes. However, after contradictory assessments of these testimonies voiced by Lebanese political figures, no one apparently thought to formally request al-Absi's extradition from Syria following this seemingly convincing "confession within a confession."

What was Fatah al-Islam to do after al-Absi's disappearance? According to Abd al-Baqi, Muhammad 'Awad (a.k.a. Abu Muhammad), the "vice-emir" (second-in-command) of Fatah al-Islam in Lebanon, based at Ayn al-Helweh, designated the Syrian regime as the next target for a terrorist operation. This prospect displeased Abd al-Baqi, who thought Abu Muhammad's planning abilities "limited." The latter wished to strike at a regime "which has shown on several occasions that it was openly fighting the group; this had become obvious, it was becoming more and more apparent everyday, and everyone was speaking of it. This had become manifest, given that the security services had killed Abu al-Layth (Shaker al-Absi's son-in-law), as well as Abu Abd al-Rahman at the border between Syria and Iraq."

Incorporating undeniable facts—such as a Syrian border patrol's fatal shooting of Abu al-Layth in early May 2007—is calculated to retroactively justify the Syrian policy toward the jihadi phenomenon. The gray area of the recent past was replaced by the affirmation of a permanent antagonism between violent Islamism and the Syrian regime. Yet, the use of repression at a given time does not of course mean that it has always been in effect. Similarly, punishing one element of a network does not equate to eliminating all of it; targeting one jihadi network does not equate to eliminating all jihadi networks. The geographic location of Abu Muhammad's decision (the Ayn al-Helweh camp, close to the city of Sidon) seems to imply that it was made under a particular political influence—namely, the Future Movement, which had a solid militant base in this area, where, according to the Abu Inad's earlier testimony, "Fatah al-Islam could move about easily."

More inconsistencies appear in Abd al-Baqi's testimony. In March 2008, he received a letter announcing that Muhammad 'Awad had been designated "emir" of Fatah al-Islam in Ayn al-Helweh. He claims to have opposed this decision and demanded to be made leader of the organization. A heated discussion ensued between him and Abu Ayman (designated as Muhammad 'Awad's main representative within the group). In the end, he agreed to acknowledge the decision formally, but he admitted to being "unable to work on this basis." This decision appears to be in line with his previously stated conviction to "not accept ambivalence in theological issues." But the remainder of his testimony contradicts his position on this principle, for he states that he played a key role in all stages of preparation for the September 27 bombing. That the leadership of Fatah al-Islam in Syria was entrusted to Abu Ayman, who formed his own consultative council (*majlis al-shura*) and did not include Abd al-Baqi in it, was another personal affront to the latter, but, oddly enough, it did not lead to his withdrawal from the group.

The end of the documentary concerns technical aspects of the car bombings, in particular how the network managed to procure the explosives that were used. Then more footage of the crime scene is shown, after which we hear the documentary's last words, spoken by Abd al-Baqi. He seems suddenly to realize how appalling his actions were and expresses regret for the death of innocent victims, "among whom could have been some of my own relatives."

This attack is a turning point in the Syrian regime's policy toward Islamist movements. Syria was now gradually reintegrating into international relations, thanks to both a more conciliatory Western diplomatic approach following the French (2007) and American (2008) presidential elections, and the Saudi regime's efforts to reconcile Arab states in the face of the Iranian threat. These developments prompted a shift in the Syrian regime's rhetoric. It announced its intention to "resecularize" Syrian society by regulating the religious expressions of Sunni Islam more strictly and banning secondary school teachers and university students from wearing the *niqab* (face veil) in public educational institutions.[49]

At the end of 2008, the Syrian regime no longer needed to advertise its ability to cause trouble in the region for several reasons. Its leaders, having endured five years of regional turbulence in Iraq and Lebanon, now had renewed confidence in their regime's longevity. The controversial election of President Mahmud Ahmadinejad in Iran had reaffirmed the country's role as a regional mediator. Syria also appeared immune to accusations by the UN international tribunal in charge of investigating the assassination of Rafiq al-Hariri. In addition, its former adversaries in the Future Movement appealed to Syria to help preempt the threat of a Hezbollah coup de force—after the latter movement had become the sole party accused in this matter, according to rumors skillfully disseminated to the Western press. American diplomats also courted Syria in preparation for the difficult resumption of the Israeli-Palestinian peace process. At this point, Syrian leaders felt their position on the regional scene had become stronger, and their vital interests were no longer threatened.

An essential factor of the regime's survival in the late 2000s was the comparison it proudly presented to foreign powers, between itself and other, worse nuisances. Not only was it no longer the "worst regional threat"—the Iranian president now had that label—but it was able to point to an "even worse threat" within its own society, the jihadi menace. If the Syrian regime were to disappear, the state would disappear along with it, inaugurating a period of chaos.

---

[49] "Syria bans the wearing of the niqab in Universities," *Le Monde*, July 19, 2010.

CHAPTER 6

The Failure to Create a Lasting Support Base for the Syrian Insurrection

To pro-independence Sunni elites in Lebanon, the Syrian uprising presented a unique chance to right the unfavorable domestic position in which they had found themselves ever since Hezbollah became the country's main political and military force in the 1990s. Sa'ad al-Hariri, whose father was assassinated by Hezbollah's operational apparatus, would benefit greatly were the Syrian regime to fall. Potentially, it could be his path back into power and a way for Lebanon to ditch the Syrian-Iranian military agenda. In 2011, at the beginning of what was then called the "Syrian revolution," many in Lebanon and abroad thought the time was ripe to help the insurgents topple the Assad regime for good.

On the other hand, for the Hariris, not acting would mean giving free rein to the radicalized religious networks of Tripoli. These sat ready to exploit the Sunni institutional elites' inaction in order to proclaim themselves defenders of their confessional community in greater Syria. If their religious enthusiasm was not contained, it might lead to excessively violent behavior by jihadis, such as would threaten the cohesion of the Sunni community. The Fatah al-Islam episode had already made clear that the Syrian regime was fully capable of exploiting the jihadi threat within Sunni ranks to discredit all of its components. So, if Tripoli's Salafis were to strike out on their own, they risked playing right into Damascus's hands, and being used to damage the legitimate concerns of the anti-Assad coalition.

Lebanese pro-independence elites had to take action, but they had to do so as discreetly as possible in order to avoid the accusation that they were importing the Syrian conflict into Lebanon. Compounding their difficulties was the fact that the Lebanese army was not a neutral participant. In fact, Hezbollah closely monitored Lebanese intelligence institutions—both the military and the General Security forces.[1] From 2005 onward, the ISF's intelligence department was the only institutional body able to elude the growing influence of Hezbollah and its Iranian backers in the country.

Finally, all protagonists, whether opponents or supporters of the Syrian regime, prioritized control over the city of Homs and its environs. For Bashar al-Assad, Homs was key because it commanded the territorial continuity between Damascus and the coastal mountains (Jabal Ansarieh), where Alawites had their geographical stronghold. For Hezbollah, there was a military need to connect the Alawite north of Syria—the mountains and the coast—with the Shi'ite south, in the Beqaa plain. Accordingly, Hezbollah's military involvement aimed at maintaining a geographic link with the Alawite region and its access to the sea. This would preserve supply routes for its weapons should Damascus fall to the rebels. Anticipating this strategy, the Syrian regime's opponents on both sides of the border tried to frustrate establishment of this strategic barrier. Their immediate concern was thus to fuse North Lebanon with the Syrian insurrection, creating a zone of Sunni militant mobilization in which men and weapons would be able to circulate freely.

These two objectives were not simply questions of military strategy. They represented existential threats for the parties involved. Establishing a sphere of Sunni solidarity between North Lebanon and Homs would threaten military corridors between the Lebanese Beqaa and the zones controlled by the Syrian regime. Hezbollah would be militarily isolated, something that the group and its Iranian ally deemed unacceptable. It would also deprive the Ala-

[1] This is why the army did not intervene when the SSNP (the Syrian Social Nationalist Party, intrinsically allied to the Syrian regime) kidnapped Syrian opposition figures in Tripoli, Wadi Khaled, or the Akkar region, in North Lebanon.

wites of any strategic depth, reducing their territory to a mirror image of the Lebanese Forces' "Christian stronghold," to which the latter retreated after the Mountain War in the Chouf in 1983. Conversely, establishing a durable Alawite power base in the northwest of *Bilad al-Sham*, connected to Hezbollah by a strategic corridor running through Homs, would surround Sunni groups in North Lebanon. Dominated by a militarized Alawite stronghold to the North, Hezbollah fighters to the East, and the Lebanese army (under Hezbollah's influence) in their own field of action, their existence would become tenuous. The Assad family's multiple natural allies in the region—the Alawites of Rif'at Eid's Arab Democratic Party, Christian militiamen affiliated to Suleiman Frangieh's Marada movement, Aounist militants, SSNP militiamen, and Hezbollah-allied Sunni networks—would further decrease their odds of survival.

A grasp of local geopolitics was thus necessary to understanding the political and military aims of the actors involved in the conflict. Through its many transnational and regional networks, North Lebanon was to play an important role in helping the Syrian insurgency in Homs in 2011 and 2012. As a consequence of its involvement, it also fell victim to radical jihadi Syrian and Iraqi networks aiming to widen the conflict to Lebanon. Fighting the Assad regime in the region once again raised the issue of who would control Sunni Islam in the Levant. In this chapter, I propose to describe and analyze how this regional game accelerated the fragmentation of Sunni politics, showing that what happened in North Lebanon could serve as a paradigm for understanding the whole Sunni predicament in Syria and Iraq.

The Beginnings of a Solidarity Movement

From the beginning of the Syrian insurrection, in spring 2011, Sunni actors close to the March 14 Movement began to mobilize in support of their Syrian coreligionists. Welcoming Syrian refugees in North Lebanon was a given from the outset, as confessional and tribal bonds of solidarity already extended across the border. Indeed, all the Lebanese families of the Wadi Khaled Valley (the Bayt Shebab, al-Muhammad, Slayman, and al-Sumaydi tribes) had relatives on the other side of the border, in Homs or Talkalakh. As the fighting spread to other areas, the refugee flows broadened to include other towns—Baniyas, Tartus, Latakia, Jazirat Arwad, Hama, Aleppo, and Rif Dimashq (the "Damascus countryside" area). Within a few months, hundreds of Syrian families flooded Tripoli's working-class areas: Tabbaneh, Qubbeh, Abu Samra, and "the market" neighborhood. Their presence has familiarized their Lebanese neighbors with the highly esteemed Syrian sheikh Adnan al-'Arour, regularly seen excoriating the Assad regime on Saudi TV channels Wisal or Safa.

The people of Tripoli readily identified with these victims of Syrian repression, being themselves all too familiar with the phenomenon. Sometimes the drama even featured the same actors. For instance, the military intelligence officer in charge of repressing Hama in the spring of 2011 was General Muhammad Muflih, who was head of Syrian intelligence in Tripoli in the mid-1980s, when he personally supervised the arrest of hundreds of the city's inhabitants. There was also much comment on the reported death of Jami' Jami' in Deir al-Zor.[2] He was the fearsome second-in-command to Rustum Ghazaleh, in charge of Syrian military intelligence in Lebanon at the time of Rafiq al-Hariri's assassination. The North Lebanese are also familiar with Abd al-Latif Fahd, in charge of the Aleppo regional branch of Syrian military intelligence since 2009. A close associate of Rustum Ghazaleh, Fahd had directed Syrian military intelligence in North Lebanon in the 2000s.

The shared experience of deprivation and social distress has brought North Lebanon's Sunnis and part of the Syrian population closer together. Muhammad, from Hama, described the uprising as a revolt of the poor, explaining that in his region "the Ba'ath party didn't help anyone any more" and "there was no healthcare to be found at all in public hospitals."[3] In addition, he mentioned the presence of Iranian soldiers among Syrian security forces as early as September 2011: "I spoke with them, I heard their accent when they spoke Arabic. They were wearing civilian clothing. It was Hezbollah who had brought them there [into Syria]." In Tripoli at the time, a rumor circulated that the Lebanese Alawite-majority

---

[2] Public Syrian TV released information about his death at the hands of a sniper on October 17, 2013, at Deir al-Zor.

[3] Interview with Muhammad, from Hama, Tripoli, September 3, 2011.

village of Mas'udiyye, in the Akkar region, had sent several dozen men across the border to fight with the Syrian *shabbiha* (Alawite pro-regime militiamen). Hezbollah fighters wounded in Syria were reportedly treated in al-Imam hospital of Baalbek, where they "were allowed no visitors." In 2011, such testimonials proliferated in the region, suggesting that the Syrian insurrection was extending to the entire Syrian-Lebanese sphere and that it was a fight against the same enemy: the Syrian regime, its ally Iran, and their local auxiliaries, *shabbiha* in Syria and Hezbollah members in both countries.

The North Lebanese with military experience took responsibility for protecting the most exposed Syrian opposition members. They did this at the beginning with the utmost discretion. Those in charge were "Sheikh" Kana'an Naji, who had been trained for clandestine action during his time in Yasser Arafat's Fatah movement (see chapter 3), and Colonel Amid Hammud, who had taken part in the formation of the Afwaj regiments in 2006, in hopes of deterring Hezbollah from armed action against the Future Movement (in vain). A former Lebanese army colonel in his fifties, Hammud had taken part in clandestine operations and was rumored to be close to the Lebanese Muslim Brotherhood. Both men prioritized efforts to protect Syrian opposition members wanted by the authorities in Damascus, such as Sheikh Anas Suwayd, a well-known Sufi figure from Homs, who was ferried back and forth between Tripoli and the Akkar region under Amid Hammud's protection. Former MP Khaled Daher, a trusted ally of Saudi Arabia in North Lebanon and a self-proclaimed opponent of the Muslim Brotherhood (he had been a member of their parliamentary bloc until he left the Brotherhood in 2000), as well as Future MP Mu'in al-Mar'abi, very close to Wissam al-Hassan, also provided protection to Syrian activists in the region.

Extending the Struggle to New Areas

Uprisings in Homs neighborhoods motivated pro-independence Sunni Lebanese to intervene decisively as early as spring 2011. Although this helped Homs resist the Assad regime's war machine for nearly two years, civilian activists from the *tansiqiyyat* (coordination groups) raised the criticism that this was a turning point in a previously peaceful protest movement. To some, this episode precipitated a series of detrimental changes for which the protagonists of the Lebanese intervention were responsible: "the militarization of protest, the sectarianization of society and the ever-more-visible involvement of Salafi groups."[4]

It is no easy task to describe the intricacies of North Lebanese involvement in Homs and its surroundings at that period, first because those activities were underground, and second because there was constant struggle for the control of the help (ammunition, medical supplies) offered among Syrians. In the first months of the insurgency, aid was conveyed to the Free Syrian Army (FSA) officers in the region. Hammud and to a lesser extent Kana'an Naji sent military aid consisting of light weaponry (Kalashnikovs, RPGs, and ammunition) to the Syrian insurgency's Khaled bin al-Walid Battalion in Homs. The battalion had been set up in Homs by Abd al-Razzaq Tlass, a former officer who defected from the Syrian army in June of 2011.[5] Tlass had grown out his beard, apparently as a manifest sign of piety, after he left the Assad regime's forces (in which any such religious markers are forbidden). He denied holding Salafi views and declared himself in agreement with Sheikh Anas Suwayd's Sufi orientation. At the beginning of the insurgency, he held significant (though not exclusive) authority over several hundred combatants, a majority of whom were army deserters. During his missions in Lebanon (carried out by night for security reasons), Tlass explained to his Lebanese contacts that his units lacked the RPGs needed to destroy regular army tanks. The price of these weapons on the local black market (over US$800 a piece) made it difficult to meet his request for more. Controversial among the insurgents, often accused of searching publicity for himself, Tlass was dismissed from the Khaled bin al-Walid battalion in November of 2011 and forced to set up the al-Faruq Battalion in

---

[4] Interviews with *tansiqiyyat* facilitators from Damascus and Idlib, conducted in Cairo in July 2012.

[5] Born in Rastan, Abd al-Razzaq Tlass was a lieutenant (*mulazim awwal*) in Der'a, in the 5th infantry division, when he deserted the army in June 2011 at the age of twenty-six after watching the military crush peaceful demonstrations. He then went to Rastan, north of Homs, where he formed *katibat* Khaled ibn Walid together with seven officers and some forty NCOs. Later defections of higher-ranking officers prompted Tlass to form *katibat* al-Faruq in July 2011. See Jonathan Littell, *Carnets de Homs* (Gallimard: Paris, 2012), 70–76.

Baba 'Amr.[6] This sequence of events became quite common. Many of the insurgents formed new battalions if they happened to lose influence in the ones to which they had formerly belonged.[7]

There is no doubt that Lebanese pro-March 14 parties had to deal with a highly divided Syrian opposition. In November 2011, the Free Syrian Army general Riyad al-As'ad (the FSA's nominal commander), whose relations with Tlass were strained, allegedly met with Amid Hammud and Kana'an Naji in Halba, North Lebanon. During their discussion, al-As'ad reportedly insisted they channel military and financial aid to the FSA to prevent the proliferation of small, uncontrollable groups. One of the FSA's initial founders, Colonel Ammar al-Wawi, who had close ties with the most secular groups in the Syrian insurgency, also met with North Lebanese backers in the fall of 2011 in order to coordinate between North Lebanon and Aleppo, Idlib, and Homs.

These relationships suggest that the first Lebanese networks formed to aid the Syrian insurrection were products of more or less well-coordinated local initiatives. But at the end of 2011, they began to benefit from the involvement of Wissam al-Hassan, the head of the ISF's intelligence department, a Hariri family confidant, and an expert on Tripoli's political scene. His department's decisive role in advancing the international investigation into Rafiq al-Hariri's assassination made him a target for the *al-Akhbar* newspaper, run by an editorial team of intellectuals close to Hezbollah and to Christian supporters of Michel Aoun, who follow a political line matching Iran's positions on Lebanon. On the sensitive issue of aid to the Syrian insurrection, al-Hassan was seconded by the efficient forty-year-old colonel Khaled Hammud (no relation to Amid), who resides in seclusion at ISF headquarters, near the Hôtel-Dieu hospital in Beirut. He does this to frustrate assassination

---

[6] Another noteworthy Syrian commander, known as Abu 'Arab (his real name is Walid al-Abdallah, from Deir al-Zor, a former colonel in the regular army), had at least equivalent responsibilities as a leader in the al-Faruq battalions until he was wounded, evacuated through Lebanon, and hospitalized in Qatar.

[7] For a meticulous description of Syrian military opposition in 2011 and 2012, see Joseph Holliday, *Syria's Armed Opposition*, Middle East Security Report 3 (March 2012), Institute for the Study of War.

attempts, such as the operations that killed his colleague Wissam Eid in 2008[8] and his boss four years later.

The very nature of clandestine operations makes it difficult to piece together an accurate picture of how they function. As General Wissam al-Hassan allocated his aid, he prioritized the most faithful and most professional actors, apparently judging that Amid Hammud, Kana'an Naji, and Khaled Daher met these criteria. Amid Hammud took charge of facilitating the armed battalion members' recognition of the Syrian National Council (SNC) (at this period, it was struggling to secure recognition in Syria). This former military man also managed diplomatic relations and valuable contacts with the embassies of Qatar and Saudi Arabia in Beirut, which suggests that he participated, in the full sense of the word, in the Sunni solidarity networks of North Lebanon and was not a passive recipient of aid from the Hariris.

In late 2011, Wissam al-Hassan decided to put young Uqab Saqr, elected to parliament on one of the Hariri's lists in 2009 in the Zahle district, in charge of an Istanbul-based operational center for weapons and funds distribution.[9] Unlike Amid Hammud, who relied on a variety of channels, Uqab Saqr worked exclusively for Sa'ad al-Hariri and Wissam al-Hassan. The choice of Istanbul for this center was probably a response to the necessity of escaping the reach of Syria's and Iran's very active allies in Lebanon. It may also be related to a perceived danger in relying exclusively upon northern Lebanese networks, whose main leaders were eager to maintain at least partial autonomy from their patron.

This ambitious operation was beyond any doubt planned under the supervision of the Saudi secret services, anxious not to be seen publicly interfering in Syrian domestic affairs. Apprised of the local realities of the revolt by the early refugees and anti-Assad combatants sheltered in North Lebanon, Lebanese Sunni officials shared their knowledge of the Syrian military situation with their Saudi counterparts in exchange for a share in the leadership of the Syrian uprising. As for the Saudi officials, thanks to their Lebanese allies,

---

[8] Wissam Eid had played a considerable role in analyzing the phone calls that led to identifying the network responsible for Rafik al-Hariri's assassination. Eid himself was murdered on January, 25, 2008, in Beirut.

[9] In its September 18, 2012 issue, *Time* magazine was the first press organ to mention a "chamber of military operations" led by Uqab Saqr in Istanbul.

they had dual access to the Syrian theater of operations. One route was coordinated by Uqab Saqr and went via the Turkish-Syrian border; the other, under Wissam al-Hassan, used the Lebanese-Syrian border. This meant that they did not have to depend solely on access through the Turkish border, already used by support networks in Qatar.

In November 2012, the pro-Iranian *al-Akhbar* started putting excerpts from Uqab Saqr's phone conversations with *katibat* commanders in the vicinity of Aleppo on their website. The paper aimed to show by this that Sa'ad al-Hariri had given up trying to "dissociate" Lebanon from the events going on in Syria, despite his public commitment to do so. Moreover, for Syrian regime sycophants, who since 2011 had been accustomed to accusing Qatar and Saudi Arabia of funding a regional and international plot to sow chaos in Syria, such revelations offered a timely confirmation of their conspiracy theories. The tapes of the various conversations successively put on line show the young MP totally absorbed in operations for the delivery of military equipment. In one conversation, probably pertaining to his efforts to secure the release of nine Lebanese Shi'ite "pilgrims" taken hostage by a Syrian *katibat*, he complains about shipments being blocked, voices Sa'ad al-Hariri's impatience and assures the party on the other end, Lu'ay al-Miqdad, media spokesman for the FSA, that he is keeping his boss Sa'ad al-Hariri informed of the situation "minute by minute, hour by hour."[10]

Uqab Saqr's choice of aid recipients soon became a topic of controversy within the ranks of the insurgency. According to *Time*, which quoted "FSA sources, prominent activists and members of the Istanbul control room," Uqab Saqr was "mainly responsible for designating the representatives of Syria's 14 provinces to whom the Istanbul center would funnel small batches of light weapons—Kalashnikov rifles, BKC machine guns, rocket-propelled grenade launchers and ammunition—to reach FSA groups operating in each area."[11]

An "influential U.S.-based Syrian activist" complained that "these representatives did not have a presence on the ground" and "were

[10] See *al-Akhbar*, December 3, 2012.
[11] *Time* (see note 9 above).

not known."[12] Criticism was thus almost instantly directed at the Lebanese MP, already inherently guilty in the eyes of some Syrian opponents due to his religious affiliation (he is a Shi'ite). The young MP had experienced the weight of regional Arab rivalries. The operations room headed by Uqab Saqr thus served as an instrument in a Saudi policy that aimed to weaken Qatar's role among existing military councils. In late August 2012, in Antakya, Saudi Arabia had moreover backed the stillborn project of forming a Syrian National Army to be led by General Muhammad Hussein Hajj 'Ali, former chief of the military academy in Damascus. Most of the military councils rejected the initiative, disputing the legitimacy of such outside authority. At first in favor of the Saudi plan, Colonel Qassem Sa'ad al-Din, chief of the Homs military council until March 2012, had to step down after sustained harsh criticism from katibat officials.

Uqab Saqr's activism coincided with Bandar bin Sultan's growing influence within the Saudi decision-making apparatus after his appointment as chief of the Saudi intelligence services on July 19, 2012. The energetic Saudi prince, known for his strong enmity toward Iran and Syria, was allegedly working closely with Wissam al-Hassan. In August 9, 2012, the latter arrested former pro-Assad minister Michel Samaha. Caught on video without his knowledge, Samaha was accused of smuggling explosives from Syria to Lebanon in league with Syrian intelligence chief Ali Mamluk, with the intent of carrying out bombing attacks in North Lebanon.

During that period, Sa'ad al-Hariri's strategy seems to have been oriented in such a way as to broaden the political spectrum of aid beneficiaries beyond Islamists. Receiving direct support from the Hariri family did not compromise one's ideological orientation. A young engineer who had worked in Damascus, originally from the Syrian village of Zabadani near the Lebanese border, was grateful for the aid he received from al-Hariri to cover his purchase of light weaponry, as it spared him having to "request aid from Qatar" and "betray his secular convictions by turning to the Islamists."[13]

---

[12] Ibid.

[13] Interview with young Syrian opposition activists, Cairo, June 2012.

Whereas Hariri's envoys privileged FSA officers, anti-Assad networks in North Lebanon supported the most effective Syrian forces on the ground. Among those who benefitted from this help was Umar al-Buqa'i (called "al-Gidr"). In his forties, al-Gidr was smuggling oil and cigarettes before the March 2011 Syrian insurrection. With others, he founded the al-Faruq *katibat* in Homs's Baba 'Amr neighborhood in July 2011. According to an inhabitant of Baba 'Amr, al-Gidr and his friends knew the trails across the border, and could easily convey guns and ammunition from North Lebanon to Homs: "This gave them an edge over defecting army officers. Those who displayed guns had an immediate effect on society."[14]

The former smugglers rapidly declared themselves Salafis, and started to enroll local youth distrustful of former army officers, even those originating from Homs.[15] One Lebanese militant who gave ammunitions to al-Gidr remembers that "the latter's group was much more organized and efficient than the others, which explained our preference for him."[16]

Growing divisions within the insurgency's ranks in Homs, as well as Naji's own preferences, might explain why, in 2012, Naji decided to help the Tawhid Brigade (Liwa' al-Tawhid) in Aleppo. This well-organized, disciplined outfit, entrenched in certain districts east of the city and much appreciated by the local population, seemed like an Aleppo equivalent of Naji's own networks in Tripoli. Its leader, Abd al-Qader Saleh, was a pious merchant close to the Tabligh, a transnational pietistic network originating in India.[17] The Tawhid Brigade was not Salafi, and its leaders had previously operated under the umbrella of the Joint FSA Headquarters in Aleppo.

Far from being outdone, Sheikh Da'i al-Islam, as well as Sheikh Salem al-Rafi'i, were relying on their own transnational Qatari and Kuwaiti Salafi networks. Both of them chose to help the "Haraki Salafism" current embodied by the Ahrar al-Sham organization

---

[14] Interview with a Syrian exile, North Lebanon, September 2013.

[15] In order to overcome this distrust, some ex-officers had no choice but to declare themselves Salafi. This was the case for Abou Arab al-Zein, an ex-lieutenant who commanded the al-Huda *katibat* in al-Qusayr.

[16] Tripoli, May 2014.

[17] He was killed in a bombing in Aleppo in November of 2013.

(Freemen of the Levant), "which by June 2012 had become one of the most powerful insurgent organizations in the country."[18] Known for its proximity to Turkey and Qatar, Ahrar al-Sham "never integrated FSA structures, but cooperated on the ground with the latter's provincial military councils."[19] Da'i al-Islam developed contacts with Ahrar al-Sham leader Hassan 'Abbud (Abu Abdallah al-Hamawi) and may have known him even before, during their common anti-US activities in Iraq after the invasion of the country in 2003. Da'i, as well as Salem al-Rafi'i, also coordinated some aid with Zahran 'Allush, a former Saydnaya prisoner who became the commander of the radical Salafi group Islam Battalion (*katibat al-islam*).

An attempt by actors close to Hariri to avoid Salafi entanglement is evidenced by their choice of those among the Syrian opponents who were accorded protection in North Lebanon. According the *amana*, in the sense of "guaranteeing the safety of a guest" (an ancient practice that goes back to tribal times in pre-Islam Arabia) could be a very sensitive matter. The question arose when Salafi sheikh Lu'ay al-Zu'bi, originally from Der'a (where the uprising began in March 2011), arrived in Lebanon in September of 2011. He combined all the attributes of the internationalist jihadi militant: a former "Arab Afghan" who had traveled to Peshawar in Pakistan as a volunteer for the anti-Soviet jihad in Afghanistan, he had next fought in Bosnia (in 1993) before spending some time in Khartoum at the same time as Osama bin Laden, in the late 1990s. In 2011, he claimed to represent a "democratic" form of Salafism, compatible with electoral practices and political pluralism.[20] He attributes this evolution to his having matured through his "experience in prison" of "cohabiting with detainees of very diverse political orientations." This sheikh had founded an organization with the rather interesting name, "The Believers Participate" (al-Mu'minun Yusharikun), and was looking for Western backing, arguing that he held a centrist position of equilibrium between opposition forces, and had "contacts in radical circles that would allow

---

[18] See Thomas Pierret, "Salafis at War in Syria: Logics of Fragmentation and Realignment," in Francesco Cavatorta and Fabio Merone, eds., *Salafism after the Arab Awakening: Contending with People's Power* (London: Hurst, 2014).

[19] Ibid.

[20] Interview with Sheikh Lu'ay al-Zu'bi, Tripoli, September 2011.

him to check the progress of al-Qaeda in Syria." He emphasized this role of containment of religious radicalism in order to obtain support from outside the country. Lu'ay al-Zu'bi has mentioned writing fatwas forbidding acts of aggression against churches in Syria (which implies that such acts did occur at the beginning of the Syrian revolution), and has approved addressing greetings to Christians on their religious holidays—while Egyptian Salafi sheikhs have mustered religious arguments to ban this practice. Thanks to a Tripolitan notable's social skills, he was invited to appear on al-'Arabiyya satellite TV on October 19, 2011, as the main guest on the program "Studio Beirut," but showed conservatism throughout the interview, never making eye contact with the presenter, journalist Gisele Khoury.

Before arriving in Lebanon, Lu'ay al-Zu'bi had been given a telephone number and told that the number's holder would give him *amana*. Unfortunately for him, the holder's name was none other than Amid Hammud, who would not jeopardize his standing by vouching for a figure with such a controversial past, in spite of his semi-repentant attitude. Hammud told his friends in the FSA and the Syrian Brotherhood that, in light of his past, Sheikh al-Zu'bi was not to be trusted.

Without any protection, the sheikh constantly risked arrest by Lebanese military intelligence and subsequent transfer to the Syrian intelligence services. It was MP Khaled Daher who finally provided him with protection until he could move on to Egypt. Lu'ay al-Zu'bi's experience shows the harsh reality of political relationships in Lebanon: one's actual arrest does not depend on being charged with a crime, on a legal investigation, or on evidence justifying an interrogation. It remains contingent on the military and political balance of power. The security services, in turn, evaluate these factors before taking (or not taking) action.

The Odyssey of the *Lutfallah II*

On April 27, 2012, the Lebanese army's marine forces stopped a ship off the coast of Tripoli and boarded it for inspection. They found a variety of weapons from Libya—mortar shells (8mm and 120mm), artillery shells, machine guns, precision rifles (Dragonovs), ammunition, RPG launchers, and an anti-aircraft system. The ship's cargo was destined for Syrian insurgents defending Homs. *Al-Akhbar* attributed this initiative "to a Tripolitan figure who went to Egypt to meet with leaders of one of the Libyan militant groups, along with some members of the Syrian National Council."[21] In fact, two Syrian entrepreneurs who had lived in Saudi Arabia prior to the insurrection had prepared the shipment, one providing the ship, the other the cargo. They obtained the weapons free of charge in Libya through the mediation of religious figures in Benghazi, including several Salafi sheikhs.[22] According to one of the organizers:

> The Lutfallah II never entered the port of Alexandria [in Egypt, on the way to its destination]; its papers were merely registered in the port. . . . The ship started out from Benghazi, heading to Mersin, Turkey. There were two ships, in fact: a passenger ship and a freighter carrying the weapons. As they reached Lebanese territorial waters near Tripoli, the passenger ship was to proceed to the port of Tripoli for repairs, although it actually needed none. As attention was focused on it, the second ship was to discreetly unload its cargo into the water . . . three containers fitted with floats . . . small fishing boats from the area were supposed to collect them. But our plan was uncovered, probably by Syrian fishermen of Baniyas who had heard of the operation from the port of Alexandria.[23]

The *Lutfallah II*'s failed journey foreshadowed what some members of the Syrian opposition were expecting North Lebanon to become: a strategic beachhead to supply humanitarian and military aid to the insurgent forces. To one of the organizers of this operation, transforming this region into "a Sunni safe zone through which arms could be conveyed, by sea," was a military necessity. If *Lutfallah II* had succeeded, it would have put the Syrian opposition brigades on equal footing with Hezbollah, supply-wise, in the fight for Homs and its environs. Syrian opposition members and

---

[21] *Al-Akhbar*, April 28, 2012.

[22] In February 2012, the Libyan capital was adorned with a multitude of slogans supporting the Syrian revolution and slamming Arab and international powerlessness to stop the massacre of civilian populations (observation by the author, Tripoli, Libya, February 2012).

[23] Interview with one of the two organizers of the weapons shipment, May 2013.

Sunni Lebanese forces agreed that Tripoli's fate was integral to al-Qusayr and Homs, in Syria. The old slogan *talazum al-masarayn* (the inseparability of the two [countries'] fates), repeated ad nauseam in the late 1990s by Syrian regime spokespersons to accelerate absorption of the Lebanese entity, was used this time to express the shared fate of the Lebanese and Syrian populations at the hands of the same dictatorship. A Lebanese protagonist in a support network for the Syrian insurrection described the "indissoluble bond" as follows:

> If al-Qusayr falls, Homs will fall too. Then Tripoli will be under direct threat. All our leaders are aware of it. We know that Hezbollah will try to take Tripoli over at all costs: by starting a war of Sunnis against other Sunnis, by sending in the army, by going in it itself.[24]

Their similar interpretations of the situation did not, however, preclude major tactical differences between Syrian insurgents and Lebanese actors. The Syrian opponents who organized the *Lutfallah II* operation did not coordinate with the Sunni operational leadership in Tripoli. Indeed, the potential for such a massive operation to shift the local status quo might well have induced leaders in Tripoli to veto it. They had made a limited, albeit vital, commitment to send light weaponry, munitions, and medication to the Syrian rebels, supplies that are of considerable military importance in urban warfare. Playing this role—limited though it was—required them to maintain a low profile inside Lebanon, and to do nothing that might justify a large-scale intervention by the army or Hezbollah. Only a substantial shift in the status quo would cause them to change their approach.

Preoccupied with open revolt, certain Syrian rebel leaders were less sensitive to maintaining internal balances of power in Lebanon. Thus, they had been advocating the opening of a Lebanese

---

[24] Tripoli, May 2013. The leader of a Syrian *katibat* (brigade) echoed this idea in the following statement of solidarity: "I am trying to get the Lebanese to understand what the fall of Homs and al-Qusayr would mean for them: it would be the fall of Tripoli, as well. . . . If Hezbollah triumphs in al-Qusayr, it will take Tripoli. This is why we must anchor this idea in their minds [the minds of the Lebanese], the idea of Tripoli, the Sunni citadel, 'Trablus al-Sham [Tripoli of Greater-Syria].' This idea has a historical reality to it. I am trying to get them to understand they are in danger, that their fate depends on Homs."

front to alleviate some of the military pressure on Homs and draw Hezbollah's men back to their own soil. A Syrian leader summarized this strategy of *tawrit* (involvement):

> My goal is to bring the Syrian and Lebanese fighters under my command to Tripoli, to open a front there. I want them to return with heavy weaponry. The war must be extended to Tripoli.[25]

Hezbollah's Role

Hezbollah's intervention in North Lebanon predated the Syrian crisis. Since the party's foundation, it has taken great care to establish friendly contacts among northern Sunnis so as to neutralize the sectarian divide within the Muslim community. An additional objective was to prevent North Lebanon from becoming a Sunni equivalent of southern Lebanon: a semi-autonomous and militarized zone that placed confessional elites in the strongest possible position from which to negotiate the community's collective rights at the national level.

Hezbollah's involvement in Syria developed gradually. The beginning of the Syrian revolt in March 2011 initially prompted its affiliates to increase surveillance in North Lebanon. This enabled SSNP cadres to abduct members of the Syrian opposition in the area. In 2012 a new phase began, in which Hezbollah forces initiated military operations on Syrian territory. The Iranian heads of the elite al-Quds unit within the Pasdaran (Iranian Revolutionary Guard) incited Hezbollah to take action, and it did so in force, following the July 18, 2012, attack on Syrian National Security offices in Damascus. That evening, the movement's secretary-general, Sayyid Hassan Nasrallah, paid tribute to the "martyred leaders" of the Syrian security forces killed in the attack—Asif Shawqat, Dawud Rajha, and Hassan Turkmani—calling them "comrades-in-arms," without whom "there would have been no Resistance in Lebanon and Palestine." In his speech at the commemoration of the sixth anniversary of the 2006 "divine victory" over Israel,

---

[25] Interview with a *katibat* leader, Cairo, May 2013.

Nasrallah recalled that Syria was not only a "strategic corridor between Iran and the Resistance in Lebanon and Palestine," but also played the active role of a "foundation on which the Resistance could rely," as demonstrated by the "Syrian-made" missiles Hezbollah fired on Haifa during the 2006 war.

On this occasion, Nasrallah revived a trope of the Resistance ideology: to *muqawimin* ("resistance fighters"), local contexts only matter in terms of their ability to preserve a regional system dominated by Iran and based on a military zero-sum game with Israel. On the other hand, the *muqatil* (combatant), as embodied in the Syrian FSA brigades, for example, is primarily concerned with the preservation of his local freedom from external threats. To Nasrallah, anyone who was not in the Resistance camp was automatically in the camp of the "Zionist entity." He had no choice but to use Gaza and Lebanon to formulate yet another legitimization of the Syrian regime, even if Syria has not allowed any semblance of democratization at home, and to gloss over his own movement's involvement in domestic repression inside Syria.

According to members of FSA brigades, Hezbollah units specializing in urban warfare then deployed to Damascus, Aleppo, and Idlib. In addition, the Party of God sent forces to guard the Shi'ite mausoleum of Sayyida Zaynab and several state buildings in Damascus, including the state television premises.

Hezbollah also paid close attention to the northern Syrian-Lebanese border. As early as spring 2012, Hezbollah combatants deployed along the frontier, from the Lebanese Hermel district to the Syrian town of al-Qusayr, situated ten kilometers away from the border and twenty-odd kilometers southwest of Homs. For the Syrian regime and Hezbollah, the objective was to reestablish control of Homs and al-Qusayr (through which vital supplies for the Homsi resistance were transported) to protect supply and communication lines between the Beqaa plain and the Alawite mountain stronghold. After for a time staunchly denying their involvement in the area, Hezbollah's media began to publicize the names of their casualties. In October 2012, the movement organized a funeral service for Commander Ali Hussein Nassif (Abu 'Abbas) in the village of Buday, west of Baalbek, "who was killed in Syria while accomplishing his jihad duty," according to the elliptic expression of the party's media.[26] Rebels allegedly planted an explosive device on a road near al-Qusayr that his convoy would travel, having received intelligence from an informant inside the regular Syrian army that an important regime figure was to follow that route. An exiled member of the Deir Ba'alba Revolutionaries' Brigade (*katibat thuwar deir ba'alba*) in Cairo confirmed that Hezbollah also played a decisive role in the fall of the neighborhood of Deir Ba'alba, northwest of Homs, to pro-Assad forces on December 28, 2012.

Syrian opposition videos also underlined the presence of Hezbollah militiamen in the region. For instance, in May 2013, the al-Qusayr Media Center (*al-markaz al-i'lami fi al-qusayr*) uploaded an account of an al-Huda Brigade ambush against Hezbollah combatants at a location that was "west of the Orontes River," according to the group's spokesperson.[27] The indefatigable Hadi al-'Abdallah himself, who has become the major satellite TV channel's chief correspondent in Syria since the beginning of the conflict, described the footage as evidence "irrefutably proving" Hezbollah's presence in the region. To support this claim, he produced identification documents taken from one of the Party of God's captured fighters, Muhammad Hassan al-Miqdad, born on April 15, 1973, and a member of Hezbollah's Liaison and Coordination Committee (*lajnat al-irtibat wa al-tansiq*). This man was also carrying a pass bearing the phrase, "To Whom It May Concern: please facilitate the safe passage of the bearer of this card," which bears witness to the freedom of movement Hezbollah's operatives enjoy enjoyed in the Syrian-Lebanese region.

This testimonial is part of a broader public relations war, which is just as ferocious as the real war. Its discourse is composed of a combination of the true and the false. According to a member of the Syrian opposition in contact with the leader of the al-Huda Brigade, the ambush actually took place much farther north, near the

---

[26] On October 1, 2012, the *al-'ahd* (The pledge) newspaper's website stated rather briefly "that Hezbollah and the inhabitants of Buday village and the surrounding area held a funeral for martyr and leader Ali Hussein Nassif (Abu 'Abbas) who was killed while accomplishing his jihad duty." The same phrase appeared on the website, http://moqawama .org/ (accessed October, 5, 2012).

[27] The video is available on YouTube. http://www.youtube.com/watch?V=HJIcltvgJs (accessed May 30, 2013). Al-Miqdad's pass and his Lebanese ID were reproduced in the Lebanese newspaper *Al-Liwa'* on May 15, 2013.

city of Hama. Moreover, Muhammad Hassan al-Miqdad was killed in the attack, a fact not mentioned in the video, perhaps in order to avoid jeopardizing any prisoner exchanges. It seems that in this case, the al-Qusayr Media Center may have shifted the geographical location of the fighting so as to soften the harsh reality of the rather bleak military situation in the al-Qusayr area. There, Hezbollah is indeed present on the ground, and was inexorably tightening its control of the surrounding villages when the video was uploaded.

Hezbollah is also involved on Syrian battlefields because of its need to secure its arms stocks on Syrian territory and maintain a strategic sanctuary in "safe" areas there. Moving the materiel to Lebanon would carry heavy risks, as demonstrated by the January 29, 2013 Israeli air strike on the Jemraya site in Syria.

Hezbollah and the al-Quds Force

Within Hezbollah, it is the Jihad Council, the command body of the Islamic Resistance, that makes military decisions. Hezbollah is but the political manifestation of the Islamic Resistance and is subordinate to it. It is fundamental to understand that the group's relationship with the Islamic Republic of Iran is military in nature. The more one focuses on the strategic and operational dimensions of the party's activities, the deeper one gets into the Islamic Resistance's functional frameworks, and the more likely one is to encounter representatives of the most ideological sectors of the Iranian Republic. The al-Quds Force of the Revolutionary Guards (*pasdaran e-sipah*) is the embodiment of these sectors, specializing in external missions.[28] The Pasdaran were behind the formation of the Islamic Resistance in Lebanon in the early 1980s, and have retained a strong influence over Hezbollah's military units. Today, General Qassem Suleymani runs the al-Quds Force as the instrument of Iranian policy in Iraq after the fall of Saddam Hussein.[29]

---

[28] For a military description of this institution, see Steven O'Hern, *Iran's Revolutionary Guard* (Washington, DC: Potomac Books, 2012).

[29] On Qassem Suleymani's importance, see Dexter Filkins, "The Shadow Commander" in *The New Yorker*, September 30, 2013.

It deployed to the Syria-Lebanon region in May 2011.[30] Yet their involvement in Syria has also created tensions in Hezbollah. The party's political bodies have reportedly taken more nuanced positions, particularly the political council (*al-majlis al-siyasi*) and the consulting council (*majlis shura al-qarar*), whose members are uneasy about risking the movement's popular support base by supporting large-scale repression in Syria.

Lebanese sources have even mentioned differences of opinion within Hezbollah's leadership during the year 2012 over the advisability of military action in North Lebanon. Deputy Secretary-General Na'im Qassem and Mustafa Badr al-Din, the substitute for the late head of operations, Imad Mughniyyeh, are said to support this option. The prospect of Assad's fall has led to a reinforcement of the Islamic Resistance's (including its Iranian members') hold on the party and of Hezbollah's hold on Lebanese institutions and territory. Khamenei's Iran cannot afford to lose its access to the northern border of Israel at a time when its relationship with the Palestinian movement Hamas has weakened as a result of the Syrian insurrection.

Inside North Lebanon, Hezbollah's representatives have been trying to win over the credible figures in the opposing camp with promises of protection or money. When the carrot does not work, the stick is used. The SSNP handles much of the "dirty work"—surveillance, intimidation, transportation of explosives—as was the case in Beirut after the May 7, 2008, power play. Actors aiding Syrian refugees constantly feel threatened and do not move anywhere without taking serious precautions. There have also been reports of Hezbollah's local affiliates purchasing plots of land and apartments in North Lebanon in order to prepare for the possibility of launching future military initiatives.

The Lebanese Army, under Various Influences

The Syrian leadership was aware that North Lebanon–based solidarity networks were key to Homs's resilience, even as the regular army had extensively shelled the city, destroying several of its

---

[30] See Will Fulton, Joseph Holliday, and Sam Wyer, "Iranian Strategy in Syria," Joint Report for AEI's Critical Threats Project and the Institute for the Study of War, May 2013.

Sunni residential areas. In January 2012, Bashar al-Assad requested that Suleiman Frangieh (head of the Marada militia and a long-time ally of the Assad family) direct his man in the government, Defense Minister Fayez Ghosn, to have the Cabinet discuss redeploying the army in North Lebanon and the Beqaa region. The armed forces' commander-in-chief, Jean Kahwaji, allegedly backed the initiative in hopes of reaching the presidency of Lebanon, in keeping with the disquieting tradition of entrusting this position to a Christian military man. Following this Cabinet debate, the army "decided" to increase its presence in North Lebanon in order to hamper anti-Assad Lebanese Sunnis' efforts to provide supplies to the pro-Syrian insurgency in Homs and its surroundings. Anti-Assad Sunni militants have also complained of the army leadership's attitude toward the SSNP militants' behavior: "Every time we stop cars packed with arms and explosives and turn them over to a Lebanese army barracks, a few hours later, we find that their drivers have been allowed to leave the premises with their arsenal intact."[31]

This non-neutral attitude is reminiscent of the army's practices in the south, where Hezbollah's military convoys pass checkpoints without a hitch, as their itineraries are known in advance, and their commanders' credentials are easily learned and remembered by military personnel. Wissam al-Hassan went so far as to describe the Lebanese army intelligence services and its chief Shi'ite officer, Ibrahim al-'Abbas, as "the instrument of Iran and Syria in Lebanon."[32] The Lebanese army's redeployment along the country's northern border facilitated the "fall" of the completely destroyed neighborhood of Baba 'Amr in Homs, since insurgent fighters ran out of ammunition to defend it. On March 1, 2012, the al-Faruq Brigade had no choice but to withdraw from this "city symbolic of the Syrian revolution."

In this context of mistrust, on May 20, 2012, Lebanese army soldiers opened fire on a vehicle as it passed through a military checkpoint at Kweikhat, killing two Sunni sheikhs from Akkar. The nebulous circumstances of the incident—Did the vehicle attempt to force its way through the checkpoint? Were the soldiers' orders unclear?—further aggravated the Sunni population's feelings of

---

[31] Interview with an important Tripolitan figure, Tripoli, April 2012.
[32] Interviews with General Wissam al-Hassan, Paris, September 2012.

alienation from the military as an institution charged with protecting all Lebanese citizens. One of the victims was Sheikh Abd al-Wahid, born in Bireh in 1969, a village imam in the Akkar region. He had also been elected at the top of the "Support for the Syrian Revolution" list in the May 6 local elections in his native village. He was close to the Future Movement and had mobilized his charity, al-Nur, to help Syrian refugees staying in the Akkar region. Both religious figures were on their way to participate in an event planned to commemorate the May 7, 2008, clashes in the town of Halba, where partisans of Khaled Daher massacred some SSNP members in retaliation for the bloodshed during Hezbollah's move that day in Beirut.[33]

To illustrate the collusion between the army and Hezbollah, Syrian opposition activists circulated a document from the Lebanese Ministry of the Interior and Local Authorities, dated October 26, 2012, the authenticity of which is unverifiable. In this letter the Lebanese Explosives Company (a state-owned company, run by a military officer) committed to deliver "50,000 tons of explosives and 51,000 meters of fuse wire" to the Syrian authorities on February 13, 2013. The letter requested that the Lebanese Internal Security Forces escort the convoy on its way to the border. According to Syrian opposition members, the convoy left from Tripoli and passed through Beirut, then made the border crossing at al-Masnaa.

The Bloody Drama of Jabal Mohsen and Bab al-Tabbaneh

The first clashes between the Tripoli neighborhoods of Jabal Mohsen and Bab al-Tabbaneh since the civil war took place in August 2008, a few weeks after Hezbollah's May 7 military takeover in Beirut and the Chouf district. In fact, the recurrent outbreaks of violence between the Alawite middle classes of Jabal Mohsen

---

[33] The lynching of the SSNP militants was the March 8 equivalent of what had happened on a much larger scale in West Beirut on March 14. However, the dreadful scene in Halba was filmed on a mobile phone and immediately broadcast on al-Manar TV (affiliated to Hezbollah), whereas Sa'ad al-Hariri's partisans' no less tragic fate in Beirut had remained unseen—Hezbollah had taken the precaution of cutting the cables of the Future Movement's TV channel.

and the Sunni working-class residents of Bab al-Tabbaneh are not caused by irreconcilable sectarian enmity, but are rather a consequence of a more cynical form of manipulation. The testimony of Rif'at Eid (who succeeded his father Ali Eid as head of the Arab Democratic Party's Alawite militia), as given at the time, was all the more credible because it directly incriminated his political allies of the March 8 Movement. According to him, it was Hezbollah sympathizers who fired rockets at the Jabal Mohsen mountain:

> After the Beirut events, the Future Movement was eliminating the Ba'ath Party and Hezbollah offices in the streets of Tripoli. To Hezbollah's allies, to draw their adversaries' attention away from this, the only solution was to create another focal point in Jabal Mohsen by re-igniting the old conflict of the 1980s. It was *abaday* (neighborhood thugs) from Bab al-Tabbaneh, whom Umar Karami and Hezbollah hired, who revived the conflict.[34]

One of these locals was Samir al-Hassan, who had gone over to Hezbollah after his release from a Syrian prison in 2000 (see chapter 3). In any case, the diversion had the desired effect, and inhabitants of Jabal Mohsen retaliated with considerable firepower, using, in part, arms from depots the Syrian army had abandoned when it withdrew in 2005. This justified the mobilization of Sunni fighters of all persuasions in Bab al-Tabbaneh—beginning with Hezbollah's Sunni affiliates, who otherwise would have been at risk of military annihilation in retaliation for the Beirut events. By manipulating sectarian violence between Sunnis and Alawites, Hezbollah proxies managed to protect their allies in the city of Tripoli. The Jabal Mohsen "front" that the Party of God initially reopened continued to serve the latter's interests during the Syrian conflict. Indeed, for allies of Bashar al-Assad's regime, igniting sectarian clashes has the effect of enlarging the Lebanese army's presence in the north of the country and, therefore, restricting the pro-Syrian revolution support networks' room to maneuver.

At the other end of the political spectrum, the Salafi sheikhs have also taken advantage of the situation to emphasize their role

[34] Interview with Rif'at Eid, Arab Democratic Party headquarters, Jabal Mohsen, Tripoli, August 19, 2008. At the time, some Tripoli leadership figures of the Future Movement agreed with his analysis.

as the vanguard of Sunni Islam confronting the "*nusayri* (Ala-wite) infidels." This particularly helps them in their dealings with funding sources in the Gulf. Thus, the so-called "war" with Jabal Mohsen disseminated a sectarian framework of interpretation of the ongoing events, fueled by scores of videos on the Internet. Sa-lafis have used this opportunity to attract more followers by trying to convince new recruits to dissociate themselves from the Future Movement—discredited due to its military weakness during the May 7, 2008, events—and to support instead those who are pre-pared to risk injury or death to defend the Sunni community.

To fickle ex-Tawhid militiamen, who now have formed small gangs composed of leaders and local heavies in Bab al-Tabbaneh, firing a rocket at the Jabal Mohsen apartment buildings is still the best way to pressure the Sunni *zu'ama'* (figureheads) for money. These community leaders cannot ignore the potential electorate Bab al-Tabbaneh represents (approximately 50,000 votes). Thus, the tensions between the two neighborhoods are not the product of a reemerging conflict that had been frozen since the end of the civil war. The Bab al-Tabbaneh/Jabal Mohsen area is not merely reflect-ing the fighting occurring a few kilometers further east, in Syrian territory. Rather, it constitutes an artificial yet deadly front line, manipulated by a multitude of actors with divergent interests, whose only shared characteristic is their disregard for the people who actually live in the two neighborhoods.

Intelligence and Jihadism: The Role of Sheikh Ghiyyeh

On November 12, 2013, two motorcycle-borne assassins targeted Sunni sheikh Sa'ad al-Din al-Ghiyyeh as he climbed into his car in a neighborhood of Tripoli. Ghiyyeh was a pivotal figure in the interface between regional jihadi networks in Tripoli on the one side, and Syrian intelligence, the *mukhabarat*, on the other side. Motivated by a deep hatred for the United States and indeed for the West as a whole, Ghiyyeh's main concern was to reconcile his jihadi "al-Qaeda type" agenda with Syrian regional policies, so as to establish a common *modus operandi* without betraying his own beliefs.

Sa'ad al-Din Ghiyyeh's biography is unusual. He was born in Takrit (in the Akkar region) in 1963, to an Alawite mother and a

Sunni father. Between 1988 and 1992, he acquired military experience in Abu Nidal's Revolutionary Council (al-majlis al-thawri). During this period, he gained expertise "on security issues," as "the point was to kill Mossad agents wherever possible."[35] He crossed paths with Abu Nidal himself in the Beqaa region, without knowing who he was. Every month, he had to carry out self-criticism sessions before the organization's leaders, as did all group members. Despite his own Islamic beliefs, he retrospectively justified staying in this radical group for years as a means of "protecting himself from potential arrest by the Syrian authorities." For Ghiyyeh, this experience was the first of many that required him to reconcile his own ideological convictions with security issues arising from the regional balance of power.

In the early 1990s, he witnessed the formation of the clandestine Jund al-Sham (Army of Syria) network, led by Palestinian sheikh Ibrahim al-Ghunaym. According to Ghiyyeh, al-Ghunaym had conceived of this project during discussions in the late 1960s with Abdallah Azzam at the "Sheikhs' Camp" in the Jordan Valley (so named because it was a military training camp exclusively reserved for Islamists). The core members of Jund al-Sham were those who attended Sheikh al-Ghunaym's lectures, "but there were Jund al-Sham representatives in Tunisia and Algeria. Zarqawi was a member, as was Shaker al-Absi, who wielded at least as much authority inside the group as did Zarqawi."[36]

In 2003, Ghiyyeh earned his master's degree at al-Hasaka University, a branch of the shari'a college (kulliya) of Damascus University. There he defended his thesis, "The Masonic Threat to Mankind and Islam." He also began giving classes in a religious studies institute in Aleppo, where he delivered religious accreditations (ijaza) to the most fervent students. In Aleppo, he met the Syrian preacher Abu al-Qa'qa', whose complete sermons he collected. In the late nineties, Sheikh Ghiyyeh and Abu al-Qa'qa' headed to Afghanistan, where they stayed with Zarqawi in Herat.[37] In Afghanistan, Ghiyyeh also met Muhammad Jarah, one of the 9/11 hijackers. In 2002, six months before the United States invaded Iraq, Sheikh Ghiyyeh—then around 40 years old—volunteered to

[35] Interview with Sheikh Ghiyyeh, Qubbeh, Tripoli, August 27, 2008.
[36] Interview with Sheikh Ghiyyeh, Qubbeh, Tripoli, August 3, 2010.
[37] Interview with Sheikh Ghiyyeh, Qubbeh, Tripoli, August 21, 2008.

go to Iraq "not to defend Saddam Hussein's regime, but to commit a martyrdom operation in God's path."[38] In Baghdad he underwent military preparation in the special college Saddam Hussein's regime had set up for Arab volunteers. He also reconnected with Shaker al-Absi and Zarqawi in Iraq and found that they all belonged to Jund al-Sham. Recognizing his propaganda value, Iraqi authorities invited him several times to appear on state television to explain his motives for fighting. He told me also that he gave the Friday sermon in several of Baghdad's mosques.

At the war's outset, Ghiyyeh was deployed to Basra in the Allahu Akbar Battalion of Saddam's Fedayin. After seven days of urban guerrilla fighting, a pincer maneuver, executed by American-British troops in coordination with local tribes hostile to the jihadis, targeted his group. In his telling, the fighting had a strong effect on him. He recalled watching as a group of plainclothes Iraqis collaborating with British troops stabbed one of his companions, a young Yemeni volunteer. Later that day, to avenge the Yemeni, Ghiyyeh's colleagues randomly planted a bomb in the district. "We blew up the bomb when civilians came by," he recounted. "Maybe we killed innocent people, but it was impossible not to react after our friend's death. This is how *fitna* began in Iraq. We knew we had to kill collaborators, especially translators without whom the Americans could not work." He continued, "At the very beginning, Zarqawi didn't want any *fitna*, but it happened this way, since most of the collaborators were Shi'ites. This is why I decided to leave Iraq after this . . . I didn't want any killing between Sunnis and Shi'ites."[39] Ghiyyeh escaped Basra and left Iraq, allegedly returning the following year to Iraqi Kurdistan, where Zarqawi was staying. He enjoyed the hospitality of the Kurdish jihadi group Ansar al-Islam, before going back to Lebanon a final time. There, the local press wrote about the "Lebanese sheikh who fought against the Americans in Iraq."

Upon returning to Aleppo he resumed teaching in an Islamic institute until Sheikh Abu al-Qa'qa' introduced him to Muhammad Dib Zaytun, the Syrian officer in charge of "political security"

---

[38] According to his testimony in *al-Mustaqbal* newspaper on April 17, 2003.

[39] Interview with Sheikh Ghiyyeh, Qubbeh, Tripoli, September 6, 2009. He might also have realized that it would have been dangerous to unleash a war against Syrians' allies in Iraq at that time.

in Aleppo (Zaytun had been the sheik's handler since the latter's military service years; see chapter 4).[40] Ghiyyeh described a *"mukhabarat* [intelligence] officer different from the others, very friendly, who very well understood the Islamist concerns, and stressed the need to put aside conflicts of the past so as to confront the challenges threatening the Islamic umma."[41] Ghiyyeh thought he knew how to handle his *mukhabarat* interlocutors: "You need to tell them what they want to hear. . . . That one has to oppose anyone who would betray the Arab nation by evoking Western intervention or [requesting] help! Then I can do whatever I want!" The Sunni preacher adopted the same tactics when he delivered sermons in the al-Mina neighborhood to gain the support of Kamal Khayr, a close Hezbollah ally: "Using this tactic, I enjoy protection from both Hezbollah and General Security (*amn al-'amm*), since Shafiq Wazzini [Director of General Security] works for the party [Hezbollah]."

In 2006, Ghiyyeh became head of security for Kana'an Naji for a few months, although the latter was known to be opposed to the Assad family. It is unclear why Naji, a former leader of the February 9 Movement, would have been trying to hire someone he thought was a Syrian agent, but perhaps he saw an opportunity to try to use Ghiyyeh for his own interests.

Ghiyyeh claims that Kana'an Naji did ask him to go to Tartus (in Syria) to talk to Ahmad Nazih, the *mukhabarat* Syrian officer in charge of Tripoli. Ghiyyeh was supposed to try to convince Nazih that he would be available to collaborate with the Assad regime to organize an operation against UNIFIL in southern Lebanon if, for example, they would provide him with "weapons and explosives." Ghiyyeh complied and did go to Tartus, but he was convinced "that Wissam al-Hassan planned this operation to entrap the Syrians."

[40] Abu al-Qa'qa' then explained to Ghiyyeh that during his military service, he had started performing the five daily prayers inside army barracks, which was forbidden in Syria. He had been spared a prison sentence through the intercession of a Sunni officer, originally from Rif Dimashq (the Damascus countryside), named Muhammad Dib Zaytun, who later became the head of security for the Aleppo region. According to Ghiyyeh, the latter allegedly convinced Abu al-Qa'qa' in 2006 to write a fatwa directing Syrian *mujahidin* to go to Lebanon instead of Iraq in order to fight the West. Muhammad Dib Zaytun, then head of the Syrian Political Security Directorate, was on the list of thirteen Syrian officials that the European Union accused in May 2011 of repressing anti-regime demonstrations. Bashar al-Assad would go on to appoint him as director of the General Security Directorate in July 2012.

[41] Interview with Sheikh Ghiyyeh, August 3, 2010.

Ahmad Nazih, whom Ghiyyeh himself allegedly informed of this possibility, did not "fall into the trap."

Later, during Fatah al-Islam events, Ghiyyeh welcomed into his home young Saudis who reportedly belonged to al-Qaeda in the Arabian Peninsula. He was in contact with Nabil Rahim, then al-Qaeda representative in Tripoli, who years earlier had graduated from his institute in Aleppo. He knew the head of Fatah al-Islam's religious committee, Abu al-Harith, as well as Abdallah al-Bishi, the Saudi sheikh who audited Fatah al-Islam's jihadi credentials. Ghiyyeh also said he met with Shaker al-Absi twice: "I told him not to entangle himself in Lebanese intricacies . . . but he was stuck in that camp. . . . The Syrians sent him there, and would probably have him arrested if he came back to Syria." According to Ghiyyeh, Lebanon, because of its confessional structure, cannot be a "land of jihad," rather it is a "land of *ribât*" (the term evokes a fortified town located at the enemy's border), from "where one should fight against the Israelis. There are many books in which al-Qaeda explains how to behave in such a land."[42]

Sheikh Ghiyyeh attempted to convince Sunni youths to rally to the cause of Resistance to Israel and the West on Hezbollah's and the Syrian regime's terms. To him, there were no words harsh enough to express the perfidy of Rafiq al-Hariri:

> an apostate [*murtadd*], worse than an infidel. He [was] responsible for the army's behavior during the Dinniyeh clashes. He signed death warrants for those who had killed Nizar al-Halabi. He had a church built in Harissa to buy the Christians' approval.[43]

Sheikh Ghiyyeh was influential among the youth of Qubbeh and had formed an armed militia in the old town's market area. He considered himself a political and military ally of Rif'at Eid, the Alawite leader of the Arab Democratic Party in Jabal Mohsen, and was ready to support him in case the Syrian conflict were to expand into North Lebanon.

After the outbreak of insurrection in Syria, Ghiyyeh began to exploit his Sunni jihadi affiliation to feed misinformation to foreign

---

[42] Interview with Sheikh Ghiyyeh, Qubbeh, Tripoli, August 19, 2008.
[43] Interview with Sheikh Ghiyyeh, Qubbeh, Tripoli, August 27, 2008.

media about the nature of the fighting. On May 22, 2012, the French daily *Le Figaro* ran an article titled "Syria, the Jihadis' New Favorite Country," in which the paper's special correspondent mostly relied on the testimony of a "veteran of jihad, Sheikh Saadedin Ghia . . . who regularly travels back and forth between his residence in Tripoli, North Lebanon and the Syrian battlefield" to fight the Assad regime. He presented "Sheikh Ghia" (Ghiyyeh) as "a Sunni Islamist who fought with al-Qaeda in Afghanistan and Iraq," and quoted his account of trips to join jihadi fighters on the other side of the Lebanese-Syrian border: "Before dawn, I cross the river that marks the border, disguised as a peasant; I return at nightfall, after I've hidden my weapon on Syrian territory." In the journalist's account of Sheikh Ghiyyeh's travels, he notes the existence of a jihadi network between Lebanon and Syria: "A hundred-odd Lebanese Salafis, like him, and 300 to 400 other non-Syrian volunteers [*sic*] have infiltrated Syrian territory to fight the partisans of Bashar al-Assad, according to several concordant sources." The Sheikh acknowledged an impending conflict with the FSA:

> The jihadis deem members of the FSA infidels opposed to the project of building a caliphate. Relations between the FSA and us will not improve. In the end, it will be them or us. But we must be patient: Syria is a place of experiments. As the chaos sets in, the regime and the FSA will both grow weaker. And in the end, people will align themselves with the jihadis.

The *Figaro* journalist uncritically passed on this testimony, apparently taking for granted most of the sheikh's information. But the latter's statements take on a different meaning in light of his past and the history of his activities and role in Tripoli. In fact, far from promoting or leading the jihadi struggle on Syrian territory, the sheikh is actually one of Hezbollah's and the Syrian intelligence services' most reliable allies in Tripoli's Sunni circles.

Since the beginning of the Syrian crisis, he had also been writing texts lambasting Saudi Wahhabism, "whose texts" he argued, were "inspired from the Jewish scriptures."[44] In Aleppo in August 2010,

---

[44] Sa'ad al-Din Ghiyyeh, "Part of the shared beliefs between Wahhabism and Judaism" [*juz' min al-tatabuq bayna 'aqidat al-wahhabiyya wa 'aqidat al-yahud*], Al-'arabiyya. http://www.alarabiyya 24.com/ar/print/6219 (accessed November 2013).

he claimed that the Iranian ambassador asked him to become Hezbollah's representative in North Lebanon. He immediately reported the proposal to the usual Syrian intelligence officers, who told him to hold back before making any decision.[45] When the Syrian crisis started one year later, he was able to continue his main task of fighting pro-Western Sunnis, until his violent death in 2013.

On the evening of November 12, the ninth night of Ashura and hours after Ghiyyeh's assassination, Hezbollah secretary-general Hassan Nasrallah denounced "those who are targeting the Resistance path, who are targeting all kinds of unity and solidarity between Muslims, who are targeting every nationalist strand anxious to preserve the common life (al-'ich al-muchtarak) between Lebanese. The [assassination] targets all the like-minded people who try to deal with questions in a manner different from certain *takfiri* and extremist factions in the region." Taking a swipe at the March 14 camp, Nasrallah feigned surprise at "those political and parliamentary forces who pretend to value security and peace among Lebanese, [who] continue, to this very moment, to ignore this morning's assassination and act as if nothing had happened."[46] Al-Ghiyyeh was also a member of the Congregation of Muslim Ulama (Tajammu'al-'Ulama' al-Muslimin), one of Hezbollah's main networks of influence with Sunni clerics. The congregation, for their part, published a press release to condemn "the *takfiri* villainy behind Ghiyyeh's killing."[47] The Iranian Embassy in Beirut likewise condemned the brutal exit "of the leading model of Resistance Islam."

As a matter of fact, and quite ironically in spite of the circumstances, Ghiyyeh seemed part of what those declarations unanimously condemned. According to young students who had attended his religious courses, Ghiyyeh reportedly sent about twenty volunteers across the border to fight in the ranks of the Islamic State in Iraq and Syria (ISIS), a jihadi militia known for killing Alawite and

---

[45] Interview with Sheikh Ghiyyeh, Qubbeh, Tripoli, August 2010. This was my fourth meeting with Ghiyyeh; he declined all further interviews.

[46] See the al-Manar website: "Al-Sayyid Nasrallah: The killing of Sheikh Ghiyyeh indicates a dangerous process and targets the Resistance path." http://www.almanar.com.lb /adetails.php?fromval=1&eid=646160 (accessed November 14, 2013).

[47] Al-Nahar, November 13, 2013.

Shi'ite civilians as well as Christians and secular Sunni Muslims.[48] This rumor is debatable, since Ghiyyeh's own mother was Alawite. But it is almost sure that the sheikh maintained contacts with jihadi groups in Syria linked to al-Qaeda, whether out of conviction or with the aim of informing Syrian officers.

For the Syrian security apparatus, using people such as Sheikh Ghiyyeh provides very useful information about jihadi networks in the region, which can be manipulated and reoriented according to their designs. It also helps them to discredit efforts to build a Sunni civilian constituency free from their influence. Introducing al-Qaeda's role in North Lebanon and Syria threatens to strip the protest movement of its popular legitimacy and lends credence to the allegation that Sunnis are unfit to rule on either side of the border. Jihadi networks are indeed a real threat to non-radical Sunnis. Less spectacular but equal in seriousness is the threat emanating from the dissemination of Salafi discourse in everyday life, which has the pernicious effect of undermining the legitimacy of political Sunni elites.

The Salafi Specter
THE SERMONS OF SHEIKH SALEM

Sheikh Salem Abd al-Ghani al-Rafi'i is one of the many taking advantage of the atmosphere of insecurity in North Lebanon to vie for local leadership. Born in 1961 in Dhahar al-Ayn, in the al-Mina neighborhood, he left Lebanon in the early 1980s with a scholarship to attend the Islamic University of Medina, where he earned his bachelor's degree with distinction in 1984. He continued his studies at the University of Punjab in Lahore, Pakistan. The return of Syrian troops to Tripoli in 1986 dissuaded him from returning to Lebanon. In 1989, he moved to Germany. The contacts he had made in the Gulf enabled him to finance the construction of the Islamic center in Neukölln, in the southeastern part of West Berlin, a neighborhood nicknamed "Little Istanbul" due to the high proportion of Turkish immigrants in its population. The center is a building several stories high, containing a mosque—the al-Nur mosque (the Light)—where al-Rafi'i became the imam. It also offers courses in German language and computing. Enrolled at the

---

[48] Interview, Tripoli, May 2014.

same time in the doctoral program at the Holy Qur'an and Islamic Science University in Omdurman, north of Khartoum, Salem al-Rafi'i devoted his doctoral dissertation to "The Rules of Personal Status of Muslims in the West" (*ahkam al-ahwal al-sharkhsiyya lil-muslimin fi al-gharb*).

Published in Lebanon in 2002, the dissertation purports to describe the incompatibility of Western positive law (with German law serving as its model) with Islamic rules governing marriage, filiation, and divorce as they are presented in classical Muslim jurisprudence.[49] The categories of judgment Sheikh Salem al-Rafi'i developed in the course of his experience can be grasped by taking a quick look through this work. He bases his analysis on "thirteen years of living in Germany" at the head of an Islamic center "which became the reference for Muslim emigrants in Berlin" (p. 7). He clearly devoted effort to counteracting the effects on his congregation of a version of Islam that advocated integration in German society, attested to in fatwas (legal opinions), "sources of perdition" that leave too much room for "people's whims and desires" (p. 7). The task of comparison forced Sheikh Salem to delve into the subtleties of German law, which posed difficulties due to his "poor command of the language."

While dealing ostensibly with the issue of the legitimacy of Muslim residency in a "land of infidels," Sheikh Salem in fact tackles the highly sensitive issue of the religious legitimacy of political authority in the "land of Islam." He believes the debate as to whether or not a Muslim must leave an infidel land to complete his *hijra* (migration) in the "land of Islam" has become largely immaterial. The real question is whether a "land of Islam" still exists, given the increasingly narrow field of application of religious law in Muslim countries, "whether in matters of politics, the economy, society, relations between states, the principle of allegiance and disavowal (*al-wala' wa al-barra'*)" (p. 44).[50]

---

[49] *Ahkam al-ahwal al-sharkhsiyya lil-muslimin fi al-gharb* [The rules of personal status of Muslims in the West] (Beirut: Dar Ibn Hazm, 2002/1423).

[50] Based on an interpretation of verses in the Koran [5/51], *al-wala' wa al-barra'*'s principle was first promoted by Suleyman bin 'Abdallah, the grandson of Muhammad bin 'Abd al-Wahhab, in order to fight Egyptians' expeditions in the Najd in 1818 on the Ottoman sultan's behalf. According this principle, the "true believer" should disavow himself from any source of authority that is not "truly" Islamic (i.e., in conformity with the relevant

This "unprecedented situation [in] the history of Islam" even prompted "some to consider that Muslim countries had also become infidel countries" (p. 45). If one were to use the criterion adopted by "most scholars"—that of the "supremacy of Islamic law (*ghalabat ahkam al-islam*)" over secular rules, the conclusion would be self-evident, because "the rules that apply in Muslim countries are the rules of infidels (*ahkam al-kufr*)." Even more, "the existence of a Islamic legal system applied to certain aspects of life, such as personal status, cannot be an exception to this observation, because an exception is not the rule. Power is in the hands of those who govern by the rules of disbelief, even in the case of the application of the rules of Islam to personal status, because the judges are subject to the power of the state and cannot apply the rules themselves. They must resort to the power of those who do not govern by the Law of God" (p. 46).

The sheikh then makes a distinction between the (infidel) leaders and their (Muslim) societies. This opposition enables him to rescue contemporary Muslim societies from the contemptible category of impiety. Of course, "Muslims cannot manage to impose the precepts of divine law (*shari'a*) on their leaders, but those in power are afraid [of their people], and dare not manifest their hostility toward religion in public nor make fun of it or disavow it" (p. 47). It is societies' attachment to their religious practices that dissuades their leaders from destroying Islam; but, "if they could, they wouldn't hesitate to do so, at least most of them wouldn't" (p. 47). This climate of "competition for power" between infidel rulers and Muslim societies brings Muslim societies closer to qualifying as belonging to the "land of Islam." Yet this quality remains incomplete. Sheikh Salem finds that the situation today in Muslim states is comparable to what was described by the legal scholar and theologian Ibn Taymiyya (1263–1328) in his "Mardin fatwa." Questioned as to whether the Turcoman emirate of Mardin was a "land of war" or a "land of peace" after it was invaded by the Mongols in 1260, the "sheikh of Islam" answered that Mardin was in a mixed situation (*murakkab*), combining elements related to the "land of Islam" and others to the "land of war." According to Sheikh Salem,

Wahhabi creed). In 2003, al-Qaeda's ideologue Ayman al-Zawahiri wrote a lampoon with this title to delegitimize Muslim leaders who followed Western norms and policies.

this description "was identical to the situation Muslim countries have arrived at today" (p. 50).[51] Once he has settled the matter of the legality of Muslim residence in the land of infidels, in particular mentioning the companions of the Prophet's stay in Ethiopia, "where the rule of polytheism (ahkam al-shirk) applied," the sheikh would repeat his remark that the issue was no longer germane today, "because 'land of infidels' and 'land of Islam' were equal in their application of these infidel laws, even if there [were] differences in the degree of their subjugation to this order" (p. 73).

By choosing to study personal status, Sheikh Salem reproduces a normative heritage essentialized by Islamic jurisprudence, according to which it would be impossible for Arab or Turkish immigrants to acculturate to German society without becoming impious. This society, out of logical opposition, is moreover placed in a relationship of total otherness, indifferently qualified as the "land of infidels (bilad al-kufr)" or the "land of polytheism (bilad al-shirk)." The West is presented as an island of many temptations, where evil spreads in the form of "fornication (al-zina), alcohol (al-khamr) and unlawful money (al-mal al-haram)." Even the European social model itself harbors great dangers. While it is more enviable than some others, "especially compared to the atrocious situation in Arab countries," it gives women the possibility of no longer obeying their husbands, because "the state can meet their needs and they will no longer need their spouses' money or protection" (p.79). The German family is in jeopardy due to the leniency of the law and an educational system that gives children "classes in sex education as early as age seven, explaining the role of sex and ways of love-making without warning them against forbidden relations" (p. 80).

While Muslims are subject to social control in the "land of Islam" "in the street, at work, and in the family," Muslims in Europe

---

[51] He qualifies this remark by pointing out that if it weren't for the impossibility posited by several prophetic hadith, of a world "without the land of Islam" after Muhammad's preaching, he would have fully subscribed to Ibn Taymiyya's position. Sheikh Salem quotes a hadith to mark Mecca's intangible attachment to the land of Islam (p. 49): "There is no hijra (migration from Mecca to Medina) after the Conquest (of Mecca)," Sahih al-Bukhari, Book 52, Hadith 42. In support of the same idea, on the same page, he also quotes the hadith: "This religion will continue to exist, and a group of people from the Muslims will continue to fight for its protection until the Hour is established," Sahih Muslim, Book 33, Hadith 248.

can give free rein to "vile deeds and vices" (p. 77). Governed by a "materialist view of life," Westerners have "allowed an uncle to marry one's brother's daughter, and a maternal uncle to marry one's sister's daughter, for their medical experts have established there is no risk" without considering "the vices that such a law gives rise to in individuals of the same family and the fear affecting one another" (p. 372). Against these institutions that "give a husband no rights over his wife, not even to ask her to pour him a cup of coffee," and refuse him the status, which Islam guarantees, of "head of the family," and that require wives "to give their consent prior to sexual intercourse" (p. 495), the sheikh advocates the right for Muslim emigrants to apply God-given Islamic rules. In this he claims to be following "international treaties and the resulting pacts that Westerners attach such importance to and that guarantee minorities the exercise of their social and cultural rights" (p. 635). The sheikh concludes with an invocation: "May God save Muslims from being absorbed (*al-dhuban*) by the mirage (*al-sarab*) of Western civilization" (p. 636).

In its own way, it is an anti-integration manual designed for the European Muslim, like the bestselling *Muslim's Path* written by one of his professors at the University of Medina, Abu Bakr al-Jaza'iri. Only strict observance of the rules taken from the Qur'an and the *sunna* enable the believer to preserve his Muslim identity in his personal life. If he does not follow them, he is plagued by "disorder and chaos (*fitna*)." The term *fitna*, used frequently throughout the book, is not defined as discord among Muslims, but rather takes on the meaning of disorder between the Muslim and his belief. Clichés flow easily from one page to the next, with Western-style marriage described as an institution in which "men are not in a position to forbid their wives from having sexual relations with other men, for like men, women are free in this regard as well."

Salem al-Rafi'i's reputation is not limited to that of a Salafi moralizer concerned with preserving the Muslim family from the pernicious influence of Western society. In 2005, on returning from a trip to Lebanon, he was turned back at the Berlin airport. The interior minister blamed him for mentioning "the victory of the mujahidin in Chechnya and in Palestine" during a sermon at the al-Nur mosque at the end of 2004, and, according to the German press, suspected him of having ties with young radicals. He resettled permanently in Lebanon in 2004 and established the Uthman bin 'Affan Islamic institute in al-Mina and the al-Taqwa center.

Sheikh Salem Abd al-Ghani al-Rafi'i became the main imam of al-Taqwa mosque and a man of considerable financial means. He is quite respected among the youth of the working-class neighborhoods of Qubbeh, Bab al-Tabbaneh, and al-Mina, some of whom attend Friday sermons in the mosque. There, he also holds a public religious event every Monday evening, during which he preaches from *maghrib* (late afternoon) to *'isha* (evening) prayers. Since 2008, he has been organizing protests in al-Nur Square in solidarity with prisoners suspected of belonging to Fatah al-Islam. He has also championed Shadi al-Mawlawi, a twenty-four-year-old man whom Lebanese security services arrested in the summer of 2012 for his alleged connections with Jabhat al-Nusra in Syria. The details of Shadi's arrest have made him a folk hero in Tripoli, helped along by Sheikh Salem's role as a sort of plebeian tribune for the Islamic populace, making a kind of religious intercession against state decisions.

Security services trapped Shadi al-Mawlawi as he was going to government minister Safadi's office in hopes of getting financial support to save his hospitalized young daughter. The information immediately spread through Islamist circles and sparked a wave of protests. This placed Tripoli's Islamist movements within the repertoire of protest action typical of the early phases of the Arab Spring uprisings, with many demonstrations and sit-ins on al-Nur Square. These various protest cycles allowed jihadi militants such as Hussam al-Sabbagh and Nur al-Din al-Ghalayani to show themselves in broad daylight and march through the streets behind the sheikh. In exchange for his protection, these two former members of Fatah al-Islam have formed armed groups in the Qubbeh and Bab al-Tabbaneh neighborhoods. A resident of the al-Mina neighborhood indicated that Sheikh Salem's partisans are showing religious intolerance in the areas under their control, and attempting to replace the state: "We are now paying the price of the Afwaj's eradication," he said.

In his March 2, 2012, sermon in al-Taqwa mosque, Sheikh al-Rafi'i commented on a hadith from the *Sahih Muslim* collection, which goes as follows:

The Prophet said: "The people of Iraq are about to receive no more *qafiz* or dirhams." We asked: "For what reason?" He answered: "Because here, the *'ajam* [Persians, in this context] will stand in the way of it." Then he added: "The people of al-Sham are near to receiving not even a *dinar* or a *mudi-un*." We asked: "For what reason?" He replied: "Because of the Rum [the Byzantines]." He was silent for a moment, then the messenger of Allah said: "At the end of my community, there will be a Caliph who will give money freely and lavishly."

The sheikh interpreted these words of the Prophet on the basis of several eschatological hadith, then extrapolated other points from this, which allowed him to confidently announce the imminent arrival of the Mahdi of the Sunnis (*mahdi al-sunna*) to the congregation.[52] In his reasoning, he also referred to another hadith describing the gradual degradation of authority in Islam: "The caliphate following mine will last thirty years, then there will be a regime of misfortune (*mulk al-'adud*), then a tyrannical power (*mulk al-jabr*)." The "times of hardship and misfortune" last "over 1,300 years."[53] The 1,300 years cover the period of Islamic empires, from the foundation of the Umayyad Empire to the end of the Ottoman caliphate, followed by the years of tyrannical modern dictatorships, "with Mustafa Kemal in Turkey and the Arab rulers in the Arab countries." In the latter phase, "men have been humiliated and the lands have been plundered," but the Arab Spring uprisings mark the "beginning of the end" of tyrannical power, which will give way to "the sun of a new Islamic Caliphate," God willing, he explained.

Current political events were of no intrinsic interest. They were to be interpreted in the future perfect, because their significance lay in what was to come, a divine intervention to save humanity. Many hadith mention the first caliphate as that of the four "rightly guided caliphs" who ruled directly after the Prophet, and announce the imminent establishment of a "second Islamic caliphate by the Sunni

---

[52] A note on translation: In Sunni Islamic eschatology, the Mahdi (literally, the "divinely guided" or "rightly guided") is "a messianic deliverer who will fill the Earth with justice and equity, restore true religion, and usher in a short golden age lasting seven, eight, or nine years before the end of the world," Encyclopædia Britannica Online, s.v. "mahdi," http://www.britannica.com/EBchecked/topic/358096/mahdi (accessed May 30, 2013).

[53] Literally speaking, the expression *'al-adud* comes from the lexical field of "to bite" (*'add*), and suggests the aggressiveness of power and the pain these rulers' subjects feel.

imam al-mahdi, peace be upon him." The sheikh then evoked a narrative transmitted by Imam al-Bazar and authenticated by Sheikh Nasser al-Din al-Albani, both considered authoritative in Salafi circles:

> The land will be filled with wicked actions and injustice. When it will be nothing but wicked actions and injustice, Allah will designate a man whose name shall be mine. He will fill the Earth with equity and justice, in equal measure to the wicked actions and injustice it had before him.[54]

He specified that "all religious scholars" concur that the man referred to here is the Mahdi; it is he who will spread justice and light to eliminate the evil surrounding humanity. Yet, according to the sheikh, the Mahdi's inevitable coming does not exonerate believers from the responsibility of jihad. He was dealing with a classical issue that arises in Marxist theory: what justifies the need for communists to act, if the superior force of historical materialism will inevitably triumph over the exploitation of the masses anyway? Just as the laws of history require party action to become reality, believers cannot remain inactive and merely wait for the Mahdi, explained Sheikh Salem:

> Beware! This does not mean that today, people must abandon their jihad! Or abandon the struggle against the unjust (*dhalimin*)—never! Fighting oppressors is a duty for the *umma*, whether the Mahdi has come, or has not yet come, whether he is late or early! But it is a sign from the Prophet [that announced] the end of the struggle against oppression for this generation will end in God, and with the end of all injustice on Earth, thanks to the coming of the Mahdi.

The second hadith regarding the Mahdi's arrival was none other than the introduction to the sermon. Sheikh Salem then explained the technical terms in the hadith to his congregation: the *qafiz* is a dry measure for grains used in Iraq at the time. By metonymy, *qafiz*

---

[54] See Nasser al-Din al-Albani, hadith 5073, 904, in *Sahih jami' al-saghir wa-ziyadatihi* (Beirut and Damascus: la Librairie Islamique, 1988). To Sheikh al-Albani, hadith 5073 narrated by al-Bazar is authentic (*sahih*).

refers to food. No longer being able to use the *qafiz* thus implies a food shortage. This is how the hadith supposedly evokes famine. To the sheikh, it was quite clear that this part of the hadith as cited by Muslim in his *Sahih* "refers to the economic embargo (*hisar iqtisadi*) imposed on the Iraqi population under their former president Saddam Hussein." He replaced the immediate reference in the text (the impossibility of using the *qafiz*) with a second reference, the appalling situation of Iraq deprived of food. As Iraq has never known such trauma before, in its entire history, this authentic hadith, "which has been traced back directly to the Prophet" (*marfu'*), must be referring to Iraq from 1991 to 2003. Sheikh Salem managed to connect religious beliefs and empirical reality in a circle: the hadith had to be true, because of the indisputable dreadful and deadly effects of the embargo on Iraqi children. Thanks to this substitution of ancient elements with contemporary ones, Sheikh Salem asserted that the Prophet had described the situation later experienced by Iraqis "barely able to receive food, medicine or milk for the children, except clandestinely" because of the strict implementation of the Oil-for-Food program. In this sermon, the hadith reverted to its initial status of speech, but to Sheikh Salem's speech rather than that of the Prophet. As Paul Ricoeur would say, "the sheikh creates a new ostensive reference" by substituting contemporary reality for the initial reference: this is the core of his interpretive work.[55] Similarly, the mention of the inhabitants of Iraq no longer being able to use their currency, the dirham, bears an apparent reference to the UN's decision to freeze their financial assets "both in the West and in the East."

The second part of the hadith refers to the embargo imposed on Syria by the *Rum*—the *Rum* meaning, Sheikh Salem explains, the Europeans and the Americans—since the beginning of the conflict in 2011. According to the sheikh, the Syrian population is under a double siege. In the first place it is beset by the Western powers, which falsely claim that their embargo on Syrian oil exports is intended to hamper state repression, as was decided by the Council of the European Union on May 9, 2011. The West's justification

---

[55] Paul Ricoeur, *From Text to Action: Essays in Hermeneutics II*, Kathleen Blamey and John B. Thomson, trans. (Evanston, IL: Northwestern University Press, 1991 [1986]), 158.

is false, he insists, because the embargo hits the people and not the regime, for the regime can rely on Iran and Russia for help in circumventing the embargo's effects. Having thus expounded the hadith's significance to so as make it coincide with current reality, Sheikh Salem also erased a part of that reality to make it coincide with the hadith. Explained in his terms, the embargo is a blow at "the Syrian people," who "are near to receiving not even a dinar or a *mudi-un* [a measure of grain used in Syria]." Furthermore, the embargo is not only international, but also internal, he added: all the insurgent Syrian cities are besieged, economically and militarily, by the regime (thus the "double siege"). These cities are deprived "of food, medicine, milk for the children, of water, gas, fuel. . . . Even the Red Crescent ambulances allowed passing and entering Baba 'Amr to help the women and the elderly, are robbed of medicine and food. . . ."

Thus, he presented the complete hadith as bearing several prophecies: an implicit anticipation of the Muslim conquest of Iraq and Syria, which had not yet occurred at the time the Prophet spoke; and an explicit description of the inhumane conditions of a double embargo to be levied thirteen centuries later. The sheikh did not fail to underline this, so as to marvel at the Prophet Muhammad's prescience. One mystery remained, however: in the case of Iraq, why did the Prophet mention the Persians (al-'ajam), whereas the embargo was imposed by the United States in 1991? Could that mean the hadith does not refer to the Iraqi embargo? Sheikh Salem covered his bases: it was the Iranians "through their allies in Iraq, who had incited the Americans to intervene militarily and implement the embargo," so the hadith unmasks the real culprit for the famine of "our people": Iraq. It also anticipates the Iranians' 2003 "coup d'état by proxy" to get rid of Saddam Hussein using the Bush administration's neocons: a third prophecy.

After the tribulations of Iraq and Syria, the Mahdi will come: "the Caliph who will give money freely and lavishly to my community." This was the moral of the sermon:

In spite of what our *umma* is enduring at the moment, in spite of the horrendous siege against our brothers in Syria, in spite of the air raids, RPG and missile strikes, in spite of the mass massacres, in spite of our brothers being abandoned by those who claim to be human rights defenders, in spite of some people's desire to halt this revolution, we announce Muhammad's promise—peace be upon him—that the Assad family's tyrannical rule (*mulk jabri*) will collapse, God willing, and a rightly guided Caliphate (*khilafa rashida*) will be built in its stead.

In his October 7, 2011 sermon about jihad's benefits for religion and for the pan-Islamic umma, Sheikh Salem lambasted those who claimed to stand for Sunni rights in Lebanon. He was responding to those "politicians and clerics" who accused al-Taqwa mosque of leading Sunnis to a precipice. In fact, they "did nothing to defend Sunnis when Hezbollah attacked on May 7, 2008, just as they [have been] doing nothing to defend Sunnis against the Assad regime" since the beginning of the revolution. The Sunnis' institutional prerogatives within the state were "disappearing one by one." Thus, he questioned the Hariris' political legitimacy and that of their supporters in the region in the most direct way possible. In essence, lacking both strength and honor, the Sunnis could not assert themselves in Lebanon. A mimetic form of rivalry with Hezbollah appeared as the counterpoint to this denunciation, since the failure of civil elites logically called for their replacement with religious elites ready to defend their religion by force of arms— according to Sheikh Salem's definition of jihad—as had been done inside the Lebanese Shi'ite community. The sheikh's fascination with contemporary Shi'ism appears in his borrowing of various ideas and practices: the eschatological belief in the Mahdi's imminent coming, the frequent use of the term *mustadh'afun* (oppressed) to designate the Sunni masses betrayed by their elites. In the same sermons, he has lamented the "growing number" of young Sunnis who "are joining Hezbollah."

Sheikh Salem Abd al-Ghani al-Rafi'i is one of the most energetic and effective preachers spreading these common ideas through Tripoli's poor neighborhoods of Qubbeh and Bab al-Tabbaneh. As in the Palestinian camp of Nahr al-Bared, it was persons first immersed in Salafism outside the region who, upon returning to their birthplaces, set up religious studies centers and mosques to disseminate their conception of Islam. This sheikh has pushed the logic of disengagement from Lebanese institutional history to extremes. Based on a religious reinterpretation of regional realities, he inserts his audience in the eschatological time frame of the coming of the Mahdi, and each believer is called upon to hasten this event. This is no longer a form of Salafism rooted in the communitarian framework, as was the case in 2005 when the balance of power inside the Lebanese Sunni community favored the Future Movement. This is an autonomous form of Salafism that perceives itself in a relationship of mimetic rivalry with the Shi'ite Hezbollah, the enemy that must be not only fought, but also emulated. By destroying Sa'ad al-Hariri's power bases in Beirut during its May 7, 2008, power play, the Shi'ite movement actually contributed to the fulfillment of Sheikh Salem's dream—that there be no one left standing between himself and Hezbollah.

When the security forces arrested of one of his partisans, Shadi al-Mawlawi, they gave the sheikh the opportunity to stage protests in al-Nur Square and denounce the unjustified imprisonment of all Sunnis. The square, with its giant portraits of Islamist detainees, then became the regular location of protest gatherings. Ex-Fatah al-Islam member Hussam al-Sabbagh took on the task of forming an armed group of several hundred men. He was then able to exploit the deadly clashes between Jabal Mohsen and Bab al-Tabbaneh to provide ammunition to combatants and recruit volunteers for this militia. Sheikh Salem also recruited Muhammad Taha. The ingenious handyman of the McDonald's network was put in charge of the sheikh's Facebook page after serving his eight years in Roumieh prison. When they heard the news of Wissam al-Hassan's assassination, men in these circles showed no sympathy for the deceased who, according to some of them, "got what he deserved."[56]

The Jihadi Risk

Sheikh Salem's activism naturally caused concern among other Tripoli actors. A meeting was held in August 2012 to attempt to negotiate a ceasefire between Jabal Mohsen and Bab al-Tabbaneh. It was attended by the city's main Sunni elites. Kana'an Naji then addressed Hussam al-Sabbagh in no uncertain terms: "There are two gangs in Tripoli, the Jabal Mohsen gang and yours. You must

---

[56] According to the testimony of a man from these social circles in January 2013.

keep quiet. No clashes with the army, we don't want a new Fatah al-Islam in Tripoli. Our only enemy is Hezbollah and the Syrian regime."

Members of the networks of support for the Syrian insurrection were anxious to avert potential problems linked to the uncontrolled presence of Lebanese jihadi militants on Syrian territory. For instance, FSA operatives executed jihadi and ex-Fatah al-Islam member Walid al-Bustani, as required by an April 2012 Free Syrian Army "tribunal" verdict. Born in 1963 at Bibnin, in the Akkar region, al-Bustani had emigrated to Denmark in the late 1980s. The path he took was identical to that of Bilal Khaz'al at the same period.[57] After an initial stage as a militant with the Tawhid Movement in Tripoli, al-Bustani shifted toward internationalist jihadism under the influence of a sheikh originally from Kuwait, who preached at the al-Tawba mosque, which was part of the Scandinavian *waqf* in Copenhagen. During this period, al-Bustani met Talal Fu'ad Qassem, one of the emirs of the Egyptian Gama'a Islamiyya, who was in exile in Copenhagen. The Egyptians' efforts to raise awareness of the idea of jihad in Bosnia affected him, and al-Bustani began collecting funds for the *mujahidin* during the war in the former Yugoslavia. Later, he allegedly fought on another jihad front, Chechnya, in 1999. Al-Bustani, now a Danish national, returned permanently to Tripoli in 2006, and joined Fatah al-Islam shortly after the group's formation was announced. During a trip to Denmark in 2007, he managed to raise several thousand US dollars for the movement. On the day the armed conflict with the military began, he was leading a diversionary operation in the Qalamoun region when an army patrol arrested him.

Walid al-Bustani escaped from Roumieh prison on November 16, 2010. In early 2012, several hostage-takings and acts of violence against residents of the village of Husn, north of Talkalakh, Syria, were attributed to him. He, along with a band of a few dozen men, had allegedly proclaimed the foundation of an "Islamic Emirate" in Husn. Some Christians from the Homs area then warned a parliamentarian from the Future Movement of the potential risks this individual could pose for the Syrian revolution:

---

[57] For an account of Walid al-Bustani's life, see Hazim al-Amin's article in *al-Hayat*, November 27, 2008.

"If Walid al-Bustani remains alive, all the Christians of Syria will become *shabbiha* [pro-regime militia fighters]!" In April 2012, after consulting political and religious leaders from Tripoli, the members of a Syrian *katibat* decided to eliminate him. The television channel OTV obtained video of al-Bustani's "trial," filmed with a mobile phone, and aired some of it during its news bulletin.[58] In it, al-Bustani, his arm in a sling, appears scruffy and disheveled as he faces his judges and fields a multitude of confusing questions, then is mowed down in several bursts of machine-gun fire.

THE BATTLE OF AL-QUSAYR, MAY–JUNE 2013

Since January 2013, the Lebanese army has withdrawn from the Hermel area, allowing Hezbollah to occupy the Lebanese villages of al-Qasr and Zaghrin, connected by an asphalt road, a few kilometers from the Syrian border. Hezbollah has set up a missile base at al-Qasr, from which it fires on FSA positions in and around the Syrian town of al-Qusayr. Hundreds of Syrian fighters have crossed the border to take up positions in Jabal Akrum, on Lebanese territory, in hopes of containing Hezbollah's activities in al-Qasr. This initiative, taken in late April 2013, was immediately followed by the redeployment of Hezbollah forces toward Jabal Akrum in response.

Hezbollah has been sending its fighters from Hermel, through the Syrian villages of al-Hammam and al-Rabla, to infiltrate the Homs region. Since early May 2013, it has occupied the Syrian villages of al-Hammam, al-Rabla, al-Burhaniyya, and Shumariyya as part of an advance intended to connect Hezbollah with Bashar al-Assad's troops garrisoned to the north and west, in the Shi'ite and Alawite villages of Sumaqiyya, al-Houz, and Tell al-Nabi Mando, near the Tartus-Damascus highway. Hezbollah is also attempting to establish its control of the road to al-Qusayr. Its fighters took the village of al-Jusiyya from Syrian opposition forces, and later

---

[58] The video is available online at http://www.youtube.com/watch?v=PEdTl0-mowI. accessed May 31, 2013). The presenter remarked that "several Future Movement operatives, including Amid Hammud, were mentioned by name in the video," leading viewers to believe these Lebanese protagonists were involved in setting off the Syrian insurrection, whereas in fact they began to support it (by sending small arms to insurgents) after its inception. This erroneous belief, fuelled by the Bashar al-Assad regime's propaganda, explains why this TV channel—which is close to General Michel Aoun and has been openly supportive of the Syrian regime—aired the footage.

that May they managed to seize the villages of Burhaniyya, Umm Hurri, and Nizariyya, the largest village in the region.

As Hezbollah combatants pushed insurgent brigades from their positions west of al-Qusayr, the regular Syrian army and *shabbiha* maintained control of Umar ibn al-Khattab and Abd al-Mun'im Riyad avenues, the main roads through the town. To the east and west of these thoroughfares, various insurgents' brigades—Ahfaz al-Rasul, al-Faruq, al-Huda—held positions in the ruined town, regularly targeted by aerial bombardment. After exhausting deliberations, these brigades agreed to form a shared military council, under the command of Abu Yazin, a former officer of the regular army originally from al-Qusayr, and a sometime resident of North Lebanon. In early May 2013, one month before al-Qusayr's fall, the two main front lines had been east of the town, near the cultural center and the agricultural school. By the middle of the month, Hezbollah had managed to take control of the west bank of the Orontes. Under pressure from both Syrian regime forces and Hezbollah, most of the FSA brigades then abandoned their positions in the ruins of al-Qusayr. Their leaders felt that the FSA's top officers had abandoned them, and some suspected that the FSA was prioritizing the Syrian Muslim Brotherhood's hidden agenda. This means there will be no efforts to liberate al-Qusayr because the Muslim Brotherhood has no significant militant base there. During this period, combatants received food supplies, weapons, and ammunition from North Lebanon through a network of underground tunnels several kilometers long, but when shelling from Hezbollah positions in Hermel destroyed the tunnels, deliveries slowed considerably. Only the al-Huda brigade, which Wahhabi Sheikh Adnan al-'Arour funds from afar, has remained in position, fueling the more secular forces' fears that Salafis would take over the battle of al-Qusayr.

THE SALAFI OFFENSIVE ON AL-QUSAYR

Several Lebanese Salafi sheikhs have taken advantage of the deteriorating military situation in the al-Qusayr area to call upon volunteers to join the jihad in Syria. Among them, Sheikh Ahmad al-Assir has played a significant role. Born in 1968, he earned a degree from the Dar al-Fatwa religious institute in Beirut and has gained notoriety since 2011 in Lebanon through his scathing criticism of Hezbollah. Speaking from his mosque in 'Abra, a suburb of Sidon, he arouses strong emotions in working-class Muslims, often Palestinians who have moved out of the Ayn al-Helweh and Miye-Miye camps nearby. In early May 2013, he was photographed holding a Kalashnikov in the Syrian village of Jusiyye al-'Ammar, a few kilometers from al-Qusayr. Partisans of the Salafi al-Huda brigade, led and funded by Adnan al-'Arour, escorted him into the war zone.

Before the Syrian uprising, Sheikh Ahmad al-Assir was already trying to broaden his audience in North Lebanon. In March 2012, individuals close to the Hariri family had managed to dissuade Sheikh Da'i al-Islam al-Shahhal from inviting Ahmad al-Assir to speak in a gathering, so as to "prevent the constitution of a Salafi front in North Lebanon." For the latter, as for Sheikh Salem al-Rafi'i, the Future Movement's political passivity and Sa'ad al-Hariri's physical absence in Lebanon (for security reasons), provided the right conditions for a political takeover in the Sunni community. The display of their presence in combat in al-Qusayr and Homs was part of a dynamic of rivalry at the Future Movement's expense—a tactic that was perfectly understood by Future Movement's leaders. A few Jabhat al-Nusra partisans were also present in al-Qusayr, telling others that belonging to the Free Syrian Army was *kufr*.[59] Similarly, the Salafi presence Hassan Nasrallah has dubbed a "*takfiri* menace," gave Hezbollah a pretext for military intervention in al-Qusayr.[60] Within the insurgent forces, the best way for any faction to regain influence in the various brigades was to ensure that their logistic networks—mainly funneling weapons and ammunition—remained functional. In late May 2013, the civilian figure in charge of al-Qusayr's "weapons supply room (*ghurfat taslih*)" was discreetly extracted from the town under siege in order to fetch weapons from North Lebanon and resupply the besieged.

This critical phase has induced some unaffiliated Syrians to consider the possibility of a strategic alternative—shifting the conflict

---

[59] Interview with an FSA militant, Akkar, November 2013.

[60] In his May 25, 2013 speech, Nasrallah acknowledged Hezbollah's military engagement in Syria for the first time, to combat "the *takfiri* movement which is present at the Lebanese border and represents a danger, not only to Hezbollah, but also to Sunnis, Shiites, the Lebanese, the state, the Resistance and coexistence itself."

westward, toward the "Sunni Mountain" of North Lebanon—to relieve the twin fronts of al-Qusayr and Homs. Some considered the possibility of creating a Lebanese equivalent of the FSA, a "Free Lebanese Army" composed of groups of Sunni would-be defectors from the national army, who were expected to leave it in protest against its lack of neutrality. As it has been noticed, many in North Lebanon resent the Lebanese national military hierarchy, seen as unreservedly supporting Hezbollah's cause.

In military terms, extending the conflict onto Lebanese territory found its justification in the need to bomb Hezbollah's bases in the Hermel district from a chain of bases in Sunni mountain villages—Sir al-Dinniyeh, al-Funaydiq, Bayt Ya'qub, and al-Bireh (home, one will recall, of the martyred Sheikh al-Wahid). In this scenario, moving the conflict to Lebanon would also be a way of "keeping the Lebanese Salafis in their own country, thus preventing them from pouring into al-Qusayr and Homs and imposing their version of Islam there," according to an anti-Salafi Syrian exile from Homs. Against this analysis, neither Tripoli's political notables nor operatives such as Amid Hammud supported military escalation in Lebanon. Hammud, in particular, was concerned with maintaining the status quo in order to avoid giving the Lebanese army or Hezbollah any excuse for a massive intervention in Sunni North Lebanon.

On the morning of May 26, 2013, two missiles hit the southern suburbs of Beirut. The same day, FSA secretary Ammar al-Wawi made a statement indicating that the firing of these missiles was to serve as a warning: "Lebanon cannot be kept out of what is happening in Syria, and Hezbollah's entrance into Syria will have extremely grave consequences."[61] Some Syrian opposition members had expressed their determination to carry out operations in Lebanon after the fall of al-Qusayr and Homs, which they viewed as inevitable in the short term. Remnants of Ba'athist rhetoric tend to resurface in their justifications for extending the battlefield to Lebanese territory:

Why should we be limited by the Sykes-Picot borders? If the regime establishes an Alawite/Shiite zone reaching across the

[61] *Al-Nahar*, May 26, 2013.

Syrian-Lebanese border, we must draw the logical conclusion and attack targets on Lebanese territory—this war now reaches from al-Anbar to Tarablus al-Sham [Tripoli]!

THE SECURITY PLAN FOR TRIPOLI

In October 2013, a "security plan" for the city of Tripoli was devised by the Second Bureau of the Lebanese army and the IFS leadership to end the recurrent violent clashes between the Ba'al Mohsen and Bab al-Tabbaneh neighborhoods. More generally, the plan reflected an agreement between Hezbollah and the main Sunni representatives (Sa'ad al-Hariri and Interior Minister Nuhad al-Mashnuk) to avert a spillover of the Syrian conflict and to prevent a sectarian escalation in Lebanon, after the various attacks that took place in Shi'ite-populated South Beirut and the devastating blast that targeted two Sunni mosques in Tripoli.[62] A warrant was issued in the Lebanese courts for the arrest in Jabal Mohsen of Alawite leaders Ali Eid and his son Rif'at for their alleged roles in the attacks on the al-Taqwa and al-Salam mosques. The two fled to Syria. Pending their arrest, the men who controlled the various fronts in Bab al-Tabbaneh surrendered to the army. Since then, checkpoints have been set up throughout the city and outlying areas, amid strong army presence. The population of Tripoli, exasperated with the scale of the violence, cheered the restoration of law and order. In Bab al-Tabbaneh, however, youths and women tried to blockade the neighborhood by setting fire to tires in protest against the brutality of arrests "that do not even leave women time to cover their heads."[63] In a press conference, Sheikh Da'i al-Islam, opposed to the "security plan," denounced "a conspiracy to humiliate the Sunni community to serve Safavid ambitions in

---

[62] On August 23, 3013, the bombing in Tripoli of two mosques—al-Taqwa, where Sheikh Salem al-Rafi'i used to preach, and al-Salam—caused the deaths of forty-six people. On August 15, 2013, a car bomb exploded in South Beirut, a Hezbollah stronghold, killing twenty-seven people. This attack inaugurated a series of blasts in the same area. On November 19, 2013, twenty-two people were killed by a suicide bombing targeting the Iranian embassy in Janah district. Other attacks took place in South Beirut—on January 2 and January 21, 2014; on February 2, 2014; and on February 19, 2014. In a Hezbollah-controlled zone in Hermel, a car bomb killed four people on January 16, 2014, and another killed two people in the same area on February 1, 2014.

[63] "Protests in Tripoli over the way the arrests were handled. Blocked roads . . . and intense negotiations to calm down the situation." *al-Hayat*, April 9, 2014.

Tehran, Baghdad and the southern suburbs. . . . We refuse to allow Tripoli or Arsaal to be treated any differently than the southern suburb of Beirut."[64]

The artificial and deadly front line between Ba'al Mohsen and Bab al-Tabbaneh has fulfilled its regional function. The need to put an end to clashes between the two neighborhoods justified deploying the army in Tripoli and throughout the area of North Lebanon. Sacrificing the Eid family—a relative sacrifice because the Alawite neighborhood has not been disarmed—was rewarded with a major advantage for party and Syrian regime allies: the closing of supply channels between Tripoli and Homs. Once they were trapped in the "defense of Bab al-Tabbaneh," the northern Sunnis found themselves in a highly vulnerable situation. Taken over by forces allied with the Resistance, the area could no longer play the role of a sanctuary for Sunni enemies of Hezbollah or the Syrian regime. Groups that helped the Syrian rebels thus lost their capacity to act regionally. The military neutralization of North Lebanon paved the way for Hezbollah and Bashar al-Assad's army to recover the last rebel bastions of Homs and the Qalamoun region in April–May 2014. Fears that North Lebanon would gradually be surrounded, expressed by anti-Assad Sunnis in 2012, were realized in May 2014. The Hariri camp now faces the same dilemma as it did in May 2008. If it is to carry through with its political ambitions, it must be capable of terminating the military status quo favorable to Hezbollah. That would mean taking responsibility for a military escalation for which it is not prepared, and for which it does not have the necessary support. Were it to take the risk, far greater Western and Saudi involvement in Syria would be required. If Sa'ad al-Hariri lowers his political ambitions in the name of realism, the country stands in danger of being overrun by radical Salafi movements that since 2008 have been accusing al-Hariri of betraying Sunni Islam.

The Syrian situation has also posed challenges to the Hariris' course of action. In 2012, Sa'ad al-Hariri partisans lent their aid to the most liberal and pro-Western elements of the Free Syrian Army, working directly with those involved from Istanbul. In Lebanon, Wissam al-Hassan wielded his influence over North Lebanese networks to encourage them to work to bolster the Free Syrian Army.

[64] Ibid.

Alerted by the previous Fatah al-Islam, the intelligence branch chief also cautioned his northern partners against the perils of jihadi radicalization. Besides the difficulties inherent in the Lebanese context, these efforts were thwarted as well by internal changes in the Syrian insurgency. Divisions within the Free Syrian Army made it impossible to convert a mere label into an actual organization. By the same token, the growing role played by Salafi-leaning Islamist brigades has diminished the relevance of Hariri's "Syria policy." Guided by their ideological preference and, even more, driven by a concern for military effectiveness, North Lebanese networks became increasingly involved in supporting Islamized *katibat* in Homs, Idlib, Aleppo, and Damascus. In October 2012, the murder of Wissam al-Hassan in Achrafieh, most likely perpetrated by Moustafa Badr al-Din, successor to Imad al-Mughnieh, also dealt a severe blow to those who were striving to control Sunni and Islamist circles both in Tripoli and in the area of Homs. Prince Bandar acknowledged the Islamist dynamics at work, thereby facilitating the creation of the Islamic Front (*al-jabhat al-islamiyya*) in November 2013, which brought together the main Salafi battalions. At about the same time, a former combatant for the Free Syrian Army hiding out in Akkar reported that in the city of Homs, Jabhat al-Nusra had offered to unite all the battalions under his authority: "I was stunned when I heard that those battalion leaders all agreed with al-Nusra's plan!"[65]

In Tripoli, Sa'ad al-Hariri's contacts have stopped receiving financial aid since the end of 2013. The growing role of Islamist groups in the ranks of the Syrian rebellion will inevitably have repercussions on the situation in North Lebanon, further weakening representatives of political Sunnism. Enjoying a favorable image in working-class circles in Tripoli, Jabhat al-Nusra is already believed to have contacts in the Tripoli area. On June 1, 2014, Sheikh Salem al-Rafi'i's Facebook page referred to the tweet of a certain Abu Hamam, Jabhat al-Nusra's military commander, asking "all sincere *mujahidin* to be prepared to take the conflict into the Shi'ite villages of Lebanon" in the event that the death penalty pronounced the day before by the Judicial Council against the three Fatah al-Islam members was carried out.

---

[65] Interview with an FSA member, Akkar, November 2013.

Epilogue

With the fall of al-Qusayr in June 2013 and the Syrian regime's reconquest of Homs, the Syrian region of Qalamoun, to the northeast of the Anti-Lebanon Mountain Range, has taken on strategic importance for belligerents in both camps. For the regime, "pacification" of Qalamoun is a prerequisite to securing the highway between Damascus and Homs and destroying any form of threat coming from Lebanon. Hezbollah also considers that groups active in the region planned the attacks that struck the southern suburb. After losing the battle of al-Qusayr, thousands of Syrian rebels defending Homs withdrew into this mountainous area, seeking to strengthen a Sunni network so as to maintain contact with anti-regime combatants in Ghouta, east of Damascus, and to prevent Bashar al-Assad from establishing a buffer zone around the capital.

In November 2013, the regime and Hezbollah conducted an initial offensive in Qalamoun, taking advantage of the weakening of support networks in Tripoli following implementation of the "security plan." Qalamoun Resistance now depends on Arsal—the main Sunni town (40,000 habitants) on the Lebanese side of the border. Arsal has since 2012 been connected with support networks developed in Tripoli—thus forming, with al-Qusayr, a "Sunni triangle" through which weapons, funds, and combatants pass back and forth across the border. The town hospital has accommodated dozens of injured survivors of al-Qusayr in appalling conditions. As a rear base and source of weapons and supplies for Sunni combatants, Arsal could also count on the aid of tens of thousands of Syrian refugees crowded into makeshift camps. The town thus became the Hanoi of a Syrian rebellion enfeebled by the loss of al-Qusayr.

From the standpoint of the Syrian regime and Hezbollah alike, victory in Qalamoun will only be complete when this rear base in Lebanon is done away with. Their objective is to put pressure on the Lebanese army to do in Arsal what was done in Tripoli and at the northern border in the spring of 2013. At the end of April 2014, joint Hezb and regime forces took Yabroud, the largest town in Qalamoun. Across the border, between August 2 and August 7, 2014, the Lebanese army managed to take control of entry points into Arsal. Twenty soldiers and some fifty Jabhat al-Nusra and Islamic State militants were reportedly killed in the fighting. Caught in a stranglehold between the Lebanese army to the west and a Hezbollah-Syrian government offensive to the east, the rebels took twenty-nine soldiers and police officers hostage. ISIS immediately demanded the release of Fatah al-Islam prisoners from the Roumieh prison.

At dawn on October 23, 2014, in an operation that left three Islamists dead, the Lebanese army stormed the hideout of the suspected leader of the Islamic State group in North Lebanon, Ahmed al-Miqati, in an apartment located in the village of Asoun in the Dinniyeh mountains. Forty-six years old at the time of his arrest, Ahmed al-Miqati had participated in the various episodes of Islamist violence that have marked the recent history of Tripoli and its vicinity.[1]

This arrest provoked intense fighting in the northern areas of Tripoli between October 23 and 27, 2014. The army resorted to heavy bombing of the Bab al-Tabbaneh quarter and several thousand civilians were forced to flee. The army commander-in-chief justified this move as necessary to thwart a plan to establish an "Islamic emirate" between North Lebanon and the Beqaa Valley.

This string of events spurred a segment of young Sunnis in the area to take radical action. A number of them—again from Tripoli

---

[1] In the early 2000s, through his Australian connections, he had put members of the McDonald's network in Tripoli in contact with a figure of international jihadism, also in the camp (see chapter 2). He was finally arrested in 2004 as he was planning an attack against Western embassies in Beirut. After his release in 2010, he quickly formed a cell of some dozen volunteers and took part in often-deadly clashes between the Sunni neighborhood of Bab al-Tabbaneh and the neighboring majority-Alawite locale of Jabal Mohsen.

or North Lebanon—have carried out suicide attacks in Iraq or Syria, while some who were soldiers made resounding announcements of their defection from the army over to Jabhat al-Nusra or the Islamic State, in the style of the Syrian soldiers who had joined the Free Syrian Army beginning in the spring of 2011. The Islamic State group's demands to release Fatah al-Islam prisoners in exchange for the soldiers abducted in Arsal in August 2014 also testifies to the long-standing ties of solidarity between the two groups, which share a common stock—going back to the time of al-Qaeda in the Land of the Two Rivers. Likewise, the current crisis has revealed how the Islamic State movement is trying to gain a foothold in the region by relying on an individual—Ahmed al-Miqati—who has played an important role in the recent history of jihadism in the country.

Suicide Bombings

Abu Hafs al-Lubnani—his real name is Mustafa 'Abd al-Hay—was twenty-two years old when, wearing a belt of explosives, he blew himself up in a restaurant frequented by customers from the Shi'a neighborhood of al-Washash in downtown Baghdad, "on 8 Ramadan 1435 [July 6, 2014]." He had been working as a carpenter in the poor neighborhood of al-Mankoubin in northeast Tripoli, where two thirds of the inhabitants live below the poverty line (making no more than four dollars per day), and where the influx of Syrian refugee families since 2011 sought refuge.[2] He went off to Syria two years ago to fight against the Bashar al-Assad regime. He had first joined the Salafi Ahrar al-Sham brigade in Syria. In 2013, he returned to his family in Tripoli, then left once again for Syria, this time joining the Islamic State movement. A tweet by the jihadi organization described his military travels between Aleppo, Deir al-Zor, and Eastern Ghouta, adding that he was in Mosul when the Islamic caliphate was proclaimed in June 2014.

On August 26, 2014, in Baghdad, Abu Talha al-Lubnani—Hisham al-Hajj is his true name—drove a car packed with explosives into

---

[2] The al-Mankoubin district, the "Unfortunate" in Arabic, initially received the families who were affected by the 1955 flood of the Abu Ali. This was followed by the rural migration of people originating from the two regions of Dinniyeh and Akkar. Dewailly, "Foncier et Immobilier" (see chapter 1, note 29).

the offices of a Shi'a militia, killing some fifteen people and injuring around thirty. The militia hit by the attack—As'aib Ahl al-Haqq (League of the Righteous)—is an Iraqi replica of Hezbollah, sporting a logo nearly identical to that of the Lebanese Shi'a organization. Under the title "Martyr Operation Using a Car Bomb in *New Baghdad*, Dozens Dead and Injured," the communiqué from "the Baghdad province (*wilayat baghdad*)" of the Islamic State, dated 30 *Shawwal* 1435 (August 26, 2014), saluted "the hero of heroes of the Islamic caliphate" and "the knight of Islam, Abu Talha al-Lubnani." In his early twenties, from the Rifa'iyya neighborhood in the old part of Tripoli, Hisham al-Hajj had vanished from the souks in June 2014, two months prior to his "martyr operation." The following day, in the televised LBC news report of the event, witnesses interviewed by the journalist plainly showed their solidarity: "He sacrificed himself to defend the Sunnis." "Glory to God, he chose the path of jihad! There are many people here prepared to do the same." "I'm a grandfather of ten children. If God asked me to, I'd do the same thing." "He didn't go to Iraq for money, for 1,000 dollars. . . . No, he was poor, he went to defend his people, those who are being massacred." A poster uploaded to jihadi websites by ISIS sympathizers shows him dressed in white, wearing the pure white head scarf (*ghutra*) of Salafi sheikhs and waving an assault rifle, with the organization's flag in the background. The poster's title in large letters—"The Makers of Life (*sunna' al-hayat*)"—is an ironic allusion to the documentary series Saudi satellite channel al-'Arabiyya produced in recent years on jihadi groups in the Arab World, entitled "The Makers of Death (*sunna' al-mawt*)."

On the same day as the suicide attack, supporters of the Islamic State movement stuck posters the walls of Rifa'iyya depicting him celebrating his martyr's wedding in paradise: "The inhabitants of Tripoli in the land of Syria (*trablus al-sham*) invite you to the wedding of their brave son who died in martyrdom in the Land of the Two Rivers (*bilad al-rafidayn*). Hisham al-Hajj. Tuesday, 30 *Shawwal* 1435. We ask God to welcome him." The poster was headed by a verse from the Qur'an: "Think not of those who are slain in Allah's way as dead. Nay, they live, finding their sustenance in the Presence of the Lord" (surah 3, Ali Imran, verse 169).

Hisham's suicide operation was preceded by another "martyr-dom operation" in the Shi'a neighborhood of al-Kadhimiya in Baghdad on 12 *Shawwal* 1435 (August 9, 2014) by Khaled al-Hajj (a.k.a. Abu Talha). He had been convinced by Hisham (with whom he had no family ties) to follow his lead and join the ranks of ISIS in Iraq. According to Khaled's mother, youth radicaliza-tion of Tripoli can be explained by both the role of the Lebanese state, which "humiliates and jails young people in our regions," and that of "the sheikhs and imams of mosques who brainwash young people."[3]

Lebanese journalist Hazem al-Amin has very aptly pointed out the significance of the Islamic State group's references in their com-munications to the national origins of the perpetrators of suicide operations.[4] Al-Qaeda communiqués were not in the habit of mak-ing such mentions. Bin Laden paid tribute to Lebanese citizen Ziad al-Jarrah, one of the perpetrators of the September 11 attacks, say-ing he was from *Bilad al-Sham*. Out of principle, the group did not recognize the borders drawn by the godless powers after the First World War. Although ISIS does not recognize the borders it claims to be erasing either—beginning with the one between Iraq and Syria—the jihadi organization nevertheless insists on mentioning national-ity from another motive: to exploit to its benefit the Sunni sectarian bitterness that has accumulated in Lebanon as Hezbollah has im-posed its conditions on the rest of the country. By adhering to the Is-lamic State movement, Lebanese Sunnis aim to settle their sectarian and political dispute with the Shi'as throughout the region.

Defections

Abd al-Qader Akkoumi was one of the three Islamists killed in the army raid on Asoun in October 2014. He had been a soldier in the army, and had not long before announced he was joining the Islamic State group. His defection was filmed and immediately posted on the YouTube video-sharing network on October 11,

---

[3] Hazem al-Amin, "Tripoli again in the Face of the 'Caliphate' . . . Young people with no past, pledge allegiance and commit suicide." *al-Hayat*, September 14, 2014.

[4] Hazem al-Amin, "Da'ich recognized Lebanon," https://now.mmedia.me/lb/ar/analysisar /555034 (accessed February 10, 2015).

2014, which made it possible to locate his apartment. Fresh out of adolescence, ill at ease in his army uniform, he droned out a speech read from somewhere outside of the video frame. The terms in which Akkoumi announced his defection may well have been composed by Ahmed al-Miqati himself:

> I announce my defection from this miscreant army of cru-saders (*al-kafir wa al-salibi*). . . . I resign for several reasons: the army shelling of our people (*li-ahlina*) in Arsal; army mis-treatment of our community in the North. The prisons are filled with young Sunnis (*chebab min ahl al-sunnat*). Sunni soldiers are tortured at the Ministry of Defense because they have dared stand up for their community. The sheikhs that fill prisons are tortured, their religion and their Lord are in-sulted. . . . Everything that is happening is happening on or-ders from Hassan the Demon (*al-shaytan*) and Bashar the pig (*al-khanzir*). . . . For that reason, I ask every Sunni soldier to defect and join his people in Tripoli, in Akkar, in Minya, in Dinnieh. I must warn the Sunni military that your families (*ahlikum*), the sheikhs and the most religiously faithful are beginning to blame you.

Another video had been posted on YouTube on July 23, 2014, depicting a soldier going over to Jabhat al-Nusra. Atif Muhammad Sa'ad al-Din speaks in a calm voice, delivering a speech that sums up the principal grievances of those who complain of Hezbollah's dominant role in the country. He announced his defection from the army's 8th infantry brigade. The detail is significant, because this brigade, made up of equal numbers of Christian and Muslim soldiers, was supposed to embody the ideal of national integra-tion after the civil war.[5] Subsequently, Atif Muhammad makes a connection between Hezbollah's hegemony and the experience at checkpoints set up by the army, tangible proof of Shi'a superiority, and thus perceived as a humiliating ordeal: "Everyone knows the army is an instrument in the hands of the Hezb. The Hezb is the one to choose where to set up roadblocks. We arrest anyone the Hezb wants to arrest. All the officers are working under Hezb

---

[5] During the final two years of the conflict, it had been the main instrument of power in Michel Aoun's war against Syria and then against the Lebanese Forces.

orders. Everyone knows what's going on, they know about the mistreatment of Sunnis during roadblock checks. They set up roadblocks that choke Sunni areas, whereas in the *dahiyyat*—[in the Lebanese political lexicon, the word *dahiyyat*, by metonymy, refers to the southern suburb of Beirut, the Hezbollah's unassailable stronghold]—there are weapons, but the army doesn't dare go in. All warrants for arrest are for Sunnis. In Tripoli, there are eleven thousand warrants against Sunnis, but there are no warrants out for the ones who blow up ministers and members of parliament. What kind of resistance is that?"

Videos in which new inductees announce their enrollment in the Islamic State are already peppered with the organization's jihadi jargon—for instance, Sergeant (*raqqib*) Abd al-Mun'im Khaled spoke of his defection from this *taghuti, rafida* army of "crusaders" and pledged his allegiance "to the emir of the believers, Caliph al-Baghdadi."[6] Such videos are plentiful on YouTube, but for lack of precise figures, it is impossible to know whether or not they attest to a groundswell movement.

These breaks with the army are calculated to demolish the institution's national legitimacy, because it cannot claim to defend civil peace unless it embodies the Lebanese model of community coexistence in its composition, its functioning, and its actions on the ground. Even though it has failed to profoundly change society by enabling national integration, the army remains, in its sociological makeup, a minimalist incarnation of the values of the national pact at the foundation of the Lebanese entity. The growing role of Hezbollah has spawned a sense of double standards in Lebanese and particularly Sunni public opinion, which jihadi militants seek to exploit to their advantage. The ambiguous behavior of its leadership since the start of the Syrian crisis (described in the final

---

[6] Posted October 13, 2014 on YouTube, https://www.youtube.com/watch?v=1MergmW Degw (accessed on November 21, 2014). According to the *Encyclopedia of Islam*, 2nd ed., *al-Taghut* conveys the general meaning of "to go beyond the measure, be very lofty, overflow, be tyrannical, rebellious, oppressive, proud, etc." In the Qur'an, it is used as a plural when applied to denote the "idols" and as a singular to name Satan "or a diviner or magician." See "Tāghūt," *Encyclopedia of Islam*, Brill Online, 2014. For jihadi ideologues, the meaning of the term has been extended to cover everything that is "worshipped" by nonbelievers: the state, political institutions, secular ideology, symbols, objects, man, etc. In this conception, the believer's duty is to destroy by all possible means the various forms representing *taghut*.

chapter of this book) has further heightened the perception of an army that is increasingly close to Hezbollah.

The exclusively northern origin of the defectors is also a signal to poor families in the north, for whom the army has long represented a traditional career opportunity (which explains the high proportion of Sunnis from Akkar among Lebanese troops). The gruesome video of ISIS beheading Sergeant Ali al-Sayyid in the Arsal mountains on August 28, 2014, serves a similar purpose, because the victim hailed from the Sunni village of Fnaydek in the Akkar district. Ahmed al-Miqati's son, Umar al-Miqati, and his nephew, Bilal al-Miqati, allegedly took part in al-Sayyid's decapitation. If the tragic nature of this event did not forbid irony, it would be tempting to remind the two cousins that their own grandfather had served in the Lebanese Army forty years previously. For ISIS leaders, a Sunni who works for the *taghut* instead of pledging allegiance to the caliphate deserves the same fate as the "impious" Abbas Medlej, the Shi'a soldier murdered in the same horrific conditions the following September 6.

The Roumieh Connection

In late August 2014, ISIS and Jabhat al-Nusra leaders demanded a swap between Fatah al-Islam prisoners jailed in Roumieh prison and the twenty-five Lebanese soldiers they held hostage in the wake of the fighting in Arsal. One month earlier, the Jabhat al-Nusra leader in al-Qalamoun, Abu Malik al-Shami, had addressed his "mujahidin brothers in Roumieh prison" and promised to "end their affliction within a few days," for "thousands of mujahidin were waiting for the authorization to enter into battle inside Lebanon and in all the *rafida* villages."[7]

Situated at the eastern gate of Beirut, Roumieh prison features regularly in Lebanese headlines due to the frequent riots that break out there and the appalling conditions in which over five thousand inmates are detained. Delays in judicial proceedings explain the

---

[7] LBC Group TV News. www.lbcgroup.tv/news/164366/audio-emir-of-jabhat-al-nusra -in-qalamoun-vows-to (accessed May 7, 2015).

high proportion of Islamist prisoners awaiting sentence.[8] Since the end of the civil war, Roumieh has thus brought together, in a single place, radical Sunnis responsible for several outbreaks of jihadi militancy (the Dinniyeh clashes, the McDonald's conspiracy, the Fatah al-Islam insurgency). Given that all these events occurred in North Lebanon, most of the Islamist detainees naturally hail from the northern part of the country. Local conditions in Roumieh fuel considerable anger among the inmates' families in Tripoli, whose complaints are usually exploited by Islamist sheikhs such as Salem al-Rafi'i to criticize Sunni political authorities. As was seen in chapter 2, new solidarities are established inside and outside the prison, potentially paving the way for the creation of new networks in the future.

The prison is divided into several buildings. Around 280 Islamist prisoners in 57 cells occupy an entire floor of Block B (most of them Lebanese, Palestinians, and Syrians). This building has been described by the Lebanese media as a place where inmates enjoy almost total autonomy. A lax atmosphere prevails, tolerated by the penitentiary administration as a means of relieving stress caused by overcrowding after the May 2011 riot. Prisoners have TV sets, there are no doors to their cells, and they even operate "a barber shop and a coffee shop."[9] With mobile phones and computers purchased from the guards, they can communicate easily with the outside world. In an atmosphere where the smuggling of drugs and other contraband prevails, Islamists have set up a "religious committee" (al-lajna al-shar'iyya) in charge of enforcing Islamic values.

In Block A, where Sunni Islamists occupy only about a dozen cells out of a total of 171 (with three to five people per cell), conflicts with Shi'a inmates are frequent. Some inmates refuse to eat the meat and poultry coming from the prison's kitchens, because they can't know whether the food is lawful (halal) and whether the cook is a practicing Sunni Muslim. In 2009, militants smashed the large wooden cross used for Sunday Mass, provoking sectarian

---

[8] Islamists complain they are victimized by these delays, while judges ascribe them to the refusal of the accused to attend court sessions. According to the Lebanese justice minister, 72 percent of those in prison in 2010 had not been tried, with the number falling to 42 percent in 2011. See International Center for Prison Studies (ICPS), 11th ed.

[9] Daily Star, April 18, 2015.

clashes with Christian inmates—aided on this occasion by their Shi'a fellow prisoners.[10]

On October 12, 2012, three prisoners managed to break out of the prison, including two former heads of Fatah al-Islam's "legal committee," Mahmud 'Awad Falah (a.k.a. Abu Bakr al-Shar'i), a Palestinian from Syria, born in Der'a in 1980, and Fayçal al-Aqleh, an Algerian national born in 1981 in Hussein Dey, an eastern suburb of Algiers.[11] Prior to his escape, Mahmud 'Awad Falah was the "emir" of Block A. As "emir," he could stand in for an infidel prison administration by imposing sanctions himself, for instance by forcing a prisoner to remain locked in his cell during recreation hour or deciding to isolate an inmate by forbidding others to speak to him.

In Roumieh, Falah harbored outright hostility toward Shi'a *rawafid*, whereas his chief, Shaker al-Absi, as mentioned previously, had always refrained from criticizing Hezbollah in public. This might explain why he asked the prison administration a number of times to be put back in Block B, where the eighty-eight Fatah al-Islam prisoners were incarcerated. Before his escape, Falah confessed his hatred for modern figures of *taghut*:

> The ancient pharaoh's body is exposed today to the eyes of tourists in Europe. The new pharaohs will meet the same end. The time of the law of God is near. The coming of the emirate, and then the caliphate, is nearly imminent. There where we find a suitable land to set up an emirate, we will do it. You Lebanese, you worship a tree [allusion to the cedar of Lebanon, associated with the pre-Islamic worship of plants and minerals], whereas you should be worshipping God.[12]

At the time of this writing (April 2015), it is not known for sure which of the two jihadi organizations—Jabhat al-Nusra or the Islamic State—Mahmud Falah chose, but all indications are that it was the IS.

---

[10] I am grateful to Elie Boudjok, third-year history student at Saint Joseph University in Beirut, for valuable information on the functioning of Roumieh prison contained in his college essay.

[11] See "Bill of Indictment in the Case of Fatah al-Islam," part 1 (see introduction, note 3).

[12] Elie Boudjok, college essay, Université Saint-Joseph, 2010.

The link between Roumieh prison and Tripoli resurfaced after a twin suicide attack on January 10, 2015, that targeted a café belonging to the Alawite Arab Democratic Party in the Jabal Mohsen district. The death toll was heavy: nine dead, and more than thirty persons wounded. According to Interior Minister Nouhad Machnouk, the attack was managed from Roumieh's Block B, which prompted Lebanese police to empty out the notorious block two days later, provoking a new wave of protest by inmate families in Tripoli.

Arsal and the Domestic Sunni Community Balance

The issue of Arsal crystallizes political and religious oppositions. For dominant Sunni sensitivities, the army's legitimacy as a national institution will be played out in this mountainous area. Many fear that the army's attempt to restore its credibility after the beheading of its soldiers conceals a strategy to reconquer the entire Arsal mountain area—in other words, that it is the Lebanese side of a move to encircle the area that Hezbollah and Syrian forces have already begun in Qalamoun. If this should happen, the ideological center of gravity of the Sunni community, which, since May 7, 2008, seems gradually to have shifted from the Future Movement toward "institutional" Salafi sheikhs, might then escape these clerics and come to rest with the jihadi combatants. Lebanese youths would then enroll en masse in the Islamic State movement, at the risk of jeopardizing the pact sealed in 1943 (and actually well before) between the Sunni community and the Lebanese state.

To prevent an outbreak of violence such as might bring this a scenario to pass, a group of North Lebanese sheikhs, among whom are Sheikhs Ra'ed Hlayhel and Salem al-Rafi'i, has formed in the hopes of reaching a negotiated solution. On August 4, 2014, just as the Committee of Muslim Ulema was about to make contact with Syrian rebels near Arsal, shots were fired on the convoy of clerics, leaving several wounded, including Sheikh Salem al-Rafi'i. During a press conference in Tripoli on August 6, 2014, Sheikh Ra'ed Hlayhel said that the committee's role was "to facilitate the return of the combatants from whence they came and in exchange that others had to leave the country they had gone into"—a transparent allusion to Hezbollah's role in Syria since 2012. He also stated, "It was not men in arms who opened fire on the convoy." The sheikh recounted that as they were returning from the failed expedition, the convoy had been stopped at a roadblock set up by military intelligence and that he himself had been treated harshly by a suspicious officer. They had to justify themselves ad nauseam, while the injured were waiting in the convoy ambulance. In short, the incident, as described by the sheikh, showed that the ulema from North Lebanon were better treated by Syrian rebels than by the population in Sh'ia villages (the convoy had been booed when it went through the Shi'a village of al-Labweh), by Hezbollah (implicitly accused of having targeted the convoy), and by army intelligence (represented by an officer who showed no compassion for the victims)—in other words by the three domestic threats to the Sunni community identified in Salafi rhetoric.

It is possible that the sheikhs' ambiguous efforts will be bypassed by much more radical forces. Alarming reports suggest that ISIS is running a *shari'a* court in Wadi Hmayyed, to the east of Arsal, where people accused of collaborating with the Army or Hezbollah are currently being tried.[13]

[13] *Daily Star*, February 7, 2015.

Conclusion

This book has examined why it was so difficult to build a Sunni political community in this part of the Middle East. According to John Dewey, building a political community requires setting up mechanisms for deliberation that allow its members to identify collective interests and define a shared response to a number of threats. It cannot emerge without freedom of access to data that directly concerns its political affairs: "inquiry" moves a group from apathy to political action.

Syria's withdrawal from Lebanon following Rafiq al-Hariri's assassination facilitated the affirmation, within the Sunni milieu, of a political community defined by a quest for the "truth" about the former prime minister's death. This mode of political identification gave expression to the Sunni community's desire to escape the regional hegemony of Hezbollah and the Syrian regime. Hariri's son and his entourage tried to conduct this inquiry through a partisan organization (the Future Movement), a media organization (a TV channel and a newspaper), and an investigative apparatus within the state (the Information Branch). In that sense, the process (inquiry) was just as important as the outcome it could achieve. Some lessons can be drawn from this Lebanese experience that may shed light on the ongoing Syrian situation.

In Lebanon, the reclamation of Sunni communal autonomy had to resist both the Syrian regime's refusal to accede to this emancipatory urge and Hezbollah's ideological, institutional, and military power. The Syrian regime knew too well how to instill radicalism within the Sunni community. The key was to discredit its political elites by facilitating the emergence of Fatah al-Islam in 2006, thus shifting the balance of power in favor of religiously radicalized elements. In Lebanon, mainly thanks to Wissam al-Hassan's efforts, Syria's objective was not achieved at that time. However, within Syria (and possibly in Lebanon in the near future), it may well succeed in the wake of the proclamation of the so-called Islamic State.

In 2005, Lebanese sovereignty was partially restored through the intervention of the international system (UN Security Council Resolution 1559, US threats against Syria, and the establishment of the UN international tribunal). Previously eclipsed by the *muqawim* (resistance fighter), the figure of the *muqatil*—a combatant willing to fight the former regional power system to defend his political freedom—remerged thanks to the changed political conditions.

The return of the *muqatil* was, however, short-lived. The Syrian regime and Hezbollah reacted to the new political scene by escalating institutional instability through street protests and political assassinations. Hezbollah was able to debilitate Sunni political expression from May 7, 2008 on, which indirectly gave rise to a Salafi contestation of Hariri's role as a Sunni leader. Therefore, the weakening of institutional Sunnism gave a free hand to Salafi expressions. Before, as during the 2005 nationalist movement, Salafi sheikhs had ceded the power to define the meaning of their struggle to secular political leaders such as Sa'ad al-Hariri or Fu'ad Siniora. After May 7, 2008, they publicly derided Sa'ad al-Hariri's poor performance and saw themselves as possible Sunni leaders on a national scale. The Hezbollah military move anticipated what would be done by the Syrian regime on a much wider scale: the elimination of any leader of secular opinion who might present a credible alternative to the regime for Syria's future.

True, part of the responsibility for such radicalization rests upon the Sunnis themselves. Whether in Lebanon or Syria, the internal mechanisms of socialization and politicization were not robust enough to withstand that religious current. In Syria, this is no surprise at all, for the regime has devoted itself to destroying all manner of political expression for the last fourteen years. In Lebanon, the political process among Sunni elites had relied on interpersonal relationships, which are unavoidably fragile and tend to favor local patronage networks.

Islamism—including its more moderate version embodied by the Muslim Brotherhood—played a role in the failure of the promise of a democratic revolution in Greater Syria. According to Syrian intellectual Yassin al-Hajj Saleh, mainstream political Islamism facilitated the transition to the military jihadism of the Islamic State and Jabhat al-Nusrat.[1] Being incapable of clearly and unambiguously denouncing the use of violence for religious ends, Islamists of all stripes nurtured the anachronistic and regressive dream of a return to an imperial structure in the area. Their refusal to envisage the political operating within the territorial framework of the Syrian nation-state was likely to lead to the exclusion not only of minorities but of non-Islamist Sunnis as well.

This failure may be explained by the decades of Assad's rule in both countries, especially in Syria, where it completely eviscerated those mechanisms. It was politics, not religion, that was the true enemy of the Syrian regime. Under the regime's rule, religiosity was widely accepted, even encouraged, as it was thought to be an efficient tool for depoliticizing people. But such expression could evolve into radical Islam if conditions prevailed. For example, it was no surprise to see that the first organization to emerge in 1982, after years of Syrian rule in Tripoli, was the Islamist Tawhid. In the 2000s, the story of the McDonald's network again demonstrated how a shift toward terrorist jihadism could readily take shape in a repressive regional political framework. In that case, images of the umma falling prey to multifarious forms of aggression helped to transform young teenagers into mujahidin apprentices, who then exploited the opportunities offered by their transnational environment to structure militant religious communities in the local sphere.

In a globalized world, unity of action is no longer connected with "unity of place." In 2006, for example, North Lebanon was open to multiple regional and transnational influences. Several militant spheres interacted in one local geography—Zarqawi's group in Iraq, the Saydnaya prison in the outskirts of Damascus, Australian and Danish Salafi militants, Syrian and Saudi intelligence centers, religious associations, institutes based in the Gulf, and the Pales-

---

[1] See Yassin al-Hajj Saleh, *fi al-da'f al-fikri lil-'itidal al-islami* [On the intellectual weakness of moderate Islam] *al-Hayat*, August 26, 2014.

tinian Authority in Ramallah. This new reality considerably complicates the possibility of coordinated nationwide mobilizations.

"Unity of time" no longer applies either. Each player has its own memories, its own sources of inspiration—Fatah's Palestinian saga, the "Arab Afghans'" epic, romanticized narratives, military training in Saddam Hussein's Iraq, the Syrian army's invasions of Tripoli. Given such a kaleidoscope of backstories, it is difficult to envisage how any effective "unity of action" could emerge in the Sunni community.

A Sunni Tragedy?

Are these events part of a Sunni tragedy unfolding in the Levant? Too weak to resist an increasingly dominant Iranian influence extending from the Gulf to the Mediterranean, Sunni civil elites are furthermore challenged from within by a jihadi movement that seeks to appropriate Sunni expression in the region.

Indeed, the latter are threatened by the diffusion of Islamist norms that directly undermine their political legitimacy. As much as Islamism has restructured Shi'a communities that were once divided and dominated by others in Iraq and Lebanon, it has had the opposite effect of destructuring the Sunni communities of *Bilad al-Sham*. The reason for this lies in the fact that Shi'a Islamism managed to domesticate a state apparatus in Iran in the wake of the 1979 revolution, whereas Sunni radical Islamism rejected the state system entirely—whether regional or international—and created its own mythology during the jihad against the Soviet Union in Afghanistan in the 1980s.

In the Levant, perhaps more than elsewhere, events confirm the Hegelian notion according to which only a community able to fight retains the freedom to make its own decisions. The problem is that most of the Sunni militants ready to fight and to die are doing so in the name of jihad "for the sake of God"—and they are joined by young Syrians and Lebanese who feel betrayed by the West's lack of reaction after the Assad regime's use of chemical weapons in August 2013.

By definition, jihadism cannot find accommodation within an existing political framework. Jihadism is the enemy of the modern secular state. The only way it can get beyond this irresolvable internal contradiction is by manufacturing a political framework of its own—hence the proclamation of an alleged Islamic State straddling Iraq and Syria. Likewise, jihadi ideologues' preferred means of imposing their hegemony over the Sunni community is to place that community in a relationship of permanent conflict with the Shi'ites, thus justifying in retrospect the seizure of the community by its jihadi warriors. The establishment of an Islamic State from Mosul to Tripoli is also the only way to avoid its becoming a powerless minority in Iraq and Lebanon. Crushed by repression exercised jointly by Iran, Syria, and Hezbollah, rendered defenseless by the West's indecision, the Syrian and Lebanese aspiration to freedom has evolved into a jihadi nightmare.

Jihadi groups are also exploiting a specifically Sunni social revolution that sees young men—little educated and socially marginalized—managing to become local chiefs, community leaders, and religious judges. Jihadi values give them the means to overturn social hierarchies, for inherent in the jihadi ideology is virtually permanent mobilization in the defense of Islam against its many enemies. This radicalization may turn into the death knell for the political *zu'ama* in the Sunni milieu, once youths are no longer willing to serve as cannon fodder for the political ambitions of others that bring them no benefit.

Today, the military struggle reactivates all these modes of action, increasing fragmentation. In a context where forty years of dictatorship has deprived Sunni society of memories of its urban political history, this effort for military emancipation has been hard pressed to find political and institutional expression. Without Western support but with an abundance of funding from the Gulf countries, those who continue fighting in the ruins of Homs, Aleppo, and Damascus are prepared to weather the horrors of enemy bombings and to die in God's name. Thus, the continuation of the war reinforces the territorial and ideological disintegration of the community. The longer the struggle goes on, the more it consolidates value systems incompatible with an enduring political community. In such conditions, Sunni elites will find it more difficult still to reconstitute the political memory of their community and incorporate it into a national framework reconciling liberalism and Arab identity.

Maps

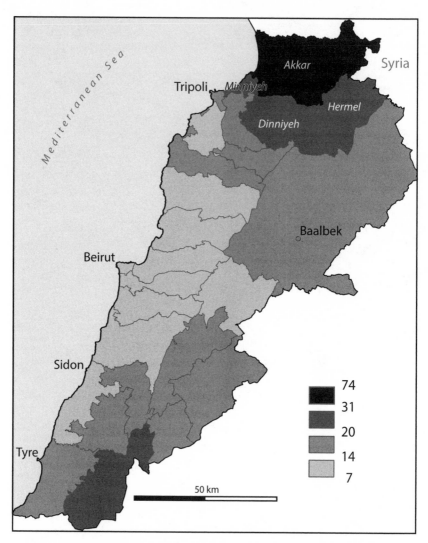

MAP 1. Proportion of illiterates aged 10 years and over in the
population (%). *Sources*: Social Affairs Ministry 1996 and *Atlas
du Liban: territoires et sociétés*, IFPO/CNRS Liban, 2007.

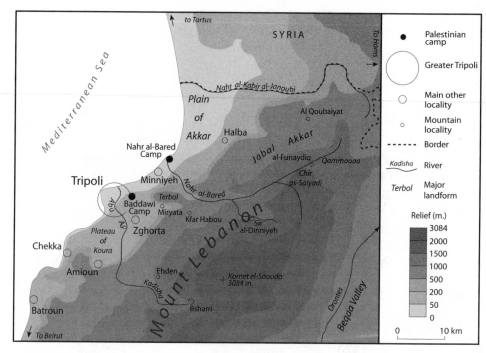

MAP 2. The North Lebanon region and its Palestinian camps

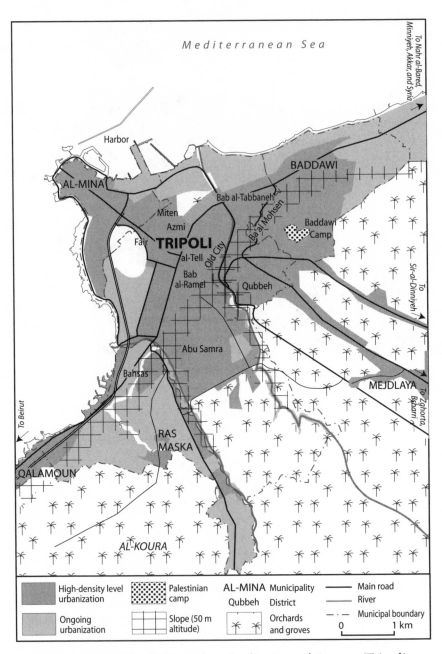

Map 3. Municipalities and main districts of Greater Tripoli

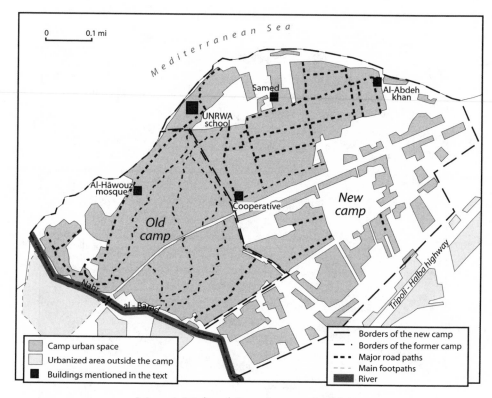

Map 4. Nahr al-Bared camp in 2007

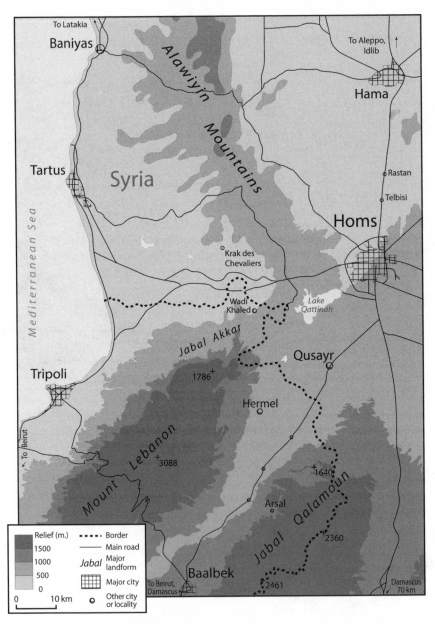

MAP 5. North Lebanon, Homs, and the border

Glossary

Acronyms

FAI (Fatah al-Islam). Name of the jihadi organization proclaimed by its leader, Shaker al-Absi, on November 26, 2006, in the Palestinian refugee camp of Nahr al-Bared, near Tripoli in North Lebanon. The organization's core is made up of former Zarqawi associates present in Iraq a few months prior to the fall of Saddam Hussein in 2003. In late 2005, it refocused its activities on Lebanon, taking control of the infrastructure (training camps, offices, buildings) left behind by the Damascus-based Palestinian organization Fatah al-Intifada, whose leaders, expelled from the PLO in 1983, had formed a special relationship with the Syrian intelligence services.

ISIS (Islamic State in Iraq and Syria). Name of the organization proclaimed in Mosul by "caliph" Abu Bakr al-Baghdadi on April 9, 2013. At first formed around the Jordanian Abu Mus'ab al-Zarqawi in 2004, then leader of the Unification and Jihad Group (Jama'at al-Tawhid wa al-Jihad), the jihadi movement in Iraq has gone by a variety of names: al-Qaeda in the Land of Two Rivers (Tanzim Qa'ida al-Jihad fi Bilad al-Rafidayn) when Zarkawi swore allegiance to Osama bin Laden (October 2004); then the Islamic State in Iraq (al-Dawlat al-Islamiyya fi al-Iraq) on October 15, 2006, when the new leaders wanted to signal their independence from the historic al-Qaeda organization. Known in Syria since 2012 as Jabhat al-Nusra, ISI became ISIS in April 2013, when Abu Bakr al-Baghdadi became eager to affirm its control over the Syrian branch of the movement. In June 2014, ISIS declared itself the "Islamic State" and henceforth considers al-Baghdadi "caliph" of the Muslims.

MUI/Tawhid (Islamic Unification Movement; Harakat al-Tawhid al-Islami). A Lebanese Islamic organization proclaimed on August 25, 1982, in Tripoli, during the Israeli invasion of Lebanon. Strongly influenced by the Iranian revolution, the Tawhid Movement, which groups together various neighborhood militias, has managed to dominate the city of Tripoli by imposing strict religious directives (bans on alcohol and mixed schools). In 1986, the Tawhid defended Tripoli against the Syrian army assault, while its chief, emir Said Sha'ban, protected by Ayatollah Khomeini, negotiated the city's surrender with Syria's president in September. On December 19,

1986, Syrian soldiers and their local Lebanese allies took revenge for Tripoli's resistance and massacred several hundred persons in the Bab al-Tabbaneh area.

SSNP (The Syrian Social Nationalist Party; al-Hezb al-Qawmi al-Suri al-Ijtima'i). Founded by a Christian Orthodox Lebanese intellectual, Antoun Sa'adeh, as an underground organization in 1932, the party refused to recognize the Sykes-Picot territorial division of the Middle East and aspired to create a secular political entity with the name "Greater Syria" that would include Syria, Palestine, Jordan, and even the island of Cyprus. Accused of fomenting a coup d'état in Lebanon, Sa'adeh was sentenced to death by a Lebanese court in 1949. With a strong foothold in the North, particularly in the al-Koura district where party affiliation is traditionally handed down within families, the SSNP welcomed the entrance of Syrian troops in Lebanon in 1976 (in Tripoli it was the only organization authorized by the Syrian army). The party has since then been an organic ally of the Syrian regime in Lebanon, systematically serving its interests. Its secret and hierarchized modus operandi, as well as its propensity to resort to political assassinations, likens it more to an armed group than a political organization. It was involved with Hezbollah in the military offensive launched against Beirut's Sunni districts on May 7, 2008.

Lebanese Political Terms

Events of May 7, 2008. Refers to the day when armed units of Hezbollah and PSNS attacked and destroyed the offices of the Future Movement in Beirut. The exact number of the operation's victims is as yet undetermined. It came in the wake of a decision by Prime Minister Fu'ad Siniora (Future Movement) to shut down Hezbollah's telecommunications network around the Beirut airport.

Future Movement. Name of the political and media network built up by the billionaire construction tycoon Rafiq al-Hariri after he was made prime minister in 1992. Backed by Saudi Arabia as well as the United States and France, al-Hariri undertook an ambitious program to rebuild downtown Beirut, which he hoped to convert into a business hub for the Middle East, in the wake of the peace process launched by the Oslo Accords between Israel and Palestine (1993). In the capital, his Future Movement list, an embodiment of the liberal Sunni and Christian middle class, prevailed in all the post-war legislative elections (1992, 1996, and 2000). During this period, he also founded a newspaper (*al-Mustaqbal*; The Future), a television station (Future TV), and philanthropic projects. Hariri's ascent was brought to a halt when Bashar al-Assad took charge of the Lebanese question in 1998. As president of Syria since 2000, Bashar unconditionally backed Rafiq al-Hariri's political opponents on the Lebanese scene (Hezbollah, as well as President Lahoud, picked by Bashar for the Lebanese presidency in 1998). Accused by the Syrian regime of having played a role in drafting UN Security Council resolution 1559 calling for Syria's withdrawal from Lebanon and the disarmament of Hezbollah, Rafiq al-Hariri was assassinated on February 14, 2005, in downtown Beirut. His son Sa'ad al-Hariri succeeded his father in politics and sought to institutionalize the Future Movement, which became a political party in 2007.

March 8 Movement. Movement in support of Bashar al-Assad and the Islamic Republic of Iran, mainly embodied by the Shiʻa and pro-Iranian Hezbollah and the Lebanese allies of the Syrian regime (Syrian Social Nationalist Party; SSNP), which organized a demonstration in support of Syria in the Lebanese capital on March 8, 2005. General Michel Aoun's movement joined the March 8 Movement after its leader returned to Lebanon from exile in France in 2005.

March 14 Movement. Movement asserting Lebanese sovereignty, composed of all forces united by their opposition to the Bashar al-Assad regime. It was named for the date of a mass demonstration against the regime, held in downtown Beirut on March 14, 2005, a few yards away from the place where Rafiq al-Hariri had been assassinated one month before.

Arab Terms Used in the Book

Al-Mujahid (literally, "the jihad combatant"). Figure of the jihadi combatant formed in the Af-Pak region in the 1980s. It embodies both transnational terrorist action (al-Qaeda) and the quest for a territorial framework in Iraq and the Levant (the Islamic State in Iraq and Syria organization).

Al-Muqatil (literally, "the combatant"). Figure used by the author to suggest the idea of local engagement, primarily intended to defend a neighborhood or a village from an outside attack.

Al-Muqawim (literally, "the resistant"). Figure used by the author to refer to combatants who are part of the regional ideological and military system of the "Resistance" (*Muqawama*), embodied by the radical wing of the Islamic Republic of Iran.

Rafida, pl. Rawafid (literally, the "refusers"). A derogatory term used by radical Sunni Islamists to refer to the Shiʻas, accused of not recognizing the legitimacy of the first three caliphs.

Biographical Notes

Jihadi Militants Who Worked with the Syrian Regime

Shaker al-Absi (1950–2007). Jihadi of Palestinian origin who took over a Palestinian refugee camp in North Lebanon in November 2006 to proclaim the birth of the Fatah al-Islam group. Born in the West Bank in 1950, Shaker al-Absi was a member of the Jordanian air force before joining Fatah, the core component of the Palestinian Liberation Organization (PLO). He defected in October 1983 and joined the dissident Fatah al-Intifada, backed by the Syrian government. His role at the time involved passing weapons into the "western sector," that is, Jordan and Palestine. In the late 1980s, he was arrested in Syria for unclear reasons and adopted a stance of ostentatious piety during his imprisonment. He was released in 1996. At the end of the 1990s, he moved in Jordanian jihadi circles and met Zarqawi, whom he followed to Baghdad in 2002. Incarcerated in Saydnaya prison in late 2003, he was released in 2005 and organized a jihadi network oriented toward Lebanon. He then set up the jihadi organization called Fatah al-Islam in the Nahr al-Bared camp in North Lebanon. After two months of violent conflict between FAI and the Lebanese army, he managed to escape from Nahr al-Bared in September 2007. He is believed to have been killed on his return to Syria.

Sa'ad al-Din al-Ghiyyeh (1963–2013). Islamist militant working as an intermediary between radical jihadi circles and Syrian intelligence services. Born in the village of Tikrit in the Akkar region of North Lebanon in 1963, he was trained by Palestinian sheikhs who staunchly opposed the PLO. In the late 1980s, he joined the Fatah Revolutionary Council (Fatah Majlis al-Thawri) and received military training in the Beqaa to avoid arrest by the Syrian army due to his Islamist sympathies. In the mid 1990s, he met the Jordanian Abu Mus'ab al-Zarqawi and the Palestinian Shaker al-Absi, with whom he formed the small group of *Bilad al-Sham* jihadis. He joined the two men in Baghdad in 2002 and took part in the fight against the US army in 2003. Through the Syrian sheikh Abu al-Qa'qa', he enjoyed a relationship of trust with Syrian intelligence officer Muhammad Dib Zaytun, as well as with Hezbollah leaders. He was murdered in Tripoli on November 12, 2013.

Abu al-Qa'qa' (Mahmud Qul al-Aghassi) (1973–2007). Syrian jihadi preacher of Kurdish origin, known for the eloquence of his anti-Western sermons. Born north of Aleppo in 1973, he was a graduate of the *shari'a* faculty of the University of Damascus. Accused of praying while fulfilling his military service in the early 1990s, al-Qa'qa' was saved from prison by a young Alawite State Security (Amn al-Dawlat) officer by the name of Muhammad Dib Zaytun, who was destined for an important position in the Syrian security apparatus. He remained Abu al-Qa'qa's main contact. Appointed imam of the al-Sakhur mosque in the eastern suburbs of Aleppo in 1999, Abu al-Qa'qa' achieved renown in Arab Islamist circles for his sermons denouncing the political, military, and cultural humiliation the Islamic umma was subjected to by the West, especially by the Americans in Iraq in 2003. In 2006, he used his influence to ask jihadi volunteers in Iraq to join Shaker al-Absi's group in Lebanon. During the same period, he altered his physical appearance, shaved his beard, and became a Hezbollah sycophant. He was murdered on September 27, 2007, outside his mosque in Aleppo, after having inveighed against the role of "mafias" in the Syrian government.

Anti-Assad Sunni Figures

Wissam al-Hassan (1964–2005). Intelligence chief in the Internal Security Force, a close associate of Rafiq and later Sa'ad al-Hariri. Born on April 11, 1965, in Beirut, to a Sunni family from the al-Koura district in North Lebanon, Wissam al-Hassan was a policeman in charge of Rafiq al-Hariri's security. Having become the former prime minister's trusted confidant, he was appointed his chief of protocol and held that post until February 14, 2005, the date of Rafiq al-Hariri's assassination in Beirut. Made head of the information branch in the Internal Security Force (ISF), al-Hassan supervised the investigation into the assassination and proved that a Hezbollah operations cell was present at the scene of the crime (the ISF officer who uncovered this network by identifying telecommunication, Wissam Eid, was killed by a car bomb on January 25, 2008, in the suburbs of Beirut). Promoted to brigadier general after his nomination, Wissam al-Hassan represented the Future

Movement—the Sunni component of the March 14 independence coalition—in the only security institution not subject to Syrian influence. He had developed support networks for the Free Syrian Army (FSA) in Syria in the fall of 2011 and ordered the arrest of Michel Samaha, a former pro-Assad minister accused of planning attacks in North Lebanon. He was assassinated by a car bomb in the Christian Achrafieh neighborhood on October 19, 2012.

Kana'an Naji (1956–). Chief of a militia in the Abu Samra neighborhood of Tripoli, trained by Fatah. Born in 1956 into a family of large landowners, Kana'an Naji became a prominent Sunni figure in the anti-Assad struggle in Tripoli in the 1980s. In 1976, with the help of Fatah, he set up a neighborhood militia that became part of the Tawhid Islamist organization in 1982. After fleeing the city when Syrian troops invaded it in 1986, he headed up a military structure financed by the PLO and Saudi Arabia that was in charge of conducting operations against the Syrian army in Lebanon. He returned to Tripoli with the Syrian withdrawal in 2005 to resume his anti-Assad activities.

Anti-Assad Tripolitan Salafi Sheikhs

Sheikh Salem al-Rafi'i (1961–). Figure of political and militant Salafism (*haraki*) from Tripoli, who since the Syrian crisis has enjoyed considerable popularity among the disenfranchised youth in the city's poor neighborhoods. Born in 1961 in the al-Mina neighborhood (the port of Tripoli), Sheikh Salem graduated from the University of Medina and holds a doctorate from the University of Omdurman (Sudan). He headed the Islamic center in Berlin in the 1990s and in his dissertation argued in favor of recognizing the Islamic specificity of Muslim populations in Europe and the United States. Turned away at the German border in the mid-2000s for his support for the "Chechen and Palestinian mujahideen," he resettled in Tripoli, where he built a huge Islamic complex. He has attracted former Fatah al-Islam members into his immediate circle and is allegedly close to Jabhat al-Nusra in Syria. His sharp criticism is directed both at the "enemies of Islam" (the Shi'a Hezbollah, the Bashar al-Assad regime) and the Hariri family, which he accuses of abandoning the Sunnis.

Sheikh Da'i al-Islam al-Shahhal (1961–). One of the main figures of militant Salafism (*haraki*) in Tripoli. Born in 1961 in the old part of Tripoli, son of Wahhabi Sheikh Salem al-Shahhal (1922–2008). In 1977, together with his father, Da'i formed the Islamic Nucleus Army, a small militia hostile to the Muslim Brotherhood and Sufism. From 1980 to 1984, like other Lebanese students from Tripoli, Da'i was granted a scholarship to study at the Islamic University of Medina. During his stay there, he befriended figures who would be prominent in the 1990s protests in the kingdom in the 1990s—sheikhs belonging to the Sahwa Islamiyya (Islamic Awakening), such as Safar al-Hawwali and Salman al-Awda. On his return to Tripoli, he founded an Islamic association—the Association for Islamic Guidance and Charity—that managed a number of religious institutions. The minister of the interior banned the association in 1996 for "incitement to religious hatred." Da'i backed the Future Movement after Hariri was assassinated in 2005, but he inveighed against the weakness of Sunni leadership in dealing with Hezbollah after the May 7, 2008 attack and criticizes the growing role of Hezbollah in Lebanon and in Syria. An ally of the Syrian Salafis, he has since 2011 backed Syrian opponents to Bashar al-Assad's regime. In December 2014, he urged young Sunnis to leave the Lebanese army.

Pro-Assad Islamists

Fathi Yakan (1933–2009). Born in Tripoli in 1933, Fathi Yakkan hailed from an old Tripolitan family. He studied engineering before turning to Islamic studies and becoming, in 1964, one of the founders of al-Jama'a al-Islamiyya, the Lebanese branch of the Muslim Brotherhood. In 1979, he advocated the establishment of an Islamic State as a solution to the Lebanese war, but carefully avoided taking sides during the civil war in Syria that pitted Hafez al-Assad against the Muslim Brotherhood (1979–1982). He remained secretary general of al-Jama'a al-Islamiyya until 1992, and then was elected to the Lebanese Parliament. A close ally of the Syrian regime and Hezbollah in Tripoli, he helped establish, in 2006, the Islamic Action Front (al-Jabhat al-'Amal al-Islam) in order to mobilize Sunni Islamists against the March 14 Movement. Teaching at the al-Jinan University set up by his wife, he was also a prolific Islamic thinker. After his death, Syrian state TV broadcast a report on his life.

Hashem Minqara (1952–). A former Tawhid emir in the port of Tripoli (al-Mina) in the 1980s, and one of the "historic" Tawhid emirs who took over the branch called Tawhid/Minqara. In October 1983, Hashem Minqara was accused of perpetrating the massacre of some thirty communist activists. He was arrested and imprisoned in Syria shortly after Syrian troops entered Tripoli in the fall of 1986. In 2000, President Bashar al-Assad authorized his exceptional release, owing to the intercession of Tripolitan billionaire Najib Miqati, who was eager to curry favor with the Islamists in the legislative elections. Minqara won some of the Tawhid cadres over to his side, without however managing to reach an agreement with Bilal Sha'ban, Said Sha'ban's son. Thus, there were two branches of Tawhid vying for the succession after the death of the organization's founder. Backed by Hezbollah, Hashem Minqara's Tawhid is one of the Syrian regime's Sunni allies in the city of Tripoli.

Tripolitan Leaders Who Acted from Abroad

Sheikh Ra'ed Hlayhel (1967–). Salafi sheikh from Tripoli who played a major role in the affair of the caricatures of Muhammad published in Denmark in 2005. A graduate of the University of Medina, where he studied from 1989 to 1993, and a sympathizer with the Saudi religious protest movement Sahwa Islamiyya (Islamic Awakening), he taught in Da'i al-Islam al-Shahhal's religious institute on his return to Tripoli. He was granted political asylum in Denmark in 2000 to avoid arrest after clashes between jihadi militants and the Lebanese army in Dinniyeh. He aroused indignation in the Muslim world after cartoons of the Prophet were published in the Danish daily newspaper *Jyllands-Posten* on September 30, 2005. On his return to Tripoli, he was one of the instigators of the demonstration that degenerated into rioting in the Christian Achrafieh neighborhood on February 5, 2005.

Bilal Khaz'al (1970–). Jihadi activist who, from Sydney, Australia, directed and financed attacks against American fast-food chains. Born in Tripoli in 1970 and influenced by a short stint in the Tawhid during adolescence, Bilal Khaz'al (Abu Suhaib) moved to Australia in 1985. He became a baggage handler for the Qantas airline company. In contact with the Arab jihadi circles in the Af-Pak region, in the early 1990s he started the bilingual (Arab/English) magazine *Nida'u al-Islam* (*The Call of Islam*), which offered a forum for the major figures of the jihadi movement, including Osama bin Laden. It was in the early 2000s that he put young jihadis in Tripoli in contact with a member of al-Qaeda in Ayn al-Helweh (Lebanon) and enabled them to attack American fast-food restaurants. Sentenced to fourteen years in prison by the Supreme Court of New South Wales in 2009, he was granted bail by the court on June 7, 2011. In mid 2012, he was jailed once again after the High Court of Australia reversed the SCNSW decision. Prior to his arrest, he frequented the al-Risalat Islamic Bookstore in Sydney, where he encouraged youths to go wage jihad in Syria.

JIHADI LEADERS IN IRAQ

Abu Mus'ab al-Zarqawi (1966–2006). Jihadi who played a fundamental role in securing a foothold for radical fundamentalist ideology in Iraq in the 2000s, infusing it as much with anti-Shi'a as anti-Western content. Ahmed Fadil Nazzal al-Khalayleh (a.k.a. Mus'ab al-Zarqawi), was born in Zarqa, fifteen miles east of Amman, Jordan, on October 30, 1966. He came from a very poor family of ten children, which belonged nevertheless to a major Transjordanian clan, the Bani Hassan, with branches that spread from the suburbs of the capital to the desert confines of the Iraqi and Syrian borders. He left school in his early teens, led the life of a local hoodlum, and then attended mosques in Zarqa. In 1989, considerably influenced by Sheikh Abdallah Azzam's jihad against the Soviet Union in Afghanistan, he went to the city of Peshawar in Pakistan, where he met the jihadi sheikh Abu Muhammad al-Maqdisi, known for his uncompromising Wahhabism and his visceral hostility toward the Saudi dynasty. On his return to Jordan, Zarqawi, together with al-Maqdisi, formed the Tawhid Group (Jama'at al-Tawhid) in 1993, with the goal of opening a front against Israel based in Jordan. Both men were arrested on March 29, 1994, and sentenced to five years in prison by the State Security Court (Amn al-Dawlat). Zarqawi served his sentence in Suwaqa prison, in the Jordanian desert some fifty miles south of the capital. Released in 1999, he traveled to Afghanistan and founded his jihadi organization—Jund Allah—in Herat, near the Iranian border. Forced to flee Afghanistan during the American offensive against the Taliban in 2001, he hid out in Iranian Kurdistan, benefitting from the support of the Kurdish organization Ansar al-Islam. In 2002, he settled to the west of the city of Anbar, where he organized combatant cells to face the coming US occupation of Iraq, recruiting most of his partisans from *Bilad al-Sham* (Jordan, Palestine, Syria, and Lebanon). He claimed credit for the attack on UN headquarters in Baghdad on August 19, 2003, and later for the murder of Shi'a political and civilian leaders. In September 2003, he founded al-Tawhid wa al-Jihad (the Unification and Jihad group) into which other former jihadi groupings merged. On May 2004, he videotaped the beheading of American hostage Nicholas Berg, introducing a new vehicle of terror to the region. On October 17, 2004, Zarqawi swore allegiance to the al-Qaeda leadership, obliging them to rely on him to establish a presence in Iraq. On this occasion he proclaimed the birth of the Organization of Jihad's Base in the Land of Two Rivers (Tanzim Qa'idat al-Jihad fi Bilad al-Rafidayn). He was killed by an American air strike on June 6, 2006.

Abu Bakr al-Baghdadi (1971–). Leader of the Islamic State in Iraq and Syria (ISIS) organization since 2010. Ibrahim al-Badri (a.k.a. Abu Bakr al-Baghdadi) was born in 1971 in the city of Samarra. He is believed to hold a doctorate in Quranic sciences earned in Baghdad. He was an imam in Samarra, Baghdad, and Fallujah prior to the occupation of Iraq in 2003. He also taught at the Islamic University in Tikrit. Arrested in 2004 by American troops, he was freed in 2006. After his release, he founded a jihadi group, the Army of the Sunna and the Community (Jaysh Ahl al-Sunna wa al-Jama'a) that was part of the Mujahidin Advisory Council (*majlis shura al-mujahidin*). He became emir of the Islamic State in Iraq (ISI) after the death of Abu Umar al-Baghdadi in April 2010. On April 9, 2013, a message from the ISI indicated that the al-Nusra Front was a cover for ISI activities in Syria and that the organization would henceforth be known as the Islamic State in Iraq and Syria (ISIS). In June 2014, Abu Bakr al-Baghdadi thus became "caliph" of an "Islamic State" with a universal mission. He traces his genealogy back to Muhammad so as to establish the legitimacy of his claim to the caliphate.

Index

PRINCETON STUDIES IN MUSLIM POLITICS